MADHUR JAFFREY'S FLAVORS OF INDIA

West 175 Publishing

GUJARAT

Ahmadabad

Palitana

Surat

Shetrunjaya
mountain

Saurashtra
peninsula

GOA

Mandovi River

Mapusa

Parra

Panaji

Zuari River

KERALA

Cranganore

Cochin

Vembanad Lake

PAKISTAN

HIMALAYAS

SIKKIM

NEPAL

Arabian Sea

Bay of Bengal

BANGLADESH

SRI LANKA

Indian Ocean

PUNJAB

Amritsar

WEST BENGAL

Ganges River

Calcutta

TAMIL NADU

Madras

Kanchipuram

Madhur Jaffrey's Flavors of India

∾

West 175 Publishing

West 175 Publishing
P. O. Box 84848
Seattle, WA 98124
Web site: www.greatfoodtv.com

Credits
West 175 Publishing Production Team
Publisher . . . . Greg Sharp
Editor . . . . Chris Rylko
Culinary Director . . . . Jenny Steinle
Production Coordinator . . . . . . Kate Terhaar
Cover Design . . . . Kathy Kikkert
Design Modification . . . . Kay Green
Proofreader . . . . Mary Rose Sliwoski

This book is published to accompany the television series entitled
Great Food which was first broadcast in 1998.

UK Version
This book was published to accompany the television series entitled
Flavours of India which was first broadcast in 1995.
First published by BBC Books, an imprint of BBC Worldwide Publishing,
BBC Worldwide Ltd, Woodlands, 80 Wood Lane, London W12 0TT.

First Published 1995
Reprinted, Hardback and Paperback 1995
© Madhur Jaffrey 1995

Designed by Barbara Mercer
Map by Linda Baker Smith
Recipe photographs by James Murphy
Styling by Jane MacLeish
Home Economist Allyson Birch
Set in Simoncini Garamond by Ace Filmsetting Ltd, Frome
Printed and bound in Singapore
Color separation by Radstock Reproductions Ltd, Midsomer Norton
Metric, Imperial and, where relevant, American cup measurements are given in the recipes.
Always follow one set of measurements only.

Library of Congress Cataloging-in-Publication Data
Flavors of India - 1st U.S. ed.
p. cm.
Includes index.
ISBN 1-884656-06-4
1. Cookery, India. I. Great food (television program) II. Title
TX724.5.I4J284 1998   98-36922
641.5954–dc21   CIP

Printed in Singapore
1 2 3 4 5 6 7 8 9 10
First U.S. Version

DISTRIBUTED BY PUBLISHERS GROUP WEST

Page 2: A temple boat in Kerala.
Pages 6-7: A Hindu wedding ceremony in Calcutta, West Bengal.

Contents

───────── ❧ ─────────

THIS BOOK IS DEDICATED TO
THOSE WHO ARE MY DEAREST
Sanford
Zia
Meera, Draig and Roban
Sakina, Frank and "Grainy"-in-the-womb

───────── ❧ ─────────

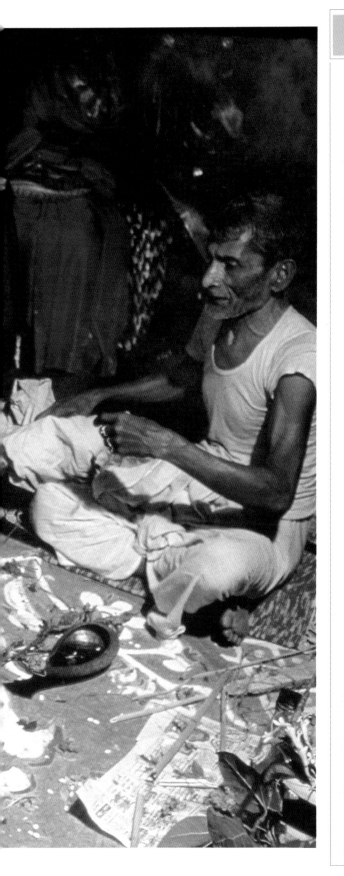

INTRODUCTION

INDIA NEVER FAILS TO surprise me. That is the least I expect of it.

This vast sub-continent, with its diverse tongues and faiths and its complex culture, is an amalgam of haphazardly arranged states that are really mini-nations. Over the last 5000 years these mini-nations, each with its own blend of historical and geographical circumstances, have evolved at their own speed, with their own influences that have come from the inside or from the outside, by land and sea.

Not even India's inhabitants know everything about their nation. Even they find gems of art, nature and culinary creativity where they are least expected. While they may know, in general, what their country holds there are millions of specifics that they may only discover with time, if they are lucky. Perhaps it is those who know India best who realize how much it is that they do not know. Like a clever, seductive paramour, India reveals itself slowly.

Perhaps all this is my way of answering a question that you may well ask me, "Why another Indian cookbook? What is there left to be said?"

A great deal, is the short answer. Every time I return to India I find new and wondrous foods. During a filming trip to Assam, near India's eastern frontier, I once found myself eating with a member of the Khasi tribe who also happened to be my designated hairdresser. She offered me two relishes – a chutney made with a fermented soybean paste, green chilies, garlic and lime juice and a bamboo-shoot pickle – both of which I had never eaten before and could not have even imagined. I immediately jotted them down in my notebook. East Asian and South Asian, compressed into one. That was over 20 years ago. Those recipes sleep in a notebook, waiting for me to find the precise spot for them.

There are other recipes that have never even made it to notebooks because I could not locate their true sources. About 10 years ago – or was it more? – when I was preparing for a trip to Kerala on India's southwestern coast, I received a detailed letter from a Keralite friend who lives in England, Norma Moss, telling me all the different foods that I should be on the look-out for in her home state. She casually mentioned a "boatman's curry" that I should try and find. It was something that was made and sold by the boatmen who ply Kerala's Venice-like network of inland waterways. Norma added that she had eaten this curry on childhood voyages and that it probably did not even exist any more.

On every trip to Kerala since then I have asked about this "boatman's curry" to no avail. I, too, was convinced that the evolution to more modern, fast-moving water buses had taken care of that particular dish. Not so. I found it this year on a rice boat in the middle of Lake Vembanad! You will find the recipe on page 30.

I always knew that the state of Gujarat had dozens of noodles – "pastas" would perhaps be a more accurate title – made out of wheat and chick-pea flour. Most of these, I thought, were fried and eaten in a dry, crisp form as snacks or made into milky, vermicelli desserts. I did not learn until this year that "pastas" here may be dropped into exquisite, savory sauces and eaten as main courses.

In all the Indian cookbooks that I have written, I have never had a recipe for the very typical, sweet and sour, cauliflower-turnip-radish pickle that is made annually in most Punjabi homes and stored in large crocks. It is never served in a restaurant. This mustardy pickle is made at home and served at home. When I was at school in Delhi and we all brought homemade lunches in tiffin-carriers, a Sikh friend from the Punjab often let us share her simple delights – thick flaky breads (*parathas*) stuffed with potatoes or grated white radish and these pickles. They were incomparable. Well, you will find the breads and the pickle in this book.

While you will find here some new variations of dishes that you already know and some easier versions of recipes in my other books, most of the dishes are new discoveries. I have had great pleasure in finding them and I hope you will have great pleasure cooking and eating them. I have looked in some depth at six of India's states – Kerala, Gujarat, Goa, West Bengal, Tamil Nadu and Punjab. In the future, I hope to look at six more and then six more . . . It is a lifelong task. India has so much.

Note to the Reader

People who love food will find great news in this new cookbook: with the addition of a few new spices, dinner can be transformed into an experience that is subtly but definitely new and exciting.

Although Indian cuisine may seem exotic taken as a whole, Madhur Jaffrey has filled this book with singular spicing ideas and ingredient combinations that are not only delicious on their own, they offer many ideas for simple variations to add to our own trusted recipes.

Of course, few people could make such an exotic cuisine as understandable and accessible to American cooks as Madhur Jaffrey. This can be verified by all of Madhur's fans who have watched her on the *Great Food* television series, effortlessly explaining a new marinade for chicken, an herb to compliment your favorite fish, corn bread that's simply baked in a different shape, relishes and appetizers that are fresh and appealing.

Flavors of India is an inspiring addition to any library, filled with the recipes that offer innumerable new ways to spice up your cooking. Enjoy!

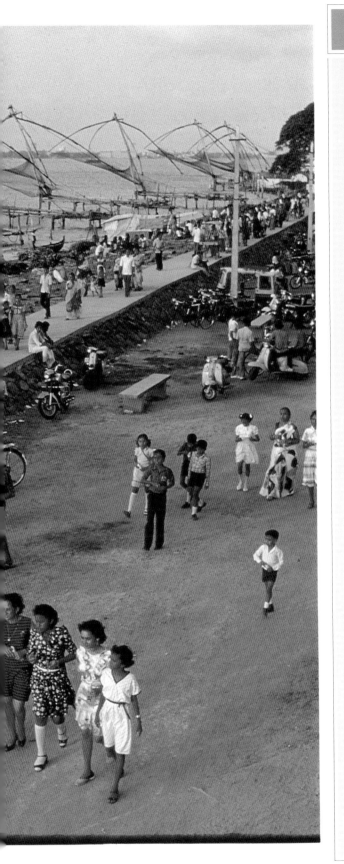

KERALA

MILLIONS OF BLACK, FLUTTERING FORMS swirl in ever-changing patterns, silhouetted against the glowing red of the setting sun. Disturbed sometimes by the sultry breezes that come off Vembanad Lake and sometimes by passing boats, these Siberian ducks will nonetheless settle down for the night on the gentle waters. They are in Kerala for the winter as any mortal in his right mind would also want to be.

Kerala, nestling along India's southwestern coast and rising skywards from the Arabian Sea to the mountainous western Ghats, is a warm, fertile heaven on earth, a sprawling Venice leavened with the lushest of tropical greenery, its land and waters proffering an endless array of delicious edibles from the "king" of spices – black pepper – to king (jumbo) prawns, the size of small lobsters.

Arching palms and paddy fields line a vast network of inland waterways that include lagoons, canals, rivers and bays. Known generally as the "backwaters," these have, over the centuries, not just yielded foods but have acted as Kerala's roads. Houses are built along them as are schools. Boats – long, slim canoes, or palm-covered "rice boats" used for transporting goods, or plain old "water buses" bursting with passengers – are often the only mode of getting from here to there.

I arrive in a canoe that has been blackened with age and water and land in front of a wrought-iron gate. Behind the gate is an old, white house. It has three wings, all supported by sloping tiled roofs, very Chinese in the way they curl up at the ends. The Chinese have traded on this coast since antiquity and left behind a rich legacy in pickling jars, cleavers and wok-like cooking vessels, to say nothing of architectural styles and fishing nets.

Two wings of the house, fronted with pillars, are right on the water. One is for the enjoyment of the men in the family, landed Syrian Christians who, as a community, claim to have been converted by St Thomas himself in the first century. The other is for the storage of coconuts from the family's many trees. They take their coconuts seriously here. The name of the state, Kerala, means "the land of coconuts." The coconut is bankable not only for its oil and its coir but also for its daily use in every single kitchen. A breakfast chutney requires it; so does the prawn (shrimp) *thoran*, prawns (shrimp) steamed with a coconut chili-paste, that is devoured at lunch; the tapioca *bonda*, a fritter nibbled at tea-time; and the country-style duck curry eaten at dinner. One local culinary authority, a Hindu and a strict vegetarian, has already told me with some firmness that for her *avial* (poached vegetables in a curry-leaf-flavored coco-nut-yogurt sauce), only coconuts from old-fashioned trees would do. None of the new hybrids for her.

The main wing of the Syrian Christian household is set back a little. There is a courtyard in front, dotted with pots of flowering bougainvillaea, then a narrow pillared veranda with beautifully carved eaves. Behind the low, central door – solid carved wood studded with brass details – is the granary. It is here that freshly harvested rice gathered from the family's fields is stored and it is here that it awaits a respectable rise in prices before it is released into the market. In the olden days, a guard slept in this room, sometimes right on top of the rice, to ensure its safety.

Rice is Kerala's premier grain, eaten at every single meal. Generally it is short-grained "boiled" (converted) rice, par-boiled, and then partially milled so that it is reddish in hue and exceedingly nutritious.

Some Kerala delicacies have already been prepared in the kitchen. As the youngsters jabber on about how they all learned to swim in the canal that fronts the house, using banana trunks as floats and often taking flying leaps straight from the house into the water, or how they loved hiding in the dark cellar where banquet-sized *uralis* (wide but shallow cooking vessels used for *payasams*, grain puddings) are stored, the older women have laid out a welcoming feast.

There is *stew*, a festive dish of lamb, potatoes and carrots simmered gently in coconut milk. It is almost always eaten to break the Lenten fast at Easter. Because it is so good and so soothing, it is also eaten at other times, whenever there is the slightest hint of a celebration. To sop up the cardamom and clove-flavored juices of the *stew*, there is a stack of creamy-white *appams* – soft, slightly cupped rice pancakes, plump and spongy in the center (the more specific name would be *kalappams* as there is a whole family of them). There is a freshly prepared rice vermicelli – *idi appam*, made by putting a rice dough through a special press and then steaming it – a dryish meat, stir-fried with tiny coconut chips (*erachi olathu*) and a delicious black *halva* made with wheat gluten and brown sugar.

Also gracing the table are cylinders of coarsely pounded rice and coconut (*pootu*) that have been steamed together in hollowed-out bamboos (these days aluminum tubing is frequently used). They are either eaten at breakfast with bananas and milk or as the starch with dishes such as the *meen vevichathu* set before us: in a bowl, sardines float in a fiery red chili and shallot sauce, soured to perfection with the judicious use of *kodampoli*, a local dried fruit of the mangosteen family.

I would happily fly to this coastal state just for its fish. A woman once said to me, "People are so lazy here. They just have to open their mouths and food falls in." There certainly seems to be an over-abundance of very fresh fish and seafood. At some beaches, such as the one near Fort Cochin where the Portuguese, Dutch and eventually the British once held sway, strollers can buy freshly caught creatures of all sizes and shapes – white salmon (*rawas*), large tiger prawns (shrimp), white and red snapper, mullet, crabs, baby sharks and pomfrets – from a fishmonger's shack and then take them to a neighboring shack to be cooked. You want a quick sauté? A blackened frying pan comes out, in goes some oil, some garlic and shallots. Meanwhile, some urchin has peeled the prawns (shrimp) and rubbed them with salt, turmeric and ground red chilies. These get thrown into the pan. A few good tosses and the contents of the pan are emptied into a saucer. A tiny spoon is stuck in. Go sit on a rock by the water and enjoy.

You want your fish fried? A more prosperous shack has a sign FAST FOOD . . . FISH FRIED BY ORDER. You could take your snapper there, if you wish. Meanwhile, in homes all across the state, squid rings are being dropped into a gingery coconut sauce, sardines are being poached with shallots, ginger and green chilies, whole pomfret are being stuffed with a paste of coconut, green chili and fresh green cilantro and then baked, crabs are being stir-fried with curry leaves and mustard seeds, and oysters are being made into fritters.

Fish are caught everywhere. Little boys begin catching them just outside their homes with crude fishing rods. Some of these youngsters will graduate to run prawn (shrimp) farms one day. The demand for more and more prawns (shrimp) by Japan as well as the West has encouraged some of the most imaginative farming. During the monsoon season, when there is plenty of fresh water falling from the heavens, precious fields are used to grow rice. Once winter comes and the only water available is from the brackish inland waterways, the fields are flooded with it nonetheless and used to farm prawns (shrimp)!

Some of these same little boys will grow up to manipulate the Chinese fishing nets that dot much of the coastline. Looking like monstrous, primeval, moving sculptures, the nets consist mainly of five solid teak poles that arch upwards to a height of at least 100 feet (30 meters). These hold and move the net. As the contraptions are lowered and raised with ropes, these lumbering giant spiders, dating from the time of Kublai Khan, scoop up all the fish that are finning by. The nets are considered so valuable that brides' families even offer them as dowries.

Some of the children might end up owning the trawlers that drag the floor of the Arabian Sea, bringing in everything from kingfish to mackerels. Some might even grow up to be *karimeen* fishermen.

The *karimeen* fishermen are unique. They work in groups of four to catch one of the most prized of fish. Flat, with black and gold stripes over a white-spotted body, the *karimeen* likes only fresh water. Vembanad Lake, a dammed lagoon, is a favored habitat.

Two of the fishermen, their skins burnished to a glowing black, tie a rope to their skimpy loincloths and dive in from their boat. The rope, with bunting-like strips of white plastic attached to it, will be pulled along the water in a wide U-shape. Its purpose is to disturb and scare the fish. The *karimeen* will look for cover in the silty bottom. A third fisherman, with steady eyes and steady hands, will dive in, find the *karimeen* in the silt, grab it with a bare hand, swim up with it and, taking careful aim, toss it into the boat.

The fishermen will do this for 5–6 hours, by which time sun and water will have taken their toll. All the black canoes that dot the lake will head to a port where the fish will be auctioned off.

Munambam Harbor, opposite Cranganore where St Thomas is supposed to have landed in AD 52 and where a wide backwater empties into the Arabian Sea, is one such port. Boats of all sizes that left home in the middle of the night begin to return in the afternoon. By the time the sun is low, casting a golden sheen on the water, the boats are five or six deep all along the harbor. As soon as the first catch hits land, the auction begins.

An auctioneer moves to the fish and yells the opening bid. Buyers yell out the price they are willing to pay. Though the need to shout seems unnecessary, the decibel level of the entire transaction, by tradition, remains high, maintaining the quality of a rough, country quarrel. The

A fish market at Trirandrum, Kerala.

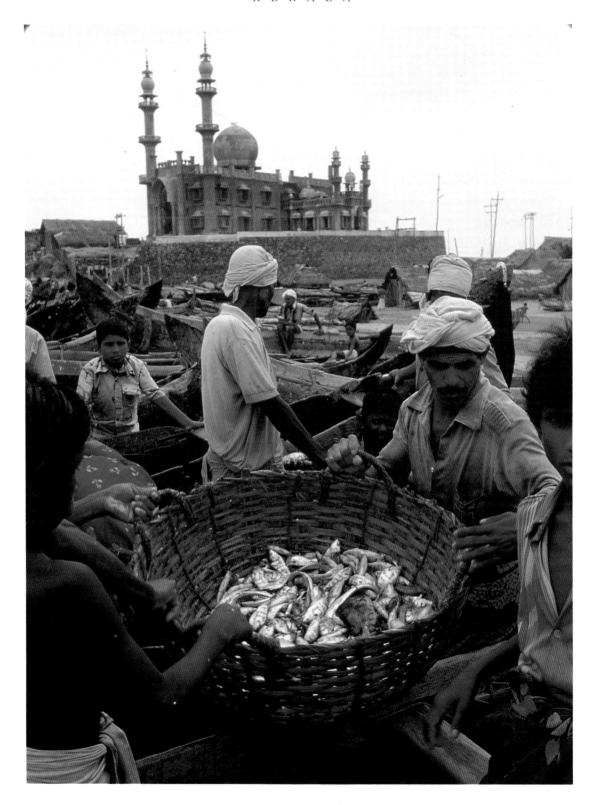

winner walks off with the baskets of gleaming prawns (shrimp) or squid or red snapper. Some of the fish, which have been earmarked for foreign markets, will go immediately for processing.

The prawns (shrimp) may end up in the prawn (shrimp) "factory" in Chavadi where truckloads seem to arrive every hour. There is no mechanization of any sort and 160 women work in long rows, squatting on flat boards that barely keep them off the wet floor. Tables were tried to enable the women to stand. The experiment failed. The women found standing uncomfortable. They preferred to squat.

Each of the mostly unmarried women, in sarong-like *pawadas* and with hair sleek with coconut oil, has seven or eight gleaming, stainless steel bowls on the floor in front of her. In their hands, the women wield sharp, single-edged blades. Their job, tedious as it may be, is to peel the prawns (shrimp) and sort them into sizes. They work with jet speed, some doing a prawn (shrimp) per second. Since they will be paid by each pre-weighed bowlful, speed means money. Skins go flying into one bowl, the peeled prawn (shrimp) into the others. As soon as a bowl – any bowl – is filled, it is taken away by one of the few males on the premises. From here the prawns (shrimp) will be taken to another factory for freezing and shipment to destinations as far away as Japan and the United States.

Most of the fish will be eaten right here in Kerala. E. X. Anthony is an attendant at the sixteenth-century St Francis' Church in Cochin where Vasco da Gama was once buried and where long matting, hand-pulled fans still run along the length of the building. Shielding himself from the heat outside, he sits on a bench in a cool corridor, his tiffin-carrier open in front of him. He is having lunch. With his white, parboiled rice, there is "*meen* (fish) curry." Did he make it himself? "Oh, yes," he says, shaking his head happily. "I ground up some coconut, red chilies, cinnamon, turmeric, cilantro, garlic and shallots. Then I added some water and cooked this sauce for 30 minutes. Then I slipped in some small fish and cooked them for a few minutes. Finally I heated some oil, put into it some mustard seeds, sliced shallots and green chilies and threw the oil and spices into the pot with the fish."

Damodaran is a boatman with even less ready cash then E. X. Anthony. He can afford no oil at all. Yet his boatman's curry (for which I have been searching, having heard of it from an old Keralite friend) is exquisite. A boat is more precious than a life to Damodaran and his family. He will accept the death of a family member more readily than the loss of his boat which provides food for them all and will do so for generations – especially *his* boat. Damodaran is the proud owner of a rice boat. These strong, sturdy vehicles, solid wood with a curving roof of waterproof matting, used for transporting rice and other goods, now cost upwards of $30,000, a fortune in Kerala. Expensive hotels display them as pretty curiosities.

I am invited inside the rice boat – a working boat – for a meal, which Damodaran prepares himself, as he does every single day of his life. I take off my shoes and climb in. The patina of the thick, dark teak wood which can take much buffeting by wind and water, would be the envy of any antique dealer. It glows with use. A plank is removed near the prow. Lo and behold, a kitchen appears. At least a stove does. On either side, neatly tucked into the hollows of bamboos so that they disappear, literally, in the woodwork, are all the spices as well as the shallots and ginger needed for cooking.

Damodaran produces a grinding-stone and grinds with swift efficiency, adding sprinklings of water as he does so. Coconut, cilantro, chilies, turmeric are all turned into a ball of paste. This goes into an earthen pot with some water and boils away. Now in go some lightly crushed shallots, some crushed ginger, green chilies, *kodampoli* (the sour tamarind), curry leaves and salt. Lastly, *karimeen* pieces are slipped in and allowed to poach. This is eaten with the local, red par-boiled rice. I cannot say if it was the boat itself or the absolute freshness of the fish or Damodaran's cooking or the watery scene replete with swaying palms on the banks and the boat slowly cutting its way through a thick carpeting of pinkish-purple water

hyacinths, but fish has rarely tasted as good.

The swaying palms on the banks give every home the coconuts it needs in its daily cooking. Except in very big cities, of which Kerala does not have too many, coconuts rarely need to be bought. Vegetarian Brahmins may use them to make *olan*, in which small cubes of vegetables (ripe cucumber, gourds, pumpkins) are poached and then mixed with par-boiled split peas and coconut milk, or to create a whole world of fudges, *halvas* and puddings. Coconut oil is the chief cooking medium and any talk of it being a saturated oil only brings derisive laughs at ever-changing Western fads, with hands pointing to healthy grandmothers and grandfathers who have eaten it all their lives.

Snacks are fried in it. A trip to Willingdon Island in Cochin takes me to a small shop, MALABAR CHIPS. Some of the finest chips, crisps really, are made here. Not potato chips but banana chips, jackfruit chips and tapioca chips. Suresh, a young man with film star looks, slices three green plantains at a time on a mean-looking mandolin. These will be fried in an enormous wok of coconut oil, cooled and then bagged in plastic to be munched on boat rides, in cinemas and while watching athletic Kathakali performers as they leap and grimace, telling the stories of Hindu religious epics in long evenings of song and dance.

Today, the state of Kerala exports frogs' legs to France, squid to Japan, prawns (shrimp) to the United States and labor to the Gulf. But none of these have made the kind of mark in world commerce, politics or history that its spices have.

This is the natural home of black pepper, which many call the "king of spices" and of cardamom, a fairly logical "queen." The teeming moist soil and the generous sun also encourage rhizomes like ginger and turmeric to spread their fingers, allowing the Western world to indulge in gingerbreads and ginger cakes and, using curcumin (the coloring matter) from high quality turmeric, to give millions of chickens in the United States and hundreds of pounds of cheeses in the United Kingdom a decidedly yellow hue.

It was the quest for these spices that brought the ships of the earliest Phoenicians, of King Solomon, of early Syrians, Egyptians, Greeks, Romans, Arabs and Chinese to the shores of India. Their interest was trade. They came and went easily. It was only in the late fifteenth century, after Pope Alexander VI had divided the "undiscovered" world between Spain and Portugal, that bloody wars began with the Portuguese, Dutch, French and British all fighting for a slice of this rich, spice-bearing coast. The British won

and set up a factory and spice depot in 1683 in Tellicherry, a name still associated with good quality Malabar pepper, each berry of which is justly renowned for its aroma, weight and size.

Today, an independent India produces about a third of the world's pepper with much of it coming from Kerala. Most families with small kitchen gardens let the vines clamber casually up their pillars and porches, even up their garden trees, but those who grow it professionally – and many conglomerates are in the business now – make the vines climb up specially spiky tree trunks so that they get a good grip and bear fruitfully. All the harvesting is done by hand. Once the green peppercorns are dried, they turn black. They are then graded and are ready for the auctions at the Pepper Exchange in Cochin and for the Futures market. They are also ready for all the *steak au poivres* we wish to eat and ready to fill pepper-grinders in millions of homes across the world. For the people of Kerala, the green ones may be pickled but what about the black peppercorns? How about roasting them and grinding them to flavor a *meen pappas*, fish poached in a sweet, sour, creamy coconut sauce?

Selvaraj's Stew

LAMB STEW

CHRISTIAN KERALITES EAT THIS at Easter and Christmas and all other festive occasions. It is particularly welcome at Easter after the Lenten Fast. It is almost always eaten with Savory Rice Breads (page 39), though plain rice would also be very good. It is a stew. To all intents and purposes it looks like Irish stew, but the sauce is enriched with coconut milk and there are cardamom pods and cinnamon for aroma and green chilies for heat.

❧

4 tablespoons vegetable oil
3 cardamom pods
1 (1 inch) (2.5 cm) cinnamon stick
3–4 cloves
About 30 fresh curry leaves (optional)
1 (1 inch) (2.5 cm) piece fresh ginger root, shredded

1 medium-large red onion, finely sliced
1 lb (450 g) boneless lamb from the shoulder, cut into 1 inch (2.5 cm) pieces, with the fat removed
2 medium-sized potatoes, cut into (1 inch) (2.5 cm) dice

2 carrots, peeled and cut into 1 inch (2.5 cm) chunks
1¼–1½ teaspoons salt or to taste
2 fresh hot green chilies
1¼ cups coconut milk from a well-stirred can or thick fresh milk (page 266)

❧

Heat the oil in a large, wide, preferably non-stick pan or wok over medium-high heat. When hot, put in the cardamom pods, cinnamon and cloves and half the curry leaves, if using. Stir once or twice. Add the ginger root and onion. Stir and fry for 4–5 minutes until the onion is soft.

Turn the heat up to high. Add the meat. Stir and fry for 8–10 minutes until the meat is just beginning to brown. Add the potatoes, carrots, salt and 5 cups water. Cover and bring to the boil.

Turn the heat to low and simmer for 1 hour.

Add the chilies and remaining curry leaves, if using. Gently simmer over medium-low heat for 10–15 minutes or until the meat is very tender and the sauce has the consistency of a puréed soup. (I sometimes need to mash 1 or 2 potato pieces against the side of the pan to achieve this.)

Just before serving, add the coconut milk, stir, and bring to a simmer.

SERVES 4

Mr A. R. Sunil's Erachi Olathu
"DRY" LAMB ENCRUSTED WITH SPICES

OF ALL THE MEAT dishes in Kerala, this remains one of my favorites. It may be that I developed a weakness for it because I first had it in the home of a close Syrian Christian friend, with a stack of *appams* as an accompaniment. The meat is first stewed with a mixture of fennel – which makes the dish unusually good – and spices. It is then stirred until all the sauce has dried up and the spices cling to it in a most delicious way.

The coconut chips are optional – they may be added for an extra Kerala taste, but you may leave them out if you cannot get fresh coconut.

FOR THE SPICE POWDER:
1 tablespoon vegetable oil
1 (1 inch) (2.5 cm) cinnamon stick
10–15 cloves
3 tablespoons coriander seeds
4–6 dried hot red chilies
1 tablespoon black peppercorns
½ teaspoon cumin seeds
1½ teaspoons fennel seeds
6 cardamom pods

YOU ALSO NEED:
5 tablespoons vegetable oil
1 cup plus 1½ tablespoons fresh coconut (page 265), first cut into thin slices and then into ½ inch (1 cm) chips
¼ teaspoon ground turmeric
1 teaspoon salt
2 teaspoons brown mustard seeds
40 fresh curry leaves (optional)

10–12 shallots, finely sliced
1 (1 inch) (2.5 cm) piece of fresh ginger root, peeled and finely sliced
3 garlic cloves, peeled and finely chopped
2¼ lb (1 kg) boneless lamb from the shoulder, cut into 1 inch (2.5 cm) dice
2 tablespoons white wine vinegar

To make the spice powder: heat the 1 tablespoon oil in a large frying pan or wok. When hot, put in all the spices. Stir until the chilies darken. Put the spices into a clean coffee grinder and grind to a fine powder. Set aside.

Heat 1 tablespoon of the remaining oil in a large frying pan or wok over medium heat. When hot, add the coconut chips, turmeric and ½ teaspoon of the salt. Stir and fry for 3–4 minutes or until the coconut is toasted. Set aside.

In a clean, large frying pan heat 3 tablespoons of the oil over medium-high heat. When hot, add 1 teaspoon of the mustard seeds. Stir until the seeds pop, a matter of a few seconds. Now add about 20 of the curry leaves, if using, 6–8 of the shallots, the ginger root and garlic. Stir and fry for 3–4 minutes until the shallots become lightly browned. Add the meat and the spice powder. Stir to coat the meat well, then add the vinegar, toasted coconut chips, ½ teaspoon of the salt and 3 cups water. Bring to the boil, then turn the heat down and cover. Simmer for about 50 minutes to 1 hour or until the meat is almost tender. Remove the lid and continue to cook for another 10–15 minutes until the sauce becomes very thick and clings to the meat, increasing the heat if necessary.

Meanwhile, heat the remaining 1 tablespoon oil in a small pan over medium heat. When hot, add the remaining mustard seeds. When the mustard seeds pop, add the remaining shallots and about 20 curry leaves, if using. Stir and fry until the shallots become golden-brown. Add the contents of pan to the meat. Mix well and remove from the heat.

S E R V E S   4

Overleaf: Lamb Stew (page 19) with Savory Rice Breads (page 39).

Mr A. R. Sunil's Taharava Kootan
DUCK CURRY, COUNTRY STYLE

DUCKS CAN BE SEEN in every paddy field and backwater. It is not surprising that they make their way into curries and roasts. Serve with plain rice.

FOR THE SPICE POWDER:

1½ tablespoons ground coriander

2 teaspoons cayenne pepper

¼ teaspoon ground turmeric

¼ teaspoon freshly ground black pepper

1 (2 inch) (5 cm) cinnamon stick

6 cloves

4 cardamom pods

YOU ALSO NEED:

4 tablespoons vegetable oil

1 small red onion, finely sliced

1 (1 inch) (2.5 cm) piece fresh ginger root, peeled and cut into long, thin slices

18 garlic cloves, peeled and finely chopped

6 fresh hot green chilies, split at one end

1 (2¼ lb) (1 kg) duck, skinned and cut into 2 inch (5 cm) cubes

1½ tablespoons white wine vinegar

1½–1¾ teaspoons salt

1¼ cups coconut milk, well stirred from a can or thick fresh milk (page 266)

1 large potato, cut into 2 inch (5 cm) pieces

1 teaspoon *ghee* (page 271)

1 teaspoon brown mustard seeds

3–4 shallots, finely sliced

About 30 fresh curry leaves (optional)

Put the coriander, cayenne, turmeric, black pepper, cinnamon, cloves and cardamom pods for the spice powder into a clean coffee grinder. Grind to a fine powder. Set aside.

Heat 3 tablespoons of the oil in a large, wide pan or wok over medium heat. When hot, put in the onion. Stir and fry the onion for 3–4 minutes or until soft. Add the ginger root, garlic and chilies. Stir and fry for another 2–3 minutes. Add the duck, spice powder, vinegar and salt. Stir once then add ½ cup of the coconut milk and 1¼ cups water. Bring to the boil. Cover, turn the heat to low and simmer

gently for 1½ hours or until the duck is almost tender. Add the potatoes and cook for 20 minutes. Add the remaining coconut milk. Stir and gently simmer for 5–6 minutes.

Meanwhile heat the remaining oil and the *ghee* in a small pan over medium-high heat. When hot, add the mustard seeds. As soon as they pop, a matter of seconds, put in the shallots and the curry leaves, if using. Stir and cook for a few minutes. When the shallots have browned slightly, empty the contents of the pan into the pan with the duck. Stir to mix.

SERVES   4 – 6

Mr Balasundaram's Nadan Kori Kootan

COUNTRY CHICKEN CURRY

THIS COUNTRY-STYLE DISH may be made with all manner of wild fowl or with ordinary chicken. It is best served with plain rice and any vegetables and salads of your choice.

If you wish to substitute unsweetened, dried coconut for fresh coconut use 1 scant cup. Barely cover with warm water and leave for 1 hour, then proceed with the recipe.

FOR THE GINGER AND GARLIC PASTE:

1 (½ inch) (1 cm) piece fresh ginger root, peeled and coarsely chopped

6 garlic cloves, peeled and roughly chopped

FOR THE SPICE POWDER:

12 dried hot red chilies

1 tablespoon cumin seeds

1 tablespoon black peppercorns

3 cloves

1 (1 inch) (2.5 cm) cinnamon stick

2 cardamom pods

½ teaspoon salt

1¼ cups freshly grated coconut (page 265)

YOU ALSO NEED:

5 tablespoons vegetable oil

1 medium-large red onion, finely sliced

½ teaspoon ground turmeric

1¼ teaspoons salt

1½ lb (750 g) chicken, skinned and cut into 2 inch (5 cm) pieces

3 medium-sized tomatoes, finely diced

6–7 shallots, peeled and finely sliced

Put the ginger and garlic for the paste into the container of an electric blender. Add 3 tablespoons water. Blend to a smooth paste. Remove from the blender and set aside.

Put the chilies, cumin seeds, peppercorns, cloves, cinnamon, cardamom pods and salt for the spice powder into a clean coffee grinder. Grind to a fine powder. Put the spice powder into the blender. Add ½ cup water and the coconut. Blend to a smooth paste. Set aside.

Heat 4 tablespoons of the oil in a wok or large, wide, preferably non-stick pan over medium heat. When hot, add the onion. Stir and fry for 4–5 minutes until golden. Add the garlic and ginger paste. Stir once, and then add the turmeric and salt. Stir once or twice and add the chicken. Stir and fry for 10–15 minutes over medium heat until the chicken is lightly browned.

Add the tomatoes to the chicken. Stir and cook for 2 minutes. Add the spice paste and fry again for 3 minutes. Now add 2½ cups water, turn the heat down and continue to simmer gently for about 10–15 minutes or until the sauce becomes thick and the chicken is tender.

Meanwhile, heat the remaining oil in a small frying pan over medium heat. When hot, add the shallots. Stir and fry for 3–4 minutes until brown and crisp. Remove with a slotted spoon, spread on paper towels and set aside. When the chicken is cooked, sprinkle with the fried shallots and stir them in.

SERVES 4

Mr A. R. Sunil's Fish Moilly
FISH STEW

THIS SIMPLE AND DELICIOUS dish may be made with cod steaks or chunky pieces of halibut or haddock fillets. In Kerala, this sauced dish is always served with rice but you may serve it with boiled potatoes and a salad.

About 1¼ teaspoons salt
½ teaspoon ground turmeric
1 lb (450 g) fish steaks or
  fillets, cut into 2 inch
  (5 cm) cubes (see above)
4 tablespoons coconut oil
  or any other vegetable oil

1 medium-large red onion,
  finely sliced
6 fresh hot green chilies,
  finely sliced
1 (1 inch) (2.5 cm) piece
  fresh ginger root, peeled
  and finely shredded

About 30 fresh curry leaves
  (optional)
1 cup coconut milk, well
  stirred from a can or thick
  fresh milk (page 266)
2 tablespoons lime juice

Mix ¼ teaspoon of the salt and ¼ teaspoon of the turmeric together. Rub over the fish. Set aside.

Heat the oil in a large, wide, preferably non-stick pan or wok over medium heat. When hot, add the onion, chilies and ginger root. Stir once or twice. Add the curry leaves, if using. Stir and fry for 3–4 minutes until the onion is soft. Add ¼ teaspoon turmeric powder and ¾ cup water. Mix well. When the mixture boils, add the fish. Spoon the sauce over the fish. Add

¾ teaspoon salt. Turn the heat down. Cover and simmer for 4–5 minutes, spooning the sauce over the fish and shaking the pan gently to prevent sticking. Add the coconut milk. Shake the pan and check the salt, adding a little more if needed. Cover and simmer for a further 3–4 minutes, shaking the pan now and then. Add the lime juice. Shake the pan gently and remove from the heat.

SERVES 4

Shoba Ramji's Meen Pollichathu

FISH BAKED IN FOIL

WHOLE FISH ARE GENERALLY "baked" in a wok lined with a banana leaf. Since we in the West seldom have access to a banana leaf, I have wrapped the fish in foil and baked it in an oven. You may use whole fish such as turbot, red snapper – as I have done here – or, for greater convenience, steaks from swordfish, salmon or cod. The timing will, of course, vary depending on the size and thickness of the fish.

If you use more than one fish, or pieces of fish, it would be a good idea to wrap them separately before putting them in the oven. Although this dish is normally served with rice, you may eat it with boiled potatoes and sautéed vegetables.

FOR THE SPICE PASTE:
2 teaspoons coconut oil or any other vegetable oil
4–6 shallots, peeled and roughly chopped
4 garlic cloves, peeled and roughly chopped
1 (½ inch) (1 cm) piece of fresh ginger root, peeled and finely sliced
15–20 fresh curry leaves (optional)

4 teaspoons cayenne pepper
½ teaspoon salt
1 tablespoon vinegar
1 teaspoon black peppercorns

YOU ALSO NEED:
3 tablespoons coconut oil or any other vegetable oil, plus extra for greasing
1 medium-large red onion, finely chopped

4–6 fresh hot green chilies
1 medium-sized tomato, finely diced
1 tablespoon sesame seeds
½ teaspoon salt
2 (1½ lb) (750 g) red snapper fish, cleaned and gutted
2 tablespoons coarsely chopped cilantro

Pre-heat the oven to 400°F (200°C).

Heat the 2 teaspoons oil for the spice paste in a small pan over medium-low heat. When hot, add the shallots, garlic, ginger root and the curry leaves, if using. Stir and fry for 2–3 minutes until the shallots begin to soften. Add the cayenne pepper and salt. Stir once or twice. Put in the container of an electric blender with

the vinegar and 2 tablespoons water. Blend.

Put the peppercorns in a small, heated pan. Stir and roast over medium-high heat for 2 minutes. Crush in a mortar and add to the

Duck Curry, Country Style (page 23) with Vegetable Rice (page 38).

shallot mixture. Put to one side. This is the spice paste.

Heat the 3 tablespoons oil in a wide pan or wok over medium-high heat. When hot, add the onion. Fry for 3–4 minutes until soft. Add the chilies. Fry for 3–4 minutes until they begin to soften. Add the tomato, sesame seeds and salt. Stir and fry for 4–5 minutes until the tomato is soft. Put to one side.

Make 3–4 shallow, slightly diagonal slits on either side of each of the fish. This will allow the flavor to infuse. Smear the fish with the spice paste.

Grease 2 pieces of foil, each roughly 12 × 12 inches (30 × 30 cm) in size and big enough to wrap a whole fish in. Sprinkle the center of the foil, where the fish is to sit, with the cilantro. Divide half of the fried onion mixture between the pieces of foil, sprinkling it over the cilantro. Place the fish on top. Put the remaining onion mixture over the fish. Wrap the fish lightly in the foil. Bake in the oven for 20–25 minutes until just cooked through. Uncover gently. Lift the fish out with a long fish spatula and place on a serving dish. Pour the extra juices over them and serve.

If you are at all worried about breaking the fish, you can loosen their undersides with a spatula and slide them onto a serving plate or else serve them directly from the foil.

SERVES 4

Shoba Ramji's Meen Patichatu
MARINATED AND STEWED SARDINES

SARDINES ARE A COMMON fish here, loved by people of all means. As one travels along the backwaters, it is not uncommon to see villagers on the banks cooking sardines in fiery red sauces.

In this particular recipe the sardines are smeared with a coconut paste and left to simmer with curry leaves. They are best served with plain rice.

Sardines that are used here range from 5 inches (13 cm) to 8 inches (20 cm) in length. They are generally cooked whole, but if they are the larger size they are frequently cut in half first. You may, if you prefer, use swordfish or halibut steaks, remembering to cook them in a single layer.

If you wish to substitute unsweetened, dried coconut for fresh coconut use 5 tablespoons. Barely cover with warm water for 1 hour. Squeeze dry then proceed with the recipe.

FOR THE SPICE PASTE:

7 fresh hot green chilies,
roughly chopped

1 (½ inch) (1 cm) piece
fresh ginger root, peeled
and roughly chopped

1 small red onion, roughly
chopped

3 garlic cloves

½ cup freshly grated
coconut (page 265)

5–10 fresh curry leaves
(optional)

1 teaspoon salt

YOU ALSO NEED:

4 fresh, whole sardines,
about 12 oz (325 g) each,
cleaned and gutted
(net weight about
9 oz (250 g) each)

3 tablespoons vegetable oil

4–5 dried hot red chilies

20 fresh curry leaves,
(optional)

2½ tablespoons tamarind
paste (page 278), diluted
with 2 tablespoons water

Place all the ingredients for the spice paste in the container of an electric blender. Add ½ cup water and blend until smooth. You may need to push the paste down with a spatula from time to time.

Take the sardines and smear each of them well with the spice paste. Set aside.

Heat the oil over medium-high heat in a pan, preferably non-stick, that is large and wide enough to cook all the sardines at once in a single layer. When hot, add the red chilies and the curry leaves, if using. Stir once then lay the sardines in the pan. Cook for 2–3 minutes on either side over low heat. Shake the pan gently now and then, spooning the sauce over the sardines. Add the tamarind paste. Shake the pan to mix. Cover and cook for another 15–20 minutes, shaking the pan occasionally.

The sauce should be quite thick and should coat the sardines.

SERVES 4

Mr Damodaran's Vallamkarnanda Meen Kootan

BOATMAN'S CURRY

THIS RECIPE WAS TAKEN from boatmen plying the inland waterways near Kumarakom. They make their living fishing and carrying goods – such as rice – and people. This is a dish they cook on their rice boats for themselves and any passengers. The fish used here was the very popular flat, freshwater *karimeen* (page 14) but steaks from any firm-fleshed fish such as cod, swordfish or salmon may be used. The *karimeen* are cleaned and then cut, crossways, into 2 or 3 pieces, head and all. Steaks will need to be cubed.

This is one of the few times that I have reduced the amount of chilies. The boatman's curry was utterly delicious but incendiary! It may be worth noting that no oil is used in the cooking.

If you wish to substitute unsweetened, dried coconut for fresh coconut use 1 scant cup. Barely cover with warm water and leave for 1 hour, then proceed with the recipe.

❧

FOR THE SPICE PASTE:
4–6 dried hot red chilies, soaked in hot water for 15 minutes
1 teaspoon cayenne pepper
1 tablespoon paprika
3 tablespoons ground coriander
1 teaspoon ground turmeric
1¼ cups freshly grated coconut (page 265)

YOU ALSO NEED:
2½ tablespoons tamarind paste (page 278)
3–4 fresh hot green chilies, split into halves
1 (1 inch piece) (2.5 cm) fresh ginger root, peeled and lightly crushed
4–5 shallots, peeled and lightly crushed
1½ teaspoons salt
1½ lb (750 g) fish steaks, about ½ inch (1 cm) thick

❧

Put all the ingredients for the spice paste into the container of an electric blender. Add ½ cup water. Blend to make a smooth paste.

Put the spice paste into a medium-sized, heavy-bottomed pan. Add ½ cup water. Stir. The paste should have a similar consistency to that of a puréed soup.

Heat the spice paste over medium-low heat. Bring to a gentle simmer. Add the tamarind paste, green chilies, ginger root, shallots and salt. Stir and simmer for 2–3 minutes. Slip in the fish. Stir once and cover. Simmer gently for 10–15 minutes until the fish is just cooked.

SERVES 4

Mr A. R. Sunil's Kannava Varitiyathu
SQUID WITH COCONUT

SQUID AND CUTTLEFISH OF every conceivable size are common to these shores and are eaten all along the coastline, although not further inland for some reason. Today, a lot of the squid is exported to Japan for a very good price. Here is one of the many ways in which it can be cooked. Serve it with plain rice.

This dish is quite hot but deliciously so. If you wish to lessen the heat, just cut down on the cayenne pepper. If you wish to substitute unsweetened, dried coconut for fresh coconut use ⅓ cup. Barely cover with warm water and leave for 1 hour, then proceed with the recipe.

❧

½ cup freshly grated coconut (page 265)
5 tablespoons coconut oil or any other vegetable oil
1 medium-large red onion, finely chopped

1 (½ inch) (1 cm) piece fresh ginger root, peeled and finely chopped
About 40 fresh curry leaves (optional)
1 teaspoon ground turmeric
1 tablespoon cayenne pepper

1 tablespoon ground coriander
1 lb (450 g) cleaned squid (page 285), sliced into ½ inch (1 cm) wide rings
1 teaspoon salt
2 shallots, peeled and finely chopped

❧

Put the grated coconut into the container of an electric blender. Add ½ cup water and blend to a smooth paste. Set aside.

Heat 4 tablespoons of the oil in a large, wide, preferably non-stick pan or wok over medium-high heat. When hot, add the onion, ginger root and about 20 curry leaves, if using. Stir and fry for 3–4 minutes until the onion is soft. Add the cayenne pepper, turmeric and coriander. Stir and fry for 2–3 minutes. Add the squid and salt. Stir and fry for another 2–3 minutes.

Now add the coconut paste. Turn the heat up and stir and fry for 5–7 minutes or until the squid is just cooked.

Heat the remaining oil in a small pan over medium heat. When hot, add the shallots and remaining curry leaves, if using. Stir and fry until the shallots are golden.

Add the shallot and curry leaf mixture to the squid. Mix well and cook for another 2 minutes. The sauce should coat the squid. Remove from the heat and serve.

SERVES 4 – 6

Mr Balasundaram's Avial
Ⓥ MIXED VEGETABLES WITH COCONUT

SOUTH INDIA HAS DOZENS of dishes in which lightly boiled or steamed vegetables are "dressed" with a sauce made out of freshly grated coconut. Each sauce is different from the next. This one has yogurt and cumin in it.

There is a story about the creation of *avial*. A sixteenth-century king ordered his kitchen to provide a feast for his subjects that would last 30 days. For 29 days the food stocks held up. On the 30th day, the chef realized that all the oil – except for a few drops – had gone and that only bits and pieces of different vegetables were left in the larder. This is the dish that he came up with.

If you wish to substitute unsweetened, dried coconut for the fresh coconut use 1¼ cups. Barely cover with warm water and leave for 1 hour, then proceed with the recipe.

∾

4 oz (100 g) okra, cut into 1 inch (2.5 cm) pieces
1 medium-sized carrot, cut into 1 × ¼ inch (2.5 cm × 5 mm) pieces
1 medium-sized potato, peeled and cut into 1 × ¼ inch (2.5 cm × 5 mm) pieces

4 oz (100 g) green beans, cut into 1 inch (2.5 cm) pieces
4 oz (100 g) green, cooking plantains or very green bananas, peeled with a knife and cut into ½ inch (1 cm) thick rounds
1¾ cups freshly grated coconut (page 265)

5–6 fresh hot green chilies, coarsely sliced
1 teaspoon ground cumin
⅔ cup natural plain yogurt
1½ teaspoons salt
40–50 fresh curry leaves (optional)
1 teaspoon coconut oil (optional)

∾

Put the okra, carrot, potato, green beans and plantains in a large pan. Cover with 1¼ cups water. Bring to the boil over high heat. Turn the heat to medium and simmer for 10–12 minutes until the vegetables are tender. Drain and put to one side.

Meanwhile, put the coconut, chilies, cumin and ½ cup water in an electric blender. Blend to a smooth paste.

In a large, wide pan or wok, very gently mix the vegetables, coconut paste, yogurt, salt and the curry leaves, if using. Set over low heat. Remove the pan from the heat before the *avial* comes to the boil.

Add the coconut oil if you wish and stir gently to mix.

SERVES 4

Shoba Ramji's Thenkapal Varadhiniya
ⓥ EGGPLANTS IN COCONUT MILK

THESE EGGPLANTS ARE perfect with rice and breads.

❧

FOR THE SPICE PASTE:
½ teaspoon ground coriander
1 teaspoon black peppercorns
¼ teaspoon cumin seeds
¼ teaspoon ground turmeric
¼ teaspoon fennel seeds
1 (1 inch) (2.5 cm) cinnamon stick
2 cloves

YOU ALSO NEED:
1 medium-sized eggplant, cut into 1 inch (2.5 cm) pieces
½ teaspoon ground turmeric
½ teaspoon cayenne pepper
¾–1 teaspoon salt
6 tablespoons vegetable oil
1 small red onion, peeled and finely sliced
1 (1 inch) (2.5 cm) piece fresh ginger root, peeled and finely chopped
1 garlic clove, peeled and crushed

8–10 fresh curry leaves (optional)
2–3 fresh hot green chilies, finely sliced
1 tablespoon white wine vinegar
½ cup coconut milk, well stirred from a can or thick fresh milk (page 266)
Extra fresh hot green chilies, slit down the middle, to garnish (optional)

❧

Grind the ingredients for the spice paste in a clean coffee grinder. Empty into a small bowl. Add 2 tablespoons water. Mix to a fine paste. Set aside.

Put the eggplant in a medium-sized bowl with the turmeric, cayenne pepper and ¼ teaspoon of the salt. Mix well.

Heat 3 tablespoons of the oil in a large, wide, preferably non-stick pan over medium heat. When hot, add the eggplant. Stir and fry for 6–8 minutes until tender and golden. Remove with a slotted spoon and lay on paper towel to remove excess oil.

Heat the remaining oil in a clean pan. Add the onion. Stir and fry over medium heat for 3–4 minutes until soft. Turn the heat to low. Add the ginger root, garlic, curry leaves, if using, and chilies. Stir for 30 seconds. Add the vinegar and salt to taste. Stir once. Add the spice paste. Stir and fry for 2–3 minutes. Add the coconut milk and ⅔ cup water. Stir and fry gently for 3–4 minutes. Add the eggplant. Stir and cook for 2–3 minutes.

The eggplant will absorb some sauce. The remainder will thicken to coat the back of a spoon. Garnish with the slit chilies, if using.

SERVES 4

Mrs Bavani's Olan

ⓥ CUCUMBER COOKED WITH LENTILS

A SIMPLE DISH OF the vegetarian Nair community. It is as nutritious as it is good. It is generally eaten with plain rice and a selection of other vegetables, beans, pickles, chutneys and yogurt dishes.

❧

⅓ cup red lentils
1¼ cups coconut milk, well stirred, from a can or thick fresh milk (page 266)

1 lb (450 g) cucumber, cut crosswise into 1 inch (2.5 cm) pieces
4 fresh hot green chilies, cut in half lengthwise

1 teaspoon salt
8–10 fresh curry leaves (optional)
1 tablespoon coconut oil or any other vegetable oil

❧

Wash the lentils in several changes of water, until the water runs clear. Then soak them in enough hot water to cover by 1½ inches (4 cm) for 3–4 hours. Drain.

Put ½ cup of the coconut milk and 1¾ cups water in a medium-sized pan. Add the lentils. Bring to the boil. Turn the heat down, cover and simmer for 10–15 minutes. Add the cucumber, chilies and salt. Cook over low heat for 3–5 minutes or until the cucumber is tender.

Meanwhile, heat the coconut oil in a small pan over medium-high heat. When hot, add the curry leaves, if using. Stir once or twice and then empty the contents of the small pan, oil and leaves, into the pan with the lentils and cucumber. Add the remaining coconut milk to the cucumber and lentil mixture. Stir and cook on a higher heat for 3–4 minutes until the sauce is medium-thick.

SERVES 4

Marinated and Stewed Sardines (page 28).

Mrs Bhavani's Manga Kalan
Ⓥ MANGO CURRY

MANGO CURRIES ARE A Kerala treat. This one may be served with all Indian meals. I serve it in individual bowls, to be eaten with a spoon.

If you wish to use unsweetened, dried coconut instead of fresh coconut use 1½ cups. Barely cover with warm water and leave for 1 hour, then proceed with the recipe.

❧

3 medium-sized ripe mangoes, peeled, pit removed and flesh cut into ½ inch (1 cm) pieces
1 teaspoon ground turmeric
1 teaspoon cayenne pepper
1–1½ teaspoons salt
⅓ cup brown sugar, if needed

2¾ cups freshly grated coconut (page 265)
3–4 fresh hot green chilies, coarsely chopped
½ tablespoon cumin seeds
1¼ cups plain yogurt, lightly beaten

2 tablespoons coconut oil or any other vegetable oil
¼ teaspoon brown mustard seeds
3–4 dried hot red chilies, broken into halves
¼ teaspoon fenugreek seeds
10–12 fresh curry leaves (optional)

❧

Put the mangoes in a medium-sized pan. Add 1 cup water. Cover and stew for 8–10 minutes over medium-low heat. Stir occasionally. Add the turmeric, cayenne pepper and salt. Stir well. (If the mangoes are not sweet enough, add the brown sugar to make the dish sweeter.)

Meanwhile, put the coconut, green chilies and cumin seeds into the container of an electric blender. Add 1 cup water and blend to a fine paste.

When the mangoes are cooked, mash them to a pulp. Add the coconut paste. Mix. Cover and simmer over medium heat, stirring occasionally, until the mixture becomes thick. This should take about 10–15 minutes. Add

the yogurt and heat, stirring, until just warmed through. Do not let the mixture come to the boil. Remove from the heat and put to one side. Check for salt.

Heat the oil in a small pan over medium-high heat. When hot, add the mustard seeds. When the mustard seeds begin to pop, a matter of a few seconds, add the chilies, fenugreek seeds and the curry leaves, if using. Stir and fry for a few seconds until the chilies darken. Quickly add the contents of the small pan to the mangoes. Stir to mix.

SERVES 4–6

Mrs K. M. Matthew's Spinach Thoran
Ⓥ SPINACH WITH COCONUT

THORANS ARE GENERALLY COOKED in woks. Vegetables, or prawns (shrimp) for that matter, are lightly sautéed or poached and then pushed to the edges of the wok. A mixture of fresh coconut and spices is placed in the center and covered over with the main ingredient. The wok is covered and the dish is allowed to cook gently. The results are light and delicious. Serve with any Indian meal. In this recipe rice is used as a spice, adding an unusual nutty flavor.

If you wish to substitute unsweetened, dried coconut for fresh coconut use ⅔ cup. Barely cover with warm water and leave for 1 hour, then proceed with the recipe.

❧

2 garlic cloves, peeled
1 small red onion or
    2–3 large shallots, peeled
    and chopped
¼ teaspoon cayenne pepper
1 cup plus 1 tablespoon
    freshly grated coconut
    (page 265)

1 teaspoon salt
1 lb (450 g) spinach,
    washed and shredded
1 fresh hot green chili,
    finely chopped, and
    1 fresh hot green chili,
    split in half
1 tablespoon coconut oil or
    any other vegetable oil

½ teaspoon brown mustard
    seeds
1 teaspoon rice
2 shallots, finely sliced
About 15 fresh curry leaves
    (optional)

❧

Put the garlic, onion, cayenne pepper, coconut and salt into the container of an electric blender. Add 6 tablespoons water and blend to a smooth paste. Set aside.

Put the spinach in a wok or large, wide, preferably non-stick frying pan over low heat. Sprinkle 3–4 tablespoons water over the top and cover. When steam begins to creep out at the sides and the spinach has wilted, remove the lid. Make a well in the pile of spinach and spoon in the coconut paste and chopped chili. Cover with the spinach and replace the lid.

Again wait until steam appears, then remove the lid.

Meanwhile, heat the oil in a small pan over medium-high heat. When hot, add the mustard seeds and rice. As soon as the mustard seeds begin to pop and the rice expands, a matter of seconds, add the shallots. Stir and fry until the shallots start to turn golden. Add the split chili and the curry leaves, if using. Stir and fry for a second. Pour over the cooked spinach. Stir to mix.

SERVES 4

Mr A. R. Sunil's Neyychoru
VEGETABLE RICE

A VEGETABLE PILAF ENRICHED with chicken stock, this may be served with all Indian meals.

~

2 cups basmati rice

1 (1 inch) (2.5 cm) mace blade

3 cardamom pods

3 cloves

1 (1 inch) (2.5 cm) cinnamon stick

1 teaspoon black peppercorns

2 fresh hot green chilies, coarsely chopped

3 garlic cloves, peeled and coarsely chopped

1 (½ inch) (1 cm) piece fresh ginger root, peeled and coarsely chopped

4 tablespoons *ghee* (page 271) or vegetable oil

1 bay leaf

1 carrot, cut in half lengthwise and finely sliced

1 medium-large red onion, finely sliced

2⅔ cups chicken stock

3 tablespoons coconut milk, well stirred from a can or thick fresh milk (page 266)

1 teaspoon salt

5 raw cashew nuts, split into halves

1 teaspoon golden raisins

~

Wash the rice in several changes of water, until the water runs clean. Drain. Cover with water. Soak for 30 minutes. Drain and set aside.

Put the mace, cardamom pods, cloves, cinnamon and peppercorns into a clean coffee grinder and grind to a fine powder. Set aside.

Put the chilies, garlic, ginger root and 3 tablespoons water into the container of an electric blender and blend to a fine paste. Set aside.

Heat 3 tablespoons of the *ghee* or oil in a large, wide, preferably non-stick pan over medium-high heat. When hot, add the bay leaf, carrot and half the onion. Stir and fry for 2–3 minutes. Add the chili-garlic-ginger root paste. Stir and fry for a minute. Add the drained rice and the ground spices. Stir gently

and fry for 1–2 minutes. Add the stock, coconut milk and salt. Stir and bring to the boil. Cover tightly, turn the heat to very low and cook 25 minutes or until the rice is tender and the stock absorbed.

Meanwhile, in a small pan heat the remaining *ghee* over medium-high heat. When hot, add the remaining onion. Stir and fry until the onion is brown and beginning to turn crisp. Add the cashew nuts. Stir and fry for a minute or until the cashews turn golden. Add the golden raisins. Stir once or twice. Remove from the heat. Spread over the rice when serving or else mix with it.

S E R V E S   4 – 5

From the home of Uma and Zac J. Zacharias: Appam
ⓥ SAVORY RICE BREADS

PANCAKE-LIKE BREADS MADE OUT of a fermented rice batter, *appams* are soft and spongy discs, perfect to eat with meats, fish dishes and at breakfast with butter and honey. They are very much a part of the traditional Syrian Christian Easter meal when the Lenten fast is broken with a meat stew (see Lamb Stew, page 19). They are made in a deep, wok-like vessel and are, as a result, fat and puffy in the center, where there is more batter, and flat, lacy and crispy brown at the edges, where there is less.

You may also cook *appams* in an ordinary, 8 inch (20 cm) non-stick frying pan. You will not get the traditional shape this way but you will get a flat, spongy pancake that will still taste wonderful. Once you pour the batter into the center of the frying pan, you will need to tilt it quickly in all directions in order to make the batter spread to about 8 inches (20 cm) in diameter. Then cover the pan and cook until the batter is set and the pancake has crisp, brownish edges.

If you wish you may use 2 cups milk, heated gently until lukewarm, instead of the coconut milk and water mixture.

❧

4 teaspoons cream of rice cereal	½ teaspoon salt	with 4 tablespoons water then heated gently until lukewarm
2 cups rice flour	1½ cups lukewarm milk	
2 teaspoons dry yeast	1 (14 fl oz) (400 ml) can coconut milk, its contents well stirred and mixed	3–4 tablespoons vegetable oil
2 teaspoons sugar		

❧

Combine the cream of rice cereal and ½ cup water in a small pan. Bring to a simmer. Cook over medium-low heat, stirring constantly, for about 10 minutes until you have a thick paste. Allow to cool.

Meanwhile, in a bowl combine the rice flour, yeast, sugar, salt and the 1½ cups lukewarm milk. Stir well until you have a smooth, thick but not stiff paste. Add the cooled flaked rice paste to the rice flour paste. Mix it in. Cover with plastic wrap and leave in a warm place to ferment for 5 hours.

Add the coconut milk mixture (or the 2 cups lukewarm milk) to this fermented paste. Mix gently. The batter should now be of a pouring consistency. Cover with plastic wrap again and set aside in a warm place for another hour.

Get everything ready to make the *appams*. Set up your wok or a non-stick frying pan, keeping its lid nearby. Have near you the oil in a small cup with a pastry brush, a 10 inch (25 cm) dish with a cover to hold the *appam*, the batter, a ladle or small cup that will hold about 6 tablespoons of the batter and a spatula, curved if possible.

Turn the heat under the wok to medium-low. When really hot, brush its inside surface lightly with some of the oil to prevent the *appam* from sticking. Stir the batter. Pour about 6 tablespoons of the mixture into the center of the wok. Pick up the wok by its 2 handles (if it has one handle, wear an oven mitt and put your second hand where the second handle would be). Swish the batter around by quickly moving your arms in a circular motion, spreading the mixture until it is approximately 8 inches (20 cm) in diameter. Cover and cook for 2–4 minutes or until the edges are crisp and golden and the center is resilient and cooked through. Remove the *appam* carefully with the spatula. If not eating immediately, put the *appam* in a deep dish and cover it while making the rest. Make all the *appams* as you did the first, rubbing a little oil on the bottom of the pan whenever necessary and stirring the batter each time.

M A K E S   1 0 – 1 2
A P P A M S

Shoba Ramji's Erachi Uruga
MEAT PICKLE

FRIENDS AND RELATIVES OF mine have, over the years, brought jars of meat pickle back to me whenever they visited Kerala. I am so grateful finally to have my own recipe and not have to rely on the kindness of others. This Syrian Christian specialty is easy to prepare and enlivens the simplest of everyday meals with its meaty fieriness. Like most pickles, it will keep for several months in the refrigerator.

Although pork is ideal, you may substitute lamb for this pickle.

FOR THE MARINADE:
2 teaspoons black
 peppercorns
2 dried hot red chilies
8–9 cloves
1 (1 inch) (2.5 cm)
 cinnamon stick
¼ teaspoon fenugreek seeds
¼ teaspoon cumin seeds
½ teaspoon salt

1 tablespoon white wine
 vinegar

YOU ALSO NEED:
1½ lb (750 g) lean pork
 from the shoulder, cut
 into ½ inch (1 cm) pieces
3 tablespoons vegetable oil
½ teaspoon brown mustard
 seeds

4 garlic cloves, peeled and
 finely chopped
1 (½ inch) (1 cm) piece
 fresh ginger root, peeled
 and finely chopped
¾–1 teaspoon salt
¼–½ teaspoon cayenne
 pepper
¼ teaspoon ground turmeric
¼ teaspoon ground cumin

Put the peppercorns, chilies, cloves, cinnamon, fenugreek seeds, cumin seeds, and salt for the marinade into a clean coffee grinder. Grind to a fine powder. Put the powder in a bowl and add the vinegar and 3 tablespoons water. Mix to a fine paste.

Rub the paste over the meat. Leave to marinate for 2–3 hours.

Heat the oil in a wide, preferably non-stick pan or wok over medium-high heat. When hot, add the mustard seeds. As soon as they start to pop, a matter of seconds, add the garlic and ginger root. Stir and fry over medium heat for 2–3 minutes. Add the marinated pork and stir and fry for 8–10 minutes until browned. Add salt to taste and the cayenne pepper, turmeric and cumin. Stir and fry for 2–3 minutes. Turn the heat to low and continue cooking and stirring for a further 2–3 minutes to reduce the sauce until it is thick and nearly dry.

Cool and store in a clean, air-tight jar.

MAKES 1¼ CUPS

Mr A. R. Sunil's Kaya Varathathu
ⓥ PLANTAIN CHIPS

PLANTAIN CHIPS, MADE FROM green cooking plantains, have always been sold all over the south. (Today, they are sold all over the north as well.) The best way to make them is to slice them directly into the hot oil using a mandolin or other slicing gadget. You may substitute green bananas if you're unable to find plantains.

∾

**2 green cooking plantains
  or green bananas**
½ teaspoon ground turmeric
¼ teaspoon *asafetida*

1¼ teaspoons salt
Oil for deep-frying
**1 fresh hot green chili,
  finely chopped**

**15–20 fresh curry leaves
  (optional)**

∾

Peel the plantains with a knife, making sure that all the skin has been removed.

Combine the turmeric, *asafetida*, salt and 2 tablespoons water in a small cup.

Heat the oil over medium heat in a wok or frying pan. The oil is suitably hot if a cube of bread sizzles nicely and turns golden-brown. Slice the plantains directly into the hot oil. The chips must be thin and round. Make just enough to have one, slightly overlapping layer. Quickly dip your fingers into the turmeric solution and sprinkle whatever liquid your fingers pick up over the chips. Stir and fry for 1–2 minutes, turning the chips halfway through this cooking time. Throw in a good pinch of chopped chili and 2–3 curry leaves, if using. Fry for another few seconds and remove with a slotted spoon. The chips should remain yellow in color. Drain on paper towels. Make all the chips this way.

Leave to cool and store in an air-tight jar. They should last a good week.

SERVES 4

Spinach with Coconut (page 37) and, from left, Cucumber Cooked with Lentils (page 34), Ginger Chutney (page 44) and Plantain Chips (above).

Shoba Ramji's Ingli Poli
Ⓥ GINGER CHUTNEY

CHUTNEYS AND PICKLES are eaten all over India. The main ingredients and combinations of seasonings vary according to the culinary idiosyncrasies of each state. Ginger is grown in Kerala. It is even exported in vast quantities. It is therefore not surprising that Keralites use it in a chutney. The use of mustard seeds, fenugreek seeds, curry leaves, coconut oil and freshly grated coconut makes it very recognizably Keralan. It is served at marriages and traditional banquets here. We can serve it at any time. It does have an exquisite flavor. If you wish to substitute unsweetened, dried coconut for fresh coconut use ½ tablespoon. Barely cover with warm water and leave for 1 hour, then proceed with the recipe.

FOR THE SPICE PASTE:
1 teaspoon coriander seeds
¼ teaspoon cumin seeds
¼ teaspoon ground turmeric

YOU ALSO NEED:
3 teaspoons coconut oil or any other vegetable oil
1 tablespoon freshly grated coconut (page 265)

¼ teaspoon brown mustard seeds
¼ teaspoon fenugreek seeds
4 dried hot red chilies
10–15 fresh curry leaves (optional)
1 small red onion, finely chopped
1–2 fresh hot green chilies, finely chopped

1 (2 inch) (5 cm) piece fresh ginger root, peeled and cut into very fine slices and then into fine julienne strips
½ cup tamarind paste (page 278), diluted in ½ cup water
1 teaspoon salt
2 teaspoons brown sugar

Put the coriander seeds, cumin seeds and turmeric for the spice paste into a clean coffee grinder. Grind to a fine powder. Put in a small bowl and mix with 1 tablespoon water to make a paste. Set aside.

Heat 1 teaspoon of the oil in a small pan over medium-high heat. When hot, add the coconut. Turn the heat to low and stir and fry for 3–4 minutes until golden. Set aside.

Heat the remaining oil in a medium-sized, heavy-bottomed pan over medium-low heat. When hot, add the mustard seeds. As soon as they pop, a matter of seconds, put in the fenugreek seeds, red chilies and the curry leaves, if using. Stir and fry for 1–2 minutes. Add the onion, green chilies and ginger root.

Stir and fry for 4–5 minutes until the onion is soft and beginning to brown. Add the spice paste. Stir and fry for 2–3 minutes until the mixture becomes dry. Add the tamarind paste, salt and brown sugar. Stir and cook for 10–12 minutes until the mixture is thick. Remove from the heat. Add the coconut and mix.

Cool and use, or store in a clean, air-tight container or jar.

This chutney will keep for many months in the refrigerator.

MAKES ⅔ CUP

Shoba Ramji's Kaitha Chaka Pachadi
ⓥ SPICY PINEAPPLE YOGURT

PINEAPPLE WAS INTRODUCED TO Kerala by the Portuguese as early as the end of the fifteenth century. At first Keralites viewed it with suspicion, calling it "the jackfruit of the donkey." It has now been incorporated in their cuisine and is very much part of the daily diet.

This is a South Indian *raita*. It is quite spicy and has a slight sweet-sour flavor. Serve it with all Indian meals or eat it as a light lunch. In Kerala, it is often served as a salad to accompany spicy fish dishes. Rice is generally served on the side. You may use the same quantity of canned, sweetened pineapple if you prefer. You will not need to stew it in sugar in that case.

If you wish to substitute unsweetened, dried coconut for fresh coconut use 1½ tablespoons. Barely cover with warm water and leave for 1 hour, then proceed with the recipe.

---

2 cups fresh pineapple, cut into 1 inch (2.5 cm) chunks
2 tablespoons sugar
3 tablespoons freshly grated coconut (page 265)

½ teaspoon ground cumin
1 cup plain yogurt, lightly beaten with a fork
3 fresh hot green chilies, finely chopped
½ tablespoon salt

1 tablespoon coconut oil or any other vegetable oil
½ teaspoon brown mustard seeds
3 dried hot red chilies
8–10 fresh curry leaves (optional)

Put the pineapple in a small, preferably non-stick pan. Add the sugar and ½ cup water and bring to a simmer. Stir and stew over low heat for 10–12 minutes until the water has been absorbed.

Meanwhile, put the coconut and cumin into the container of an electric blender. Add 1 tablespoon water (or more, if needed) and blend to a smooth paste.

Add the coconut paste to the cooked pineapple. Stir and stew over low heat for 2–3 minutes. Remove from the heat and allow to cool.

Put the yogurt into a bowl. Add the green chilies and salt. Mix. Add the pineapple mixture. Stir to blend.

Heat the oil in a small, clean pan over medium-high heat. When hot, add the mustard seeds. As soon as the mustard seeds begin to pop, a matter of seconds, put in the red chilies and the curry leaves, if using. Stir and fry over low heat for a few more seconds or until the chilies darken. Remove from the heat and mix with the pineapple yogurt.

S E R V E S   4

Mr A. R. Sunil's Pazham Roast
Ⓥ PLANTAIN ROAST

EVEN THOUGH THIS IS called a "roast" the green plantains here are peeled, stuffed with a gorgeous mixture of coconut, raisins and cardamom, dipped in a batter and then deep-fried. They are a dessert and uncommonly good.

If you wish to substitute unsweetened, dried coconut for fresh coconut use 7 tablespoons. Barely cover with warm water and leave for 1 hour, then proceed with the recipe.

FOR THE BATTER:
A good pinch of saffron
   threads
1½ tablespoons rice flour
   (also called ground rice)
½ cup all-purpose flour
¼ teaspoon sugar
¼ teaspoon ground
   cardamom

¼ teaspoon salt
1 tablespoon beaten egg

YOU ALSO NEED:
⅔ cup freshly grated
   coconut (page 265)
5 raw cashew nuts, finely
   chopped
1 tablespoon raisins

¼ teaspoon ground cumin
½ teaspoon ground
   cardamom
1½ tablespoons sugar
4 green cooking plantains,
   or green bananas peeled
   with a knife
Oil for deep-frying
2 teaspoons honey
   (optional)

To make the batter: soak the saffron in ½ teaspoon hot water for 10 minutes. Put the rice flour, flour, sugar, ¼ teaspoon cardamom and salt in a small bowl. Mix well. Add ¾ cup water, the egg and the saffron. Beat to a smooth, frothy batter. Set aside.

In a separate bowl, mix the coconut, cashew nuts, raisins, cumin, ½ teaspoon cardamom and sugar. Set aside.

To prepare the plantains: make 2 parallel incisions along the length of the plantains about ½ inch (1 cm) apart. Remove the plantain flesh from between the cuts to make a groove, being careful not to break the plantain. Fill the groove with the coconut mixture.

Heat the oil for deep-frying in a large frying pan or wok over medium heat. The oil is hot enough when a cube of bread sizzles nicely and turns golden-brown.

Dip the plantains in the batter and slip into the hot oil. Deep-fry the plantains for 4–5 minutes until crisp and golden. Serve immediately, either whole or sliced, and drizzled with honey, if you wish.

SERVES 4

MADHUR JAFFREY

From the home of Uma and Zac J. Zacharias: Payasam
Ⓥ MOONG DAL PUDDING

LIKE THE *KHEER* OF northern India, *payasam* is the grain or bean pudding of the south. As Kerala is the land of coconuts, it is not surprising that both coconut milk and small fried coconut slivers are used in it as well. Fried cashews may be substituted for the coconut slivers. If you like, you may use both.

❧

1 cup *moong dal* (page 260)
1 cup dark brown sugar
2½ cups coconut milk, well stirred from a can or thick fresh milk (page 266)
½ teaspoon ground ginger

½ teaspoon ground nutmeg
½ teaspoon ground cumin
½ teaspoon ground cardamom or the seeds from 5 pods, well crushed
2 tablespoons *ghee* (page 271) or unsalted butter

2 tablespoons fresh coconut, cut into fine ½ inch (1 cm) slivers or 2 tablespoons dried coconut

❧

Set a heavy, preferably cast-iron frying pan or wok over medium-high heat. When hot, put in the *moong dal*. Stir and roast it until it turns reddish, about 5 minutes. Wash the *dal* in several changes of water. Drain. Empty the *dal* into a heavy, medium-sized pan. Add 3 cups water and bring to the boil. Turn the heat to low, cover partially and let the *dal* cook for 40–50 minutes or until tender.

Meanwhile, combine the brown sugar with ½ cup water in a small pan. Heat, stirring, over medium heat until the sugar has dissolved and you have a syrup. Add this syrup to the *dal*. Also add 2 cups of the coconut milk, stirring it

well before you pour it in. Stir and bring to a simmer. Cook over low heat, stirring frequently, until you have a thick, porridge-like consistency. This might take 20–30 minutes.

Add the remaining coconut milk as well as the ginger root, nutmeg, cumin and cardamom. Stir the spices in. Cook, stirring, for another 5 minutes.

Heat the *ghee* or butter in a small frying pan over medium heat. When hot, put in the coconut slivers or dried coconut. Stir and fry until lightly browned. Scatter over the *payasam* before serving.

SERVES 8

GUJARAT

I CAN SAY THIS unequivocally. If there is an *haute cuisine* for vegetarians – ancient, traditional foods with astounding flavors and textures, all based on sound nutritional principles – it can be found in the Indian state of Gujarat: delicate, silken "pasta" rolls made out of a cooked chick-pea flour batter (*khandvi*); a savory, baked "cake" made with a mixed batter of beans and vegetables (*handva*); fried chick-pea flour noodles with a tomato-garlic sauce (*sev tamate*); and steamed diamonds of crushed peanuts with a rich ginger and chili sauce – these are just some of the fine foods found here.

Part of this state, which runs along India's upper west coast, is desert and part is semi-desert, making water so valuable that medieval kings in the region, once they discovered an underground spring, would house it protectively in an elaborately carved structure known as a stepwell. Instead of rising upwards towards the sky as most Indian palaces do, the stepwell, a mini-palace, went downwards, whirlpool fashion, story by story, burrowing its way elegantly into the earth to the very source of the cool, precious liquid.

In a land where camels ply the caked earth (did I have any recipes for camel's milk, I was asked many times) and hedges are formed by closely planted cactus, most of this valuable water has, traditionally, been used to grow staples – grains and beans. It is with these staples, and a smattering of fresh vegetables or fruit and nutritious seasonings such as sesame seeds and peanuts, that most vegetarian Gujaratis make their delicacies.

Let me describe to you a few meals eaten at the homes of Gujarati friends in Ahmadabad.

When I had gone to bed the night before at the house of a friend in Ahmadabad (Gujarat's most populous city and now adjacent to Ghandhi Nagar, the newly built capital), I had found fresh jasmines in a basket lined with a dampened cloth, placed strategically next to my pillow. Even on that steaming, hot summer's day, I was lulled to a cool and aromatic sleep, well in keeping with the Gujarati way of life which believes in taking care of the whole human being, body and soul. I woke up, bathed, and swung for a while on the carved wooden seat suspended in my room with ornate brass chains (all Gujarati homes seem to have such swings – to cool the body and calm the mind).

Breakfast was light and came to my room on a tray, my early rising hosts mindful that I had traveled a long distance – some chick-pea flour pancakes (*pudlas*), which are rather like the chick-pea flour "pizzas" of southern France only much more delicate, well-drained yogurt that had been flavored with green onions, fresh cilantro and peanut chutney, some green

chili and lime pickle (*marchanu athanu*) and *khakra*, a very thin, crisp wheat bread rather like the breads eaten by Scandinavians but much more wafer-like.

Then, after a morning of sightseeing at the Calico Museum of Textiles, easily one of the best in the world (Indian fabrics, both ancient and modern, are to my mind quite incomparable) and the collection of Indian miniature paintings housed in a private Le Corbusier-designed museum, I returned to my hosts for lunch.

The dining-room had been planned to have a small, indoor pond at one end. (It was not exactly the stepwell of a medieval king but I was in the home of a modern noble, a textile magnate, who could get his architects to hint subtly at the symbols of past power as they installed cooling, decorative elements.) The table was set nearby.

As soon as we sat down, waiters came in bearing silver *thalis*, each with its array of small silver bowls (*katoris*) arranged neatly near the rim. The freshest of seasonal mango purée was in there to be eaten with thin, dainty, fluffy, white split pea diamonds (*idada dhokla*). Made with a batter of ground rice and *urad dal*, which is left overnight to ferment and then steamed with coarsely crushed black pepper, this dish belongs to a whole family of *dhoklas* found only in the state of Gujarat. My host, dipping a piece of the soft white sponge into the orange-gold liquid said, "Many of us like to eat just this for lunch, all summer long – at least as long as the mangoes last.

Sometimes we eat mango purée with little *pooris* (deep-fried, puffy breads), sometimes we put it in our *kadhi* (a chick-pea flour and yogurt soup) – it provides the little sweetening we crave – and sometimes we put it into our thickened yogurt dessert (*shrikhand*). Mangoes do wonders for the eyes. You eat them throughout the summer and their goodness will last you all year."

Of course, there was much more on the *thali* than just the mango purée and *dhoklas*. There were little potatoes cooked with tomatoes (*batata nu shak*), young cabbage stir-fried with peas (*kobi vatana nu shak*), *moong dal* cooked rather like rice so that each grain was separate, spinach steamed with ginger root, a "salad" of bananas and yogurt flavored with crushed mustard seeds, delicate millet breads smothered with *ghee*, and, for dessert, some fresh litchis and a sweet coconut roll (*coco pista pasand*) which, shaped like a sponge roll, had sweetened coconut on the outside and chopped pistachios on the inside. The entire meal was vegetarian, but I was hardly conscious of this as I ate.

Another friend, belonging to the Sarabhai family that owns the Calico Museum – as well as textile and pharmaceutical industries – once offered me the most delightful of poolside lunches. In a bowl was an artfully created rice salad – soft, freshly cooked rice and yogurt blended together with fresh cilantro and then given a *tarka* (or *baghar*, a seasoning in oil) of

cumin seeds, mustard seeds and fresh curry leaves. The top of the salad had been carefully dotted with fresh, pinky-red pomegranate seeds which were firmly moored but still exposed. Also stuck into the salad by their tips were a few green chilies that had been rubbed with yogurt and salt, dried in the parched Gujarati air and then quickly fried to a crisp just before use. Adding texture and fire, they were to be nibbled at as we ate. Served with this was a large shallow bowl filled with *khandvi*, the silken "pasta" rolls described earlier, and simple glasses of fresh watermelon juice. Nothing else was needed.

The art of making *khandvi* – which I have to admit I have not yet perfected (hence no recipe in this book but maybe in the next one) – combines the technique of making choux pastry in its first stages – it is a cooked, batter-like dough – with the rarer art of spreading the very hot dough out by hand until it is paper thin. I watched the Sarabhai cook, the maharaj, as he is respectfully called, do this. For my comfort, he cooked outdoors, under the generous shade of large trees.

"It is best to use fresh chick-pea flour," the cook began as he sifted some of this into a pan. Small chick-peas (*chanas*), grown on Sarabhai land, had been ground into flour at their own mill. Double the volume of liquid, a mixture of yogurt and water, was mixed in with the flour as well as some turmeric, salt, *asafetida* and lime juice. The pan was put on the fire and then stirred and stirred until the batter thickened enough to come away from the sides.

Now came the hard part. Dipping his hands into boiling hot batter, the maharaj removed just enough to spread very thinly on the back of a *thali*. He had to do this with great speed as more *thalis* waited to be covered and the batter had to remain hot or it would not spread. "Your hands should get red when you finish," the maharaj informed me.

The batter set almost instantly into a thin film. Now it needed to be rolled up tightly. This, too, was difficult as the *thalis* were a good 15 inches (30 cm) in diameter and the thin "crêpe" formed on the *thalis* was exceedingly delicate. The roll was then cut into 1 inch (2.5 cm) segments and placed in a single layer in a shallow bowl. The next step was to heat some oil, throw into it some mustard seeds, some fresh curry leaves, some asafetida, a touch of red chili powder and ground turmeric, and a few drops of water and pour this over the *khandvi*. Finally, some fresh cilantro and freshly grated coconut were sprinkled over the top and these flimsy silken masterpieces were ready to be devoured. "I make these at least two to three times a week," the cook said proudly. Clearly, much practice was needed to prepare them with his consummate skill.

As we sat eating our lunch in a leafy arbor (another Le Corbusier house, designed to have no front door), a shady oasis in a dried-up city, this host talked about the importance of dried beans in balancing the good and bad cholesterol in our bodies and of how the family of dried beans and split peas were such an under-rated source of protein in the Western world but so highly valued here and used on a daily basis, sometimes several times in the same meal. In fact, all his beans, as with most land-owning families, are grown on his own farms, harvested, then rubbed with castor oil (to keep bugs away) and stored for the year in large barrels that are kept near the kitchen. Drawing upon the pastas that already exist here, he is even experimenting with the production of dried, all-bean pastas for the West. Gujaratis are nothing if not a forward-looking people, envied all over India for their great business acumen. He will probably succeed.

To confirm how grains and beans have been traditionally integrated into the daily lives of Gujaratis, I had only to visit the home of Surendra Patel. A designer, restaurant owner and dreamer, he found a mango grove in a village on the outskirts of Ahmadabad some years ago and built his house smack in the center of it. Using mud as mortar, cow dung and clay as plaster for the walls, traditionally carved wood – some antique, some new – for window frames, shutters, lintels and doors, and regionally crafted quilts for cushions and divan

Cloth being dried in Ahmadabad, Gujarat.

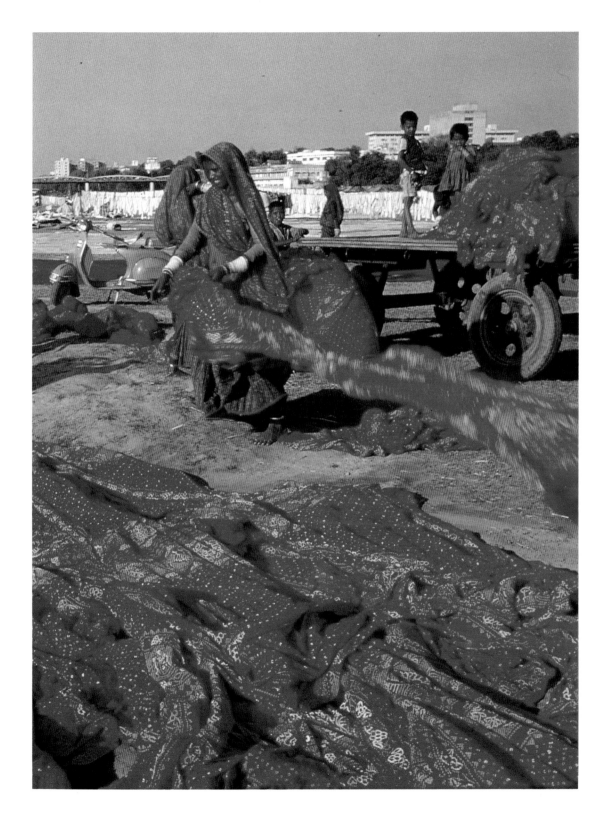

covers, just as neighboring villagers do, he came up with a modern yet ancient dwelling, fronted with formal, criss-crossing tanks replete with fountains, and backed with a freshwater pool. It is here that he lives and entertains.

It was here that he offered us an all-homemade, typically Gujarati breakfast of rice *papar* (*poppadom*), *cheewra* (a spicy, granola-like *mélange* of nuts, puffed rice, roasted split peas, dried fruit and chick-pea flour noodles) and *leeli chai* (green tea) made with lemon grass and mint. The first and last are impossible to find outside Gujarati homes. The second, though now sold by Indian grocers the world over and a cousin to the so-called "Bombay Mix," is still best when made at home using "grandmother's recipe."

Smita Patel, Surendra's wife, explained that the deliciously crunchy, sesame-seed-encrusted *papar* were made by boiling green chilies, salt, baking soda and ajwain, cumin and sesame seeds in water, adding rice flour to this water, stirring and cooking, then kneading all this into a dough, rolling out fine discs and drying them in the sun. Whenever anyone wished to eat them (friends were always dropping in), the *poppadom* were quickly roasted over charcoal and served to guests lolling on the quilt-covered divans on the veranda. White, crisp, crunchy and encrusted with sesame seeds, these homemade *poppadom* were not only exquisitely delicious, but unlike anything I had eaten in other parts of India.

They were complemented, perfectly, by the milky lemon grass tea topped with fresh mint, which was served to us in generously sized, hand-crafted bowls.

India's vegetarianism comes mainly from some of the Hindu sects and castes scattered across the land, but it also comes from Jains who may be fewer in number but are fervent in their faith. Many of these Jains are Gujaratis.

Jainism developed about the same time or earlier than Buddhism, starting around the eighth century BC and becoming quite formalized by the sixth century BC. Like Buddhism, it grew as a protest movement against some of the excesses of the Vedic faith (which later became Hinduism), including the custom of animal sacrifices. The Jains believe in kindness to all life, from insects up. To this end, the strictest believers wear masks over their noses and mouths so as not to accidentally inhale or swallow the humblest of creatures. Not only do they refrain from eating meat but some will not eat root vegetables as pulling out a root kills a whole plant. They even have hospitals for injured birds.

Traditionally, there has been enormous wealth in the Jain community. Today, a disproportionate number of India's successful millionaire industrialists are devout Jains, who, like those of earlier centuries, have crowned their successful lives with the building of temples.

Pilgrimages to places such as the temples atop Shetrunjaya mountain at

Palitana are undertaken by the faithful at least once in their lifetimes, sometimes once a year. Journeys can start from quite a distance. But first, there is food to be packed. *Farsan* is easy to carry. This is the name for savory snack foods, often made out of chickpea flour as well as other grains, nuts and beans, sometimes pastry-like and sometimes not, often crisp, but sometimes not, that are eaten at breakfast and tea-time, and all other times in between. They may be made at home but can be bought from special shops that prepare large selections several times a day.

There is much hustle and bustle in these shops as families stroll in and out. Large chunks of yellow *khaman dhokla*, looking like wet Greek sponges, are piled high on one tray, dotted with mustard seeds and sprinkled over with fresh coconut; squiggly chick-pea flour noodles (*sev*) of all sizes are arranged in neat hillocks on other trays; *khasta kachoris*, deep-fried, flaky, stuffed breads, may be bought with a choice of a sour mint chutney or a sweet one made with dates and tamarind. In the front of the shop, to lure customers with their cooking aromas, are the chefs manning their woks, churning out all manner of lasagna-like flat chick-pea flour "pastas": there is *papri* (crinkled ribbons made by pushing dough through a many-slitted griddle) and *fafra* (long, flat ribbons made by dragging the dough by the heel of a practised hand).

With the *farsan* all tied up in a cloth bundle, the pilgrims can begin their journey by car, by camel cart or even by scooter. The Gujarati women, quite traditional in their saris, oiled hair and red *tika* in the middle of their foreheads, will nonetheless think nothing of donning a baseball cap and speeding along, curving their way in and out of traffic, on scooters. Sometimes a whole family, man, woman and child, will travel on a single scooter.

Along the road, the travelers will surely come across an encampment of Rabaris from Kachchh (northeastern Gujarat). These are the local gypsies, goatherders and shepherds on their never-ending search for water and pasture. Loaded with silver jewelery – even little infants have seven earrings down the lobes of each ear – they are easily recognizable. The men, in short white shirts that are flared and pleated from the armpits down, spend most of their time with their animals. The women, tattooed prettily on their hands, cheeks and chins, embroider and cook – and what embroidery! Exquisite mirror work that is sold in trendy European boutiques for thousands of rupees more than these poor itinerants were ever paid for it, simple quilts and blankets that are in the chic collections of international designers and backless blouses that can be seen on rich young nymphs in Bombay and Calcutta. The Rabaris' cooking, because of severe financial constraints, is much more basic.

One woman, squatting on the caked earth, is making a patty out of a lightly salted millet dough. The dough looks very much like the earth. She adjusts the long scarf that falls back from her head, makes sure that her toddler daughter is within view and then flattens the patty with her hands into a thick, flat bread. No rolling pins seem to be required here. The bread is slapped on to a curved, earthen *tava* which has been heating over twigs from the thorny, desert *keekar* tree, the only fuel at hand. On good days, this bread (*bajri no rotlo*) is eaten with *doongri nu shaak*, a simple onion curry made with chili powder and turmeric. On most days, however, what accompanies it is a raw onion, peeled and smashed with a fist (raw onion gives protection from the heat, they believe) and an incendiary chutney made with garlic, salt and plenty of red chilies (*lasun chutney*).

The traveling Jain pilgrims on their way to Palitana frown upon onions and garlic (which are not only live bulbs but are said to arouse base passions), but they may pick up some dried red chilies if they happen to be passing the village of Shertha. Fields upon fields have been producing chilies here for the last 200 years. Mountains of them, red and brilliant and all freshly dried, ooze their pungency into the air as vendors at roadside stalls grind and crush them. The soil, it is said, gives the chilies such a bright color that it acts as an enticing natural dye in the food. The air, it is believed, is quite perfect for drying the chilies to a crisp.

If it is summer and they are passing through Ahmadabad, the pilgrims may stop and pick up egg-free ice creams. Perhaps cardamom-saffron or saffron-pistachio. Perhaps the baby would like mango-grape?

If, on the other hand, it is late winter and the pilgrims are going through the countryside near Surat, the port where the British gained their first toehold in India in 1612, they may decide to feast on *paunk*. In a harvest ritual which must go back to antiquity, fresh grains of wheat or millet are roasted and then combined with balls of young brown sugar made from the thickened juice of newly harvested sugar cane, to produce a snack that is best devoured with tall glasses of salted buttermilk.

If they are passing the village of Vartal, where little babes swing from cloth hammocks, they may pick up some flat, wholewheat noodles drying in coils on outdoor cots. Anthropologists today believe that noodles probably originated not in China or Italy but wherever there was wheat. This, they feel, points mainly to the Tigris-Euphrates valley in the Middle East and to the Indus valley now mostly in Pakistan but extending into northern Gujarat as well.

As towns dating back to the second millennium BC have been discovered here (with evidence of both wheat and sugar cane), it is likely that the wheat noodles in Vartal are completely indigenous, going

Men at a wedding in Gujarat.

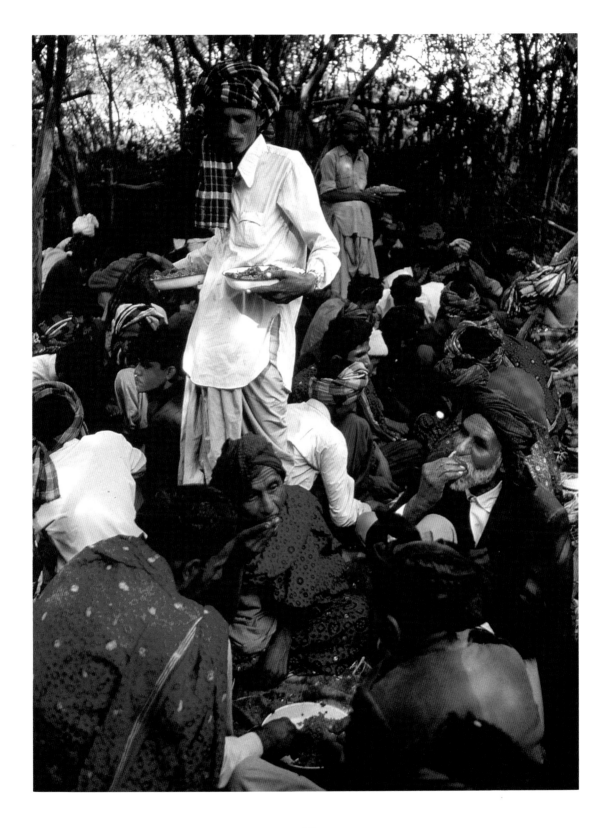

back perhaps 4000 years.

The village preparation is very simple. Wheat dough is rolled out very thin and cut into ⅛ inch (3 mm) thick strips. These are wrapped into small coils and dried in the sun. At the harvest festival of *Holi*, the coils are thrown into boiling water, drained and then eaten with melted *ghee* and sugar. The use of noodles is widespread in Gujarat. Apart from the chick-pea flour *farsan* and the *khandvi* mentioned earlier, there is also that superb creation *dal dhokli*, in which 1 inch (2.5 cm) wide strips made from a fresh whole-wheat dough are dropped into a spicy split pea soup. This is very much a noodle-eating state.

As the pilgrims near Saurashtra, the land turns increasingly brown and barren. River beds meander aimlessly. There is not a drop of water in them. The flat earth is broken up with single hillocks that arise eerily from the ground without support from sisterly ranges. Finally, Palitana appears at dawn. It lies at the foot of Shetrunjaya, another vertical rise that seems to come without warning. On top of it perches a rising crescendo of 863 temples built over 900 years.

The sky glows red but a pale pink moon, egg shaped and obstinate, refuses to leave. Mindful of the day's heat, dawn seems the only rational time to attempt this climb. There are over 4000 steps and only those in the best of shape can manage them without resorting to the flimsy *palanquins* that are available for hire. There are a few

water stops but very little shade.

The climb is arduous and takes two slow hours (young Jain nuns, it must be said, heads shaven and staff in hand, go leaping up the steps like young gazelles). But there are rewards for those who stagger to the top. Seated under a tree at the entrance are several women crying "Eat yogurt. Eat yogurt." This is some of the best yogurt you can ever hope to find. Made out of rich buffalo's milk and set in shallow terra cotta bowls, it is served with a light sprinkling of coarse salt or sugar and, of course, a liberal dash of divinity.

It would be highly improper to limit Gujarati food to that of vegetarians alone. As Islam spread from the Middle East in the eighth and ninth centuries, India was among the first places it came to. Gujarat, on India's northwest coast, was easily accessible by sea. Indeed, Arabs had traded their horses and pearls here for spices and textiles since antiquity.

Among the early converts to Islam in the eleventh century was the community of Bohris. Mohammad Kassim and his brothers are Bohris. They live in the heart of Ahmadabad, in the old walled city founded by the Muslim ruler Sultan Ahmed Shah in 1411. For the last seven generations, their family has made a good living selling china, glass and crockery. Today, they sell all those same items and have also become the biggest dealers in antique chandeliers and hanging lamps.

Narrow lanes, blocked now and then

by goats and drying, blocked-printed fabrics, lead to their front door. This opens into an enormous room whose ceiling is completely covered with row upon row of hanging lamps – blue, green, pink, ochre and, of course, the trendiest clear ones with delicate etchings. The family's trade is also their passion.

Two Gujarati swings with seats large enough for three or four people are also suspended from the ceiling. The women, their heads covered with scarves, swing and talk about the children and family recipes.

Lunch is served on a common metal plate (a *thal*) large enough to seat eight people around it. It is set upon a stool. Diners sit on the floor. All food is placed in the center for the family to share. *Laganya sheek* is made with spicy minced lamb that is packed into a baking pan, covered with a layer of beaten egg and then with sliced tomatoes. It is cut into squares and served

as the kebab course. To follow, there is an unusually delicious chicken cooked with a pesto-like green chutney containing fresh cilantro, mint, green chilies, garlic, ginger and coconut (*chutney ni murghi*). Liver, too, may be cooked this way, I am informed. There is a scrumptious lamb smothered in a most unusual sauce containing ground cashews, roasted peanuts, roasted chickpeas and watermelon seeds (*kari*). It is to be eaten with a special black pepper pilaf. And there is the absolutely mouthwatering *khichra*. For this, meat, wheat and split peas are all cooked with spices and ground up into a porridge-like paste. This is spread out on a plate. Next you dribble a little garlic-flavored *ghee* over the top. Then you sprinkle some crisply browned onion slivers, some chopped up green chilies, some fresh cilantro, lemon juice and *garam masala* over the top. Then you dig in. I could just live on that!

Mrs Kumud Kansara's Sev
Ⓥ CRISPY CHICK-PEA FLOUR NOODLES

GUJARAT HAS MANY VARIETIES of pasta although they are not called by that name. *Sev* are crisp, fried noodles prepared from chick-pea flour. To make them, a special press, a *sev*-maker, is used. Most serious Indian grocers sell them.

If you cannot find one, use a potato-ricer instead. *Sev* are generally eaten as a snack, at breakfast and at tea time. They can also be turned into an appetizer or main course by clever additions of seasonings or sauces. See the next recipe and page 80 for these magical variations. They may be made several days ahead of time.

---

3 cups plus 3 tablespoons chick-pea flour, sifted
½ teaspoon ground *asafetida*

¼ teaspoon ground turmeric
2 teaspoons cayenne pepper
2½ teaspoons salt

½ cup peanut oil or any other vegetable oil, plus oil for greasing and deep-frying

---

Put the flour, *asafetida*, turmeric, cayenne pepper and salt into a large bowl. Stir to mix.

Put the ½ cup oil into a small bowl or jug with 1 cup water. Mix well with a spoon or whisk so that the oil and water combine. Add the water and oil to the flour mixture. Mix and knead, using your hands, to form a soft, sticky dough. Set aside to rest for 15 minutes.

Meanwhile, heat the oil for deep-frying in a large frying pan or wok over medium heat. Fit a *sev*-machine with the disc that has the smallest holes or use a potato-ricer. Lightly oil the inside of the gadget you are using.

With lightly oiled hands, make a tangerine-sized ball out of the dough and put it into the *sev*-making gadget. When the oil is hot, hold the *sev*-maker or potato-ricer over it. Moving the machine in a circular motion over the oil, push out the noodles so that they fall in a continuous stream and cover the surface in a single layer. Let this layer fry for 15 seconds and then turn it over. Fry for a further 15 seconds until the noodles are crisp but not browned. Remove with a slotted spoon. Drain on paper towels. Make all the noodles this way, spreading each batch out on fresh paper towels to drain. Once the noodles have cooled, break them up slightly and store in a tightly lidded jar or tin. They will keep for several weeks.

SERVES 10-15

Mrs Kumud Kansara's Sev Masala

ⓥ CRISPY CHICK-PEA FLOUR NOODLES WITH ONIONS AND CHILIES

THIS IS BEST SERVED with drinks, hard or soft. Stick spoons into the bowl of noodles so that people can pick up spoonfuls as they want them. The mixture should be put together at the last minute or the noodles will get soggy.

2½ cups Crispy Chick-Pea Flour Noodles (opposite)
1 small red onion, finely chopped

4–5 fresh hot green chilies, finely chopped
2–3 tablespoons finely chopped, fresh cilantro

2 tablespoons lime juice
A little salt (optional)

Put the noodles into a bowl. Break them with your hands so that they are in approximately 1 inch (2.5 cm) pieces.

Add the onion, chilies, cilantro, lime juice and salt, if desired. Toss with the noodles to mix. Serve.

SERVES 4

Nishrin Attarwala's Kari
LAMB IN A CASHEW NUT SAUCE

THE BOHRIS OF GUJARAT, a Muslim community, cook some of the best meat dishes on the west coast of India. This is one of their specialities. It is served with Black Pepper Rice (page 84), which helps to absorb the absolutely wonderful sauce. It is really the sauce that makes the dish. Rich with a ground mixture of nuts – cashews, the hazelnut-like *charoli* nut (sold by Indian grocers) and roasted peanuts – seeds such as watermelon seeds and spices such as star anise and cloves, it is both uncommon and good. If you cannot get any of the more unusual nuts or seeds, just increase the cashews or peanuts by a similar amount. This dish may also be made with chicken, which should be skinned and cut into 2 inch (5 cm) pieces. Each of the two cooking stages would be 12-15 minutes.

FOR THE NUT, SEED AND SPICE MIXTURE:

2 tablespoons raw cashew nuts, split or broken
2 tablespoons *charoli (chironji)*
1½ tablespoons roasted peanuts
1½ tablespoons roasted chick-peas, or roasted *chana dal* (page 260)
1½ tablespoons peeled watermelon seeds
1 teaspoon cumin seeds
7–8 cloves
1 teaspoon black peppercorns
1 teaspoon ground coriander
1 (1 inch) (2.5 cm) cinnamon stick, broken
6–7 dried hot red chilies
2 star anise
¼ teaspoon ground turmeric

FOR THE FIRST COOKING STAGE YOU NEED:

4 tablespoons vegetable oil
2 medium-large red onions, finely sliced
1 (1 inch) (2.5 cm) piece fresh ginger root, finely chopped
5–6 garlic cloves, peeled and finely chopped
4 fresh hot green chilies, finely chopped
1 lb (450 g) boned lamb from the shoulder, cut into 1½ inch (4 cm) cubes
½ teaspoon salt

FOR THE SECOND COOKING STAGE YOU NEED:

3 tablespoons vegetable oil
1 teaspoon cumin seeds
20–30 fresh curry leaves (optional)
1 (1 inch) (2.5 cm) cinnamon stick
2–3 cloves
½ teaspoon black peppercorns
2–3 garlic cloves, peeled and chopped
2 large ripe tomatoes, puréed in an electric blender
1¾ cups coconut milk (page 266), from a well-stirred can, thinned with 1¼ cups water
½ teaspoon salt
3 tablespoons lemon juice
3 tablespoons finely chopped, fresh cilantro

Put the ingredients for the nut, seed and spice mixture into a clean coffee grinder. Grind to a fine powder. Empty into a bowl. Add 5–6 tablespoons water to make a thick paste. Set aside.

For the first cooking stage: heat the 4 tablespoons oil in a large, wide, preferably non-stick pan or wok over medium-high heat. When hot, add the onions. Stir and fry for 3–4 minutes or until they turn brown at the edges. Add the ginger root, garlic and chilies. Stir and fry for a minute. Put in the lamb and ½ teaspoon salt. Stir and fry for 2–3 minutes. Add the spice paste and 2 cups water. Bring to the boil. Cover, turn the heat to low and cook for 55 minutes.

For the second cooking stage: heat the 3 tablespoons oil in a clean, wide pan or wok over medium-high heat. When hot, add the cumin seeds, curry leaves if using, cinnamon, cloves and peppercorns. Stir for 10 seconds. Add the garlic. Stir and fry until the garlic starts to brown. Now add the lamb and the sauce from the first pan, along with the tomato purée, stirred coconut milk, salt and lemon juice. Stir to mix.

Cook over medium-high heat for about 10–15 minutes until the lamb is tender and the sauce has become thick.

Sprinkle with the fresh cilantro to garnish.

SERVES 3 – 4

Kumud Kansara's Gajar Marcha No Sambharo

ⓥ CARROTS STIR-FRIED WITH GREEN CHILIES

GUJARATIS EAT MANY VEGETABLES that are very lightly stir-fried. Rather like Chinese vegetables, they are expected to remain crunchy even after they are cooked. These carrots go well with all Indian meals. You may also serve them with a roast chicken or with plain sausages.

❧

3 tablespoons peanut or any other vegetable oil
½ teaspoon brown mustard seeds
¼ teaspoon ground *asafetida*

1¼ lb (550 g) carrots, peeled and very coarsely grated
6 fresh hot green chilies, slit in half and cut into long slivers

½ teaspoon salt
¼ teaspoon ground turmeric
½ teaspoon ground coriander
½ teaspoon lime juice

❧

Heat the oil in a large, wide, preferably non-stick pan or wok over medium heat. When hot, add the mustard seeds. As soon as they pop, a matter of seconds, add the *asafetida*. Stir to mix. Add the carrots, chilies, salt, turmeric, coriander and lime juice. Stir and fry for 2–3 minutes. Remove from the heat. The carrots should remain slightly crunchy.

SERVES 4–6

Mrs Kumud Kansara's Batata Nu Shak
Ⓥ SPICY POTATOES WITH TOMATOES

THESE POTATOES ARE HOT – and quite delicious. They are best served with Indian breads but may also be served with store-bought pita bread. They can be a part of any Indian meal.

∽

4 tablespoons peanut or any other vegetable oil

½ teaspoon brown mustard seeds

½ teaspoon cumin seeds

2 dried hot red chilies

2 bay leaves

¼ teaspoon ground *asafetida*

10 fresh curry leaves (optional)

4 small-medium potatoes, peeled or unpeeled, cut into ½ inch (1 cm) pieces

1½ teaspoons cayenne pepper

½ teaspoon ground turmeric

2 teaspoons salt

2 fresh hot green chilies, finely chopped

1 (1 inch) (2.5 cm) piece fresh ginger root, peeled and finely grated

2 tablespoons finely chopped, fresh cilantro

2 medium-sized tomatoes, chopped into 1 inch (2.5 cm) dice

1½ tablespoons unsweetened, dried coconut

½ tablespoon ground coriander

2 teaspoons brown sugar

¾ tablespoon thick tamarind paste (page 278)

∽

Heat the oil in a large, wide, preferably non-stick pan or wok over medium-high heat. When hot, put in the mustard seeds. As soon as they pop, a matter of seconds, add the cumin seeds, red chilies, bay leaves and *asafetida*. Stir for 4–5 seconds and add the curry leaves. Stir once and add the potatoes, cayenne pepper, turmeric, salt, green chilies and ginger. Stir to mix. Add ⅓ cup water. Cover and simmer for

10 minutes over low heat. Now add the fresh cilantro, tomatoes, coconut, ground coriander, brown sugar and 1½ cups water. Stir to mix, then cover again and leave to simmer for a further 10 minutes. Add the tamarind paste. Simmer for a further 2–3 minutes.

Remove from the heat.

S E R V E S   4 – 6

Mrs Kumud Kansara's Mugh Ni Dal
ⓥ "DRY" SPLIT PEAS

THE GRAINS OF *MOONG DAL* cook quite separately here and look, to all intents and purposes, like rice. Gujaratis like to eat them with Sweet and Sour Chick-Pea Flour Soup (page 79) and plain rice. You may serve this with any Indian meal.

❧

1 cup *moong dal* (page 260)	**½ teaspoon cumin seeds**	**4 fresh hot green chilies,**
5 tablespoons peanut oil or	**¼ teaspoon ground**	**finely chopped**
any other vegetable oil	**asafetida**	**¾ teaspoon salt**
		¼ teaspoon ground turmeric

❧

Wash the *moong dal* in several changes of water until the water runs clear. Drain. Soak in lukewarm warm water to cover by 1 inch (2.5 cm) for 3 hours. Drain.

Heat the oil in a heavy, medium-sized pan over medium-high heat. When hot, add the cumin seeds. Let them sizzle for 10 seconds. Add the *asafetida*. Stir once. Quickly add the *moong dal*, chilies, salt, turmeric and ½ cup water. Stir to mix and bring to the boil.

Cover very tightly, turn the heat to very, very low and cook for 15 minutes or until the water has been absorbed.

SERVES 4

Lamb in a Cashew Nut Sauce (page 64) with Black Pepper Rice (page 84) and Carrots Stir-fried with Green Chilies (page 68).

The Rajmata of Jasdan's Mugphali Nu Shak

Ⓥ STEAMED PEANUT DIAMONDS IN A GARLIC-ONION SAUCE

I GOT THIS RECIPE several years ago from the mother of the Darbar Sahib of Jasdan, a formerly royal kingdom in Saurashtra. The main ingredient here is a kind of homemade pasta cut into diamonds and then steamed. Perfect for vegetarians, it is made out of a nutritious mixture of chick-pea flour and roasted peanuts. The sauce, flavored with onions, garlic and mustard seeds, is as rich as many of the sauces for meat dishes.

∾

FOR THE STEAMED PEANUT DIAMONDS:
1 cup roasted, shelled peanuts
1 cup chick-pea flour
2 fresh hot green chilies, finely chopped
1 (½ inch) (1 cm) piece fresh ginger root, peeled and finely grated
¼ teaspoon ground turmeric
½ tablespoon cayenne pepper
½ tablespoon ground cumin
1 tablespoon chopped, fresh cilantro

½ teaspoon salt
1½ tablespoons peanut oil or any other vegetable oil

TO MAKE THE SPICE PASTE:
2 small red onions, roughly chopped
5 garlic cloves, peeled and roughly chopped
¼ teaspoon ground turmeric
2 teaspoons ground coriander
1 teaspoon ground cumin
1 teaspoon cayenne pepper

YOU ALSO NEED:
3 tablespoons peanut oil or any other vegetable oil
½ teaspoon brown mustard seeds
½ teaspoon cumin seeds
½ teaspoon fenugreek seeds
3 dried hot red chilies
2 small red onions, finely chopped
5 garlic cloves, finely chopped
4 tablespoons plain yogurt, lightly beaten
1 medium-sized tomato, finely chopped
¼–½ teaspoon salt

∾

Make the steamed peanut diamonds: put the peanuts into a clean coffee grinder. Grind to a fine powder. Put the ground peanuts and remaining dry ingredients into a bowl. Mix well. Add about ½ cup water and ½ tablespoon of the oil. Mix to make a moist, coarse paste.

Lightly grease a 12 inch (30 cm) *thali* (see page 283) or shallow cake pan with the remaining tablespoon oil. Put the peanut mixture into the *thali* and spread out evenly until you reach the edges. Press down firmly. The thickness of the pasta should ideally be a little less than ¼ inch (5 mm).

Get your steaming equipment ready. Heat a large, wide pan or wok with 3–4 inches (7.5–10 cm) water in the bottom. Set the *thali* or cake pan with the peanut mixture over the water, resting it on a trivet or a bowl so that it stays above the water. Cover the pan or wok tightly with a lid and steam for 25 minutes. The steamed pasta should be firm and moist. Allow it to cool and then cut it into 1 inch (2.5 cm) diamonds.

Put the spice paste ingredients into the container of an electric blender. Add 4 tablespoons water. Blend to a paste. Set aside.

Heat the 3 tablespoons oil in a large, wide, preferably non-stick pan or wok over medium-high heat. When hot, add the mustard seeds, cumin seeds, fenugreek seeds and chilies. As soon as the mustard seeds pop, a matter of seconds, add the onions and garlic. Stir and fry for 3–4 minutes until the onions darken. Reduce the heat to low. Gradually add the yogurt, a tablespoon at a time, stirring it into the sauce each time. Add the tomato and salt. Stir to mix. Add 1¾ cups water and bring to a simmer. Simmer gently for 10 minutes, stirring frequently. Add the steamed peanut diamonds. Cover and simmer for a further 10 minutes.

SERVES 4

Mrs Kumud Kansara's Khaman Dhokla
Ⓥ SPONGY, SPICY, SAVORY DIAMONDS

BELONGING TO THE GENERAL family of *dhoklas*, this is known locally as just plain *khaman*. *Dhoklas* are spongy, savory cakes which can be cut into squares or diamonds. Wonderfully sweet, sour and slightly hot, all at the same time, they may be served as part of a meal or eaten as a snack with tea.

All *dhoklas* need to be steamed. (For more on steaming, see page 287.) It is important that you check your steaming apparatus before you start. A large wok, with a cover, is the ideal steaming utensil. The ideal steaming tray is an Indian *thali* (see page 283), about 12 inches (30 cm) in diameter, with sides that are about 1½ inches (3 cm) high. The steaming time varies according to the size of the steaming tray and the thickness of the batter. If you are using a large wok for your steaming and your steaming tray is the *thali* suggested above, your steaming time will be about 30 minutes. However, if your steaming gadget is smaller and you can only fit in an 8 inch (20 cm) tray with 1 inch (2.5 cm) high sides, the steaming would take about 15 minutes and you will have to steam in two batches. The way to test if a *dhokla* is done is to insert a toothpick into it as you would for a cake. If it comes out clean and the *dhokla* feels spongy and resistant, then it is ready.

If you are cooking a *dhokla* in two batches, divide all the ingredients in half. It is best to have two steaming trays. Make one batch and put it to steam. Then make your second batch from scratch, beating in the water and the baking soda just before you are ready to steam. It is important that the batter be frothing and bubbling as you are putting it in to steam.

To start with, measure out all your dry ingredients, as you would for a cake, and grease your steaming trays. Get the water boiling in your steaming utensil and have extra boiling water ready in case you need it to refill the utensil.

FOR THE BATTER:
1 tablespoon peanut oil or any other vegetable oil
1¾ cups chick-pea flour, sifted

¼ cup plus 1 tablespoon sugar
2 teaspoons salt
½ teaspoon citric acid (sold by Indian grocers and some pharmacists)

1 teaspoon baking soda

YOU ALSO NEED:
4 tablespoons peanut oil or any other vegetable oil

½ teaspoon brown mustard
   seeds
¼ teaspoon ground
   asafetida

6 fresh hot green chilies,
   roughly chopped
1 tablespoon sugar
¼ teaspoon citric acid

½ teaspoon salt
2 tablespoons finely
   chopped, fresh cilantro
1 tablespoon fresh or
   dried coconut

Get everything ready for steaming (see left). Pour approximately 3 inches (7.5 cm) of water into the wok. You should be able to fit the *thali* or tray near the top of the wok. You may need to rest it on a small dish so that it is secure rather than wedged in. It should sit above the water level. Bring the water in the wok to the boil. Grease the tray or trays with the 1 tablespoon oil.

If you are steaming the batter in one batch, put the chick-pea flour, sugar, salt and citric acid into a mixing bowl. Slowly add 1½ cups water as you beat the mixture to a thick, smooth batter. The color should become lighter and the mixture double in volume. Add the baking soda. Gently beat for a further 1–2 minutes. The mixture should bubble. Quickly pour the batter into the baking tray, place the tray in the wok, cover the wok and steam for 30 minutes or until a toothpick inserted into the cake comes out clean and the cake has a light, fluffy, sponge-like texture.

Cut into 1 inch (2.5 cm) squares or diamonds.

(If the *dhokla* is to be cooked in 2 separate batches, divide the flour mixture into 2 equal parts. Add only half the water to each lot and beat it in just before steaming it. Follow general directions.)

Meanwhile, heat the 4 tablespoons oil in a small pan over medium-high heat. When hot, add the mustard seeds. As soon as they pop, a matter of seconds, remove the pan from the heat. Add the *asafetida*, chilies and ¾ cup plus 1 tablespoon water. Return the pan to medium-high heat. Add the sugar, citric acid and salt. Bring to the boil. Boil for 2 minutes or until you have a light syrup. Remove from the heat.

Pour the syrup evenly over the cooked *dhokla*. Sprinkle the fresh cilantro and dried coconut over the top.

MAKES 20–30
DIAMONDS

Mrs Kumud Kansara's Handva
ⓥ SAVORY GRAIN CAKE WITH MUSTARD AND SESAME SEEDS

A SAVORY, ALL-VEGETARIAN CAKE, encrusted with sesame seeds. Serve as a snack, with drinks or at teatime.

❧

FOR THE BATTER:
2 cups long-grain rice
¾ cup *chana dal* (page 260)
¾ cup *toovar dal* (page 261)
¾ cup plus 2 tablespoons plain yogurt
1 teaspoon baking powder
⅔ cup peanut or vegetable oil plus a little extra for greasing a cake pan
1 teaspoon brown mustard seeds
1 teaspoon sesame seeds
¼ teaspoon ground *asafetida*
8–10 fresh curry leaves (optional)

1 (3 inch)(7.5 cm) piece fresh ginger root, finely grated
4–5 fresh hot green chilies, finely chopped
1 tablespoon cayenne pepper
¼ teaspoon ground turmeric
2¼ teaspoons salt
3 tablespoons sugar
1 teaspoon citric acid
2–3 tablespoons finely chopped, fresh cilantro
2 medium-sized carrots, peeled, cut into ¼ inch (5 mm) dice, boiled for 5 minutes and drained

1¾ cups shelled green peas, boiled briefly until just tender and drained (frozen peas may be used)

FOR THE FINAL SEASONING:
4 tablespoons peanut oil or any other vegetable oil
1½ teaspoons brown mustard seeds
1½ teaspoons sesame seeds
¼ teaspoon cayenne pepper
¼ teaspoon ground *asafetida*

❧

Wash the rice, *chana dal* and *toovar dal* in several changes of water until the water runs clear. Drain. Soak the rice and *dals* in water to cover by 2 inches (5 cm) for 3 hours. Drain.

Put the drained rice and *dals* into the container of an electric blender. Add 2½ cups

water. Blend to a smooth paste. You may need to do this in stages, pushing the mixture down with a spatula from time to time.

Put the rice and *dal* paste into a large bowl. Add the yogurt. Stir to mix. Leave for 1 hour. Add the baking powder and mix it in.

Pre-heat the oven to 400°F (200°C). Lightly oil a large 12 inch (30 cm) square or round cake pan with 3 inch (7.5 cm) high sides.

Heat the ⅔ cup oil in a large, wide, preferably non-stick pan or wok over medium-high heat. When hot, add the 1 teaspoon mustard seeds and 1 teaspoon sesame seeds. As soon as the mustard seeds pop, a matter of seconds, put in the ¼ teaspoon *asafetida*. Stir once and put in the curry leaves, if using, ginger and chilies. Stir and fry for 2 minutes. Add the 1 tablespoon cayenne pepper, turmeric, the ground rice and *dals*, salt, sugar, citric acid, cilantro and ⅔ cup water. Bring to the boil, stirring frequently. Reduce the heat to medium. Simmer gently and stir for 10 minutes. Add the carrots and peas and continue to stir and cook for another 5 minutes

or until you have a thick mixture. Pour the batter into the oiled cake pan. Press down firmly.

Heat the 4 tablespoons oil for the final seasoning in a small pan or wok over medium heat. When hot, add the 1½ teaspoons mustard seeds and the 1½ teaspoons sesame seeds. As soon as they pop, a matter of seconds, add the ¼ teaspoon cayenne pepper and ¼ teaspoon *asafetida*. Stir once. Remove from the heat and pour over the rice and *dal*.

Put the cake pan into the pre-heated oven. Bake for 1¼ – 1½ hours or until the cake is cooked. Check after 1 hour and make sure it does not darken too much. Turn the oven down to 375°F (190°C) if it does. Leave for 10 minutes and cut into 2 inch (5 cm) squares.

S E R V E S   1 0

Mrs Kumud Kansara's Kadhi

(V) SWEET AND SOUR CHICK-PEA FLOUR SOUP

THIS IS NOT A soup in the sense that you can drink it as a first course. It is soupy, however, and is usually eaten with rice. As an unusual variation, you may put in 3 tablespoons of fresh mango pulp instead of the sugar.

❧

FOR THE SOUP BASE:

2 cups plus 1 tablespoon plain yogurt

2 tablespoons chick-pea flour

1 (1 inch) (2.5 cm) piece fresh ginger root, peeled and finely grated

4 fresh hot green chilies, finely chopped

1 tablespoon chopped, fresh cilantro leaves

YOU ALSO NEED:

1 tablespoon *ghee* (page 271) or vegetable oil

½ teaspoon cumin seeds

¼ teaspoon ground *asafetida*

1 (1 inch) (2.5 cm) cinnamon stick, broken into 2–3 pieces

5–6 cloves

2 bay leaves

1–1½ tablespoons sugar

¾–1 teaspoon salt

❧

Make the soup base: put the yogurt and chick-pea flour into the container of an electric blender. Add 3 cups water. Blend thoroughly. Add the ginger root, chilies and cilantro. Blend to mix. Set aside.

Heat the *ghee* or oil in a large pan over medium-high heat. When hot, add the cumin seeds. As soon as they begin to change color, a matter of seconds, add the *asafetida*, cinnamon, cloves and bay leaves. Stir and fry for a few seconds or until the bay leaves darken in color. Quickly add the soup base, sugar and salt. Stir and bring to the boil.

Reduce the heat to very low and leave to simmer gently for 15 minutes. Remove from the heat.

SERVES 4

Spongy, Spicy, Savory Diamonds (page 74) and, left to right, Green Chili and Lime Pickle (page 86) and Cilantro and Peanut Chutney (page 86).

Mrs Kumud Kansara's Sev Tamate
Ⓥ NOODLES WITH TOMATO

IN THIS DRY STATE, where vegetables do not grow with ease, a bag of crisp noodles can quickly be changed into a main dish with the addition of a sauce. Here the sauce is made with tomatoes spiced with ginger root, garlic and green chilies. This is a very popular dish at all the vegetarian truck stops that line the state's highways. It is amazingly delicious as well. Although it is best made with homemade noodles, you may use the store-bought variety sold by Indian grocers. Look for medium-thick or thin *sev*.

❧

- 2½ tablespoons peanut oil or any other vegetable oil
- ½ teaspoon cumin seeds
- 5–6 garlic cloves, finely chopped
- 1 fresh hot green chili, finely chopped
- 1 (1 inch) (2.5 cm) piece fresh ginger root, peeled, very finely sliced and then very finely chopped
- ¼ teaspoon ground *asafetida*
- ¼ teaspoon ground turmeric
- ½ teaspoon cayenne pepper
- 2 medium-sized ripe tomatoes, coarsely chopped
- 3 tablespoons finely chopped, fresh cilantro
- ¾ teaspoon salt
- 2½ cups plain Crispy Chick-Pea Flour Noodles (*sev*) (page 62)

❧

Heat the oil in a wok or large, wide, preferably non-stick pan over medium-high heat. When hot, add the cumin seeds. Let them sizzle for 10 seconds. Add the garlic, chili and ginger. Stir and fry for 2–3 minutes or until the garlic begins to turn light brown. Add the *asafetida*, turmeric and cayenne pepper. Stir once quickly and put in the tomatoes as well as 1⅔ cups water. Bring to a gentle boil and cook for 2–3 minutes over medium-low heat, stirring frequently. Add the cilantro and salt. Simmer for 2–3 minutes or until the tomatoes are tender. Add the noodles. Stir to mix. Cook for 30 seconds to heat the noodles through and just barely soften them. Serve immediately.

SERVES 4

Mrs Kumud Kansara's Pudla
Ⓥ CHICK-PEA FLOUR PANCAKES

THIS NUTRITIOUS CHICK-PEA flour pancake may be served with all Indian meals just as a bread might be. It can also be eaten at breakfast or as a snack with chutneys, pickles and other relishes.

❧

1¼ cups chick-pea flour, sifted

½ teaspoon salt

½ teaspoon cayenne pepper

½ teaspoon *ajwain* seeds (page 259)

1 small red onion, very finely chopped

1 (2 inch) (5 cm) piece fresh ginger root, peeled and very finely chopped

4 fresh hot green chilies, very finely chopped

5 garlic cloves, peeled and very finely chopped

2 tablespoons very finely chopped, fresh cilantro

About 3 tablespoons vegetable oil

❧

Put the chick-pea flour into a large mixing bowl. Slowly add 1 cup water mixing with a wooden spoon to make a smooth batter. Add the salt, cayenne, *ajwain* seeds, onion, ginger, chilies, garlic and cilantro. Stir to mix. Set aside for 15 minutes.

Smear a large, wide, non-stick frying pan with 1 teaspoon of the oil and set over lowish heat. When very hot, stir the batter and pour about ⅓ cup onto the center of the pan. Quickly tilt the pan in all directions as you would for a crêpe, spreading the batter to make an 7–7½ inch (18–19 cm) pancake. Cover and cook for 3 minutes or until the pancake is reddish-brown at the bottom. Dribble another teaspoon of oil around the edges of the *pudla*. Turn the *pudla* over and cook, uncovered, for a further minute or until golden. Remove from the heat and keep covered between 2 plates. Repeat with the remaining batter. Always remember to stir the batter before you use it.

(Left-over batter may be covered, refrigerated and re-used).

MAKES 5 PANCAKES

Mrs Kumud Kansara's Thepla
ⓥ FLAT BREADS STUFFED WITH CABBAGE

THESE ARE SIMPLE, FLAT, wholewheat breads stuffed with cabbage. Serve with almost any Indian meal, especially a vegetarian one. You could also eat them by themselves with pickles and chutneys or any yogurt relish.

∾

1½ cups finely shredded white or green cabbage

1¼ teaspoons salt

1 cup whole-wheat flour, 1 cup all-purpose white flour, plus extra for dusting

¼ teaspoon ground black pepper

½ teaspoon ground coriander

⅓ teaspoon ground turmeric

⅛ teaspoon ground *asafetida*

½ teaspoon white sesame seeds

1–3 fresh hot green chilies, finely chopped

1 (1 inch) (2.5 cm) piece fresh ginger root, peeled and very finely chopped

2 tablespoons peanut oil or any other vegetable oil, plus extra for frying

∾

Put the cabbage in a small bowl. Add ½ teaspoon of the salt. Put aside for 30 minutes so that some water is drawn out from the cabbage. Squeeze out the water and pat dry.

Meanwhile, sift the flours into a large mixing bowl. Add the black pepper, coriander, turmeric, *asafetida*, sesame seeds, chilies, ginger and remaining salt. Mix well. Add the cabbage, oil and ⅔ cup water. Mix to make a medium to soft dough. Knead for 10 minutes. Cover with a damp cloth and rest for about 10 minutes.

Divide the mixture into 9 equal balls or *theplas*. On a lightly floured surface, roll each ball into a 6 inch (15 cm) round. Heat a large,

wide, cast-iron frying pan or *tava* over medium heat. When very hot, slap on a rolled-out *thepla*. Leave for 10 seconds. Dribble a teaspoon of oil around the *thepla* so that it runs under the edges. Turn the *thepla* over. Cook for 10 seconds. Turn the *thepla* over and dribble another teaspoon of oil around the edges. Now cook, turning every 10 seconds, until the *thepla* is golden on both sides and has a few brownish spots. Remove to a plate. Cover with another plate. Cook the remaining *theplas* in the same way.

MAKES 9 BREADS

Noodles with Tomato (page 80).

Niranjana Row Kavi's Leeli Chutney
ⓥ CILANTRO AND PEANUT CHUTNEY

THIS NUTTY GREEN CHUTNEY may be served with all Indian meals.

〜

3 tablespoons roasted, salted, shelled peanuts

2¾ cups fresh cilantro, finely chopped

6–7 fresh hot green chilies, finely chopped

1 (¼ inch) (5 mm) piece fresh ginger root, peeled and finely chopped

½ teaspoon salt

¼ teaspoon sugar

1 tablespoon lime juice

〜

Put the peanuts into a clean coffee grinder. Grind to a coarse powder.

Put the cilantro, chilies, ginger root, salt, sugar and lime juice into the container of an electric blender. Add 4 tablespoons water. Blend to a fine paste.

Put the peanuts and cilantro mixture into a bowl. Mix well.

The chutney will keep for at least 2 days if covered in the refrigerator.

S E R V E S   4 – 6

Samina Hakimji's Marchanu Athanu
ⓥ GREEN CHILI AND LIME PICKLE

IN GUJARAT, PICKLES ARE eaten with snack foods and with all meals. The chilies are pale green, mild in their heat and somewhat squat. You may use any green chilies such as cayenne as long as they are not the very small, fiery ones.

〜

1½ tablespoons salt

½ teaspoon ground turmeric

½ teaspoon ground cumin

16-24 fresh hot green chilies, wiped with a damp cloth and dried off

2 limes, each lime cut into 12 pieces

3 tablespoons mustard oil

1 cup plus1 tablespoon hulled and split mustard seeds (page 273)

1½ teaspoons white wine vinegar

Coconut Pistachio Sweetmeat (page 88).

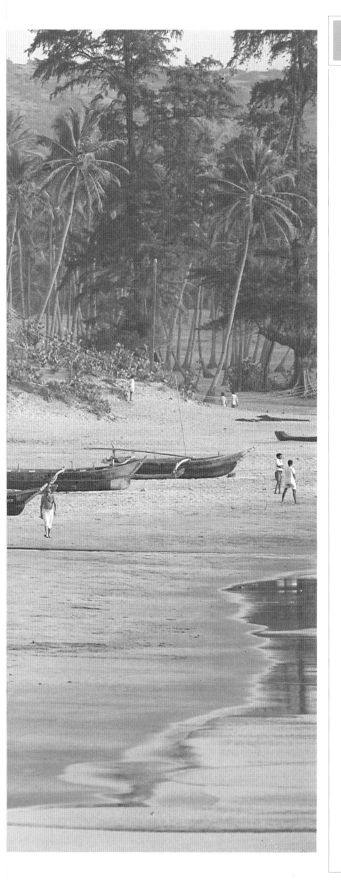

GOA

SOPHIE GONSALVES' HANDSOME, COLONIAL Goan home with its tiled roof sits on a sloping hillside of brick-red earth in the pretty township of Parra. There is a dappled arbor of passion fruit on one side. The sweet-and-sour pulp of this yellow, golf-ball-shaped fruit will be used as part of the dressing for the fresh fruit salad served on Christmas Day. A dog snoozes in the arbor's shade.

Behind the arbor, beside a well, is the kitchen garden which produces everything from curry leaves, cinnamon, black pepper, mangoes, coconuts and guavas to jackfruit and bananas. (Sophie carries a cluster of bananas into the dining-room, saying "You must try these – they are so sweet.") Stretching on the hillside at the back is a grove of cashew nut trees.

The cashews are a major local crop along with rice. There are rice fields everywhere. Even the local, whitewashed church, where a midnight Mass will be held on Christmas Eve, seems to sit in the midst of a rice field.

Sophie's cashews have just been harvested and are being roasted over wood fires in her semi-outdoor kitchen so that their hard, bitter and toxic outer shells can be cracked and removed. The nuts inside, now licked lightly by wood smoke, will be stored inside old cans in old cupboards and will taste somewhat like chestnuts. They will be served to the large family that will gather at Christmas-time.

of mixed race Catholic Goans. The original *vindalho* soon had added to it ginger, cumin, cloves, cardamom and an enormous number of dried red chilies which, rather like the red pepper used to make paprika, had more color than bite. The chilies came from the New World with the conquerors. Goa took to them in a way Portugal never did.

Today, the *vindaloo* is treated as a festive dish (pork, like all red meats, is more expensive than some of the everyday fish) and is often made in earthen vessels several days in advance. The vinegar still preserves it though, with their tropical climate, Goans without refrigerators do take the precaution of bringing it to a boil once a day and refrain from touching it with soiled spoons. It is served either with the local "red" rice, a short-grained, partially-milled, protein-rich variety, or with what is considered superior: a pilaf.

The pilaf, or *pillau* as they say here, is a possible throwback to Muslim times, or borrowed from Muslim India. It is made with basmati rice, flavored with whole spices such as cardamom and cooked in stock. *Pillaus* here may be made with the abundant prawns (shrimp), with local sausages or only with stock. The more Portuguese risotto (*arroz refogado*), on the other hand, is now made like Indian pilaf with basmati rice, though it can contain very un-Indian pilaf ingredients such as sausage or duck!

A *vindaloo* is just one of the pork dishes served on these balmy shores. If you hear the exuberant strains of a brass band coming from under a canopy of palms, a wedding is in progress and an *assado de leitoa*, a roast suckling pig, is being readied. It is cleaned and washed, then stuffed with a mixture of mashed potatoes, the chopped-up heart and liver, green chilies, curry leaves and parsley. (The stuffings vary but this is a popular one.)

The piglet is then sewn up and brushed with a mixture of turmeric water and oil as it roasts. This somewhat Eastern roast is served in proper European style, sitting on a large silver tray with an apple ensconced in its mouth!

Ask any blue-collar Goan what he is going to eat at Christmas and he is likely to reply, "*Sorpatel* with *sannas*." *Sorpatel* is another pork stew, traditionally made out of the shoulder, neck, kidneys, liver, tail and ears of the pig, though today people such as Sophie Gonsalves tend to do without the tail and ears!

Sophie likes to cook her *sorpatel* and *sannas* in the outdoor kitchen over wood. "It tastes much better this way," she says with conviction as she huffs and puffs at the fire, poking at it knowledgeably at appropriate intervals. First she cuts her meat into small cubes and boils it. Then she grinds her spices – red chilies, cumin seeds, turmeric, cloves, peppercorns and cinna-

A woman in traditional dress in Goa.

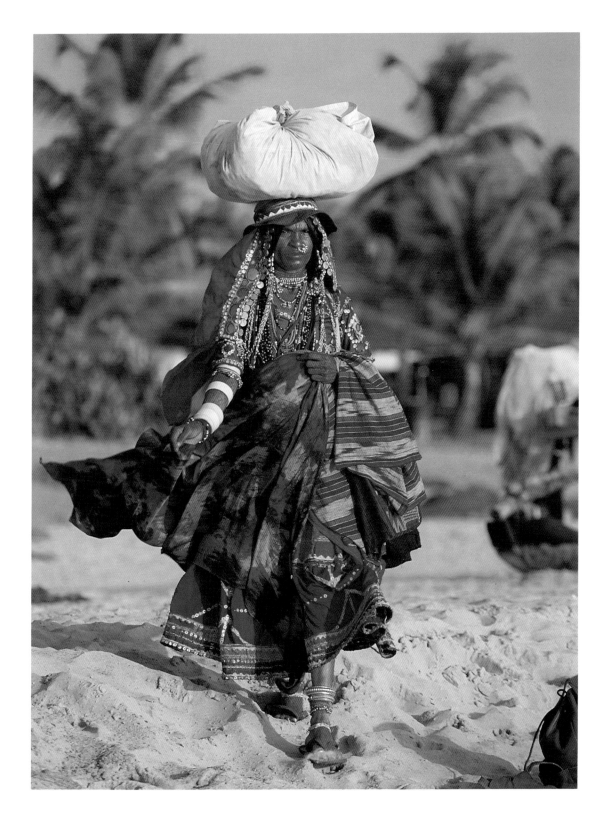

mon – in vinegar. After some onions, garlic, ginger and green chilies have been sautéed, in goes this spice paste and finally the meat. All simmers gently on the wood fire, stirred every now and then by Sophie's capable hands, until flavors meld and the meat is red, hot and sour. And what are the *sannas* that the sorpatel is eaten with? They are springy, crumpet-shaped steamed breads made in molds with a batter of ground "red" rice, ground coconut, salt, a little sugar and toddy.

Toddy is the sap collected from a palm before dawn. As the day progresses, it begins to bubble and ferment. All along this coast it is used as yeast.

Vinegary spice pastes, common to much of coastal Goan Catholic cooking, also go into the making of *chouricos*, the local sausages. Tart and spicy, they are made into curries to eat with rice, cooked along with red beans to make a glorious *feijoada*, and, best of all, eaten plain on the beach, sandwiched, along with a thin slice of onion, inside one of the local breads, the *pao*, which is a rectangular bun of white flour, or the *kunechi poee*, a butterfly-shaped, pita-like, flatter bread that is quite heavenly, both in taste and its chewy texture. The best sausages are sold in select places. "Try the blue-painted stall near the bridge over the Zuari River," you might be told, or "Go to such and such a shop in Mapusa market." Here the shopkeeper will count the links, wrap them in newspaper and hand them to you. The hungry can have a sandwich made

and gobble it up on the spot.

If you wish to see the sausages prepared from scratch, you may visit a special house in the town of Mapusa. A country road winds around a lush hill. The house sits just below the road. You enter through a gate and see nothing but an exquisite tropical garden and dozens of songbirds in cages. Just when you think that you might have entered the wrong compound, you see a sign, TASTY GOAN PORK SAUSAGES BY JOAO INACID DE SOUZA. At the back, in a series of sheds with wall signs that say "Do Not Spit" and "No Smoking," there is nothing but pork meat. Pork being cut; pork marinating in its very red spice mixture (vinegar, red chilies, cumin, pepper, cloves, garlic, turmeric, cinnamon, ginger and *feni*, the liquor distilled from either the cashew fruit or the palm); pork being pushed by machines into parchment-like casings; and sausages drying on palm-leaf mats in the sun, guarded by ferocious dogs including a Doberman. You wonder if the dogs are perhaps guarding not the sausages but the sausage recipe – the owner, who knows he is onto a good thing, will not part with it.

Besides pork dishes, Goan Catholics make a delightful beef pot roast (*bife assado*). Beef is pricked and then left to marinate in a mixture of chilies, ginger, garlic, cumin, cinnamon, pepper, vinegar, salt and turmeric. Onions are fried and the meat and marinade put into the pot along with a little water and, later, some potatoes. Nothing more is needed for a meal other than some *pao* and a simple Goan salad which tends to consist of shredded lettuce, tomatoes and cucumber dressed with just lime juice, a touch of *feni* vinegar and salt. To precede it, there might be some *caldo verde*, a mild, almost purely Portuguese soup made with potatoes, onions, dill and a touch of imported olive oil if there is any to be had.

Another example of East–West cuisine with origins dating back several hundred years is the *xacuti*. It is as popular here as the *vindaloo*. Spelled with an exotic "x" (and pronounced "sha-koo-tee") this is generally made with chicken although rabbits and the herons that stand on long legs in the paddy fields may also be snatched and thrown into the pot. Goan catering students, now studying their own culinary history with avid interest, seem to feel that the dish originated in northern Goa. It was a vegetarian (*shak* means "vegetable," *kooti* means "cut small") dish of small-cut vegetables or greens cooked with the same spice mixture that is used today for chicken pieces: roasted shredded coconut combined with a long list of spices that must be roasted first and then ground on a heavy grinding-stone, giving the dish a unique flavor – spices such as chilies, coriander seeds, fennel seeds, peppercorns, cardamom, cloves, cinnamon, mace, poppy seeds and, surprisingly, star anise. Perhaps the use of star anise, common to Chinese cooking, should not be so surprising. China began trading with India's west coast well before the start of the Christian era. In fact,

the antiques that grace the grand homes of wealthy Goans are either of Portuguese or Chinese ancestry. The exceedingly spicy *xacutis* were considered almost medicinal and offered to farmers returning from long wet days in the paddy fields during the monsoon planting season. The spices helped flush out their coughs and colds.

Pork, beef and poultry are all very well but the basic, daily diet of most people consists of vegetables, dried beans and the local "red" rice plus fish for the non-vegetarians. Breakfast could be a bowl of congee or rice gruel. It could also be *pao* and *chanyacho ros* (dried peas cooked with mustard seeds, curry leaves and roasted coconut). Lunch and dinner, on the other hand, would most likely be rice, and perhaps a vegetable such as *tamari bhaji* – a dish of red spinach from the fields, flavored with onions, green chilies, freshly grated coconut and, for souring, the dried fruit called *kokum*. The beans could be *osanay samaray* (red beans cooked with coconut and sour mango seeds). There might be *sookhi bhaji* (potatoes cooked with mustard and cumin seeds) or *bibo upkari* (cashews cooked with cumin, mustard and chilies) as well as *bharli vaangi*, small eggplants stuffed with a paste of sesame seeds, peanuts, palm sugar and onions.

Fish is what coastal Goans thrive on. Pomfret, mackerel, kingfish, sardines and squid from the sea, prawns (shrimp), crabs and lobsters from the coastal waters and river estuaries. The fish could be cooked in one of many ways. The cheapest might be a handful of tiny dried prawns (shrimp) cooked with a paste of coconut, chilies, coriander, cumin, turmeric, garlic, ginger and dried green mango slices. This makes a flavorful, slightly sweet, slightly sour and very hot sauce to put over rice. An aristocratic, Portuguese-speaking family might eat *carangrejo recheado* (crabs stuffed with onions, garlic, tomatoes and green chilies then dusted with breadcrumbs and baked) or *quisado de peixe* (fish and potatoes on a bed of onions and tomatoes). The flat fish, pomfret, might have deep slits cut on both sides of its backbone, the slits stuffed with a special spice paste called the *"Rechad"* masala and the whole fish is then fried in a frying pan.

The *rechad* spice paste, ground on stone, sits in jars in almost every home. Because the red chilies, cinnamon, cardamom, cloves, peppercorns, onion, garlic and ginger that make up the paste are ground in vinegar, it lasts for months.

The same spice mixture is used to cook squid (*ambot tik*). Fresh, juicy prawns (shrimp) may be curried (*samar codi*) with coconut milk. Tourists who are regulars in Goa order this as soon as they land. They hasten to one of the thatched, beach restaurants, order a cool cashew *feni* to drink, let the soft breeze waft through their hair and wait for their order of prawn (shrimp) curry and rice. Prawns (shrimp) can be cooked with green chilies and poppy seeds (*caldin*), they may be made into soup (*sopa de camarao*), made into a pie where the "crust" is made of rice (*apa de camarao*) or made into a preserve (*balchao*). They can be cooked with okra and pumpkin too. The more oily fish, such as mackerel and sardines, are often cooked with *teflam*, which is none other than Sichuan pepper. It is reputed to "cut" the oiliness. The spice is so well liked that one island, Divar, devotes a whole day to its celebration. Flags of all the villages are hoisted and young men load bamboo "guns" with the peppercorns to shoot at the girls of their choice!

There is a billboard on the way to Panaji from Goa's airport that says, "8 Layer Bibinca. Don't Leave Goa Without It." It is advice to be heeded. The *bebinca* is a "cake" of layered pancakes that uses coconut milk in the batter. The traditional recipe once began, "Take forty egg yolks" and ended "preparation time: 10 hours," a nightmare not only for those who tremble at the word "cholesterol" but for most ordinary, faint-hearted chefs. Such recipes were developed by once-cloistered nuns in places such as the Convent of Santa Monica where there were many quiet moments. Today's recipes are easier on the working family. Just ten egg yolks are required and only 2 hours of time. It is a smaller cake. As only thin wedges are eaten (many people are tempted to eat several thin wedges), not too much damage is done. *Bebinca* is not made every day. It is a festive cake for Christmas, so the minor damage is seasonal. The cake is so good, it is worth it.

Other desserts worth carrying out from

Goa are the coconut cake (*batica*), the coconut-stuffed pancakes (*alebele*) and *culculs*, tiny cookies that are pressed against a comb and allowed to roll into the shape of cowrie shells. This way you will be carrying away tasty memories of sunny, balmy Goa, its swaying palms and its warm sea.

A fishing scene in one of Goa's many harbors.

Jude Sequeira's
BEEF OR LAMB CHILI-FRY

THE GOANS HAVE BORROWED most recently from the Chinese and this is now a new local delicacy, found in most of the thatched shacks along the beaches.

❧

**12 oz (340 g) tender beefsteak or boned lamb from the leg or shoulder
2 medium-sized onions, peeled and finely chopped
5 garlic cloves, peeled and coarsely chopped**

**1 (1 inch) (2 cm) piece fresh ginger root, peeled and coarsely chopped
½ teaspoon cayenne pepper
½ teaspoon ground turmeric
1 teaspoon ground coriander
1 teaspoon ground cumin**

**¾ teaspoon salt or to taste
5 tablespoons vegetable oil
3–4 fresh hot green chilies, seeded and cut into long strips**

❧

Cut the beef into thin strips as you would for Chinese food. Put half of the onion, the garlic and ginger into the container of an electric blender with 2–3 tablespoons water. Blend. Add the cayenne pepper, turmeric, coriander and cumin. Blend to a paste. Rub the beef with 2 teaspoons of this paste and ¼ teaspoon of the salt.

Set aside for 10 minutes.

Heat 2 tablespoons of the oil in a wok or large, preferably non-stick frying pan over high heat. When hot, put in the remaining onion. Stir and fry until lightly browned. Put in the beef and stir and fry over very high heat until the meat begins to lose its raw look. Remove the beef and onion.

Wipe out the wok or frying pan and put in the remaining 3 tablespoons oil. Set over medium-high heat. When hot, put in the chilies and stir and fry them for a minute until lightly browned. Put in the spice paste and stir and fry for about 5–6 minutes until it is lightly browned. Now put in the beef and onion, ½ teaspoon salt and 6 tablespoons water. Stir over high heat for 1–2 minutes. Taste to check the salt and add more if necessary.

SERVES 4

Jude Sequeira's Beef Xecxec
BEEF WITH MUSHROOMS

A GOAN FIVE-SPICE MIX, very similar to the north Indian *garam masala*, is used to give aroma to this hot and sour Goan dish. It is normally served with local "red" rice but you may serve it with any rice, even a pilaf.

FOR THE GOAN FIVE-SPICE MIX:

10 cardamom pods
½ teaspoon cloves
1 teaspoon broken-up pieces of cinnamon stick
1½ teaspoons cumin seeds
1 teaspoon black peppercorns

YOU ALSO NEED:
1½ lb (675 g) lean stewing beef, cut into 2 inch (5 cm) cubes

1 teaspoon salt or to taste
2 tablespoons lime or lemon juice
1 (2 inch) (5 cm) piece fresh ginger root, peeled and coarsely chopped
6 garlic cloves, peeled and coarsely chopped
3 fresh hot green chilies, coarsely chopped
1 teaspoon ground turmeric
3 tablespoons vegetable oil

1 large onion, peeled and finely sliced into half-rings
2 medium-sized tomatoes, chopped
4 cups mushrooms, sliced
2 tablespoons tamarind paste (page 278)
Salt to taste

Put all the ingredients for the Goan five-spice mix in a clean coffee grinder and grind. (Any leftovers you have may be stored in a tightly lidded jar.)

Mix the beef with the salt and lime or lemon juice and marinate for 1 hour.

Meanwhile, put the ginger, garlic and chilies into the container of an electric blender. Add 3 tablespoons water and blend to a paste. Add 2 tablespoons of the Goan five-spice mix and the turmeric. Process briefly to mix. Take half of this spice paste and add it to the meat. Rub in

well and set the meat aside for another hour.

Heat the oil in a large frying pan over medium-high heat. When hot, add the onion. Stir and fry until the onion is medium-brown. Add the tomatoes. Fry for a further 2–3 minutes. Add the remaining spice paste. Continue to fry for 3–4 minutes, then add the marinated meat. Stir and fry to seal the meat. Then add 2½ cups water. Bring to the boil, turn the heat down to low and cover tightly. Simmer gently for 1½ hours or until the meat is tender. Add the mushrooms.

Cook for a further 5 minutes then add the tamarind paste. Stir to mix and bring to a simmer. Adjust the seasoning and serve.

SERVES 4

Jude Sequeira's Pork Vindalho
PORK WITH VINEGAR AND GARLIC

A DISH OF PORTUGUESE ancestry, *vindalho* (or *vindaloo* as it is known throughout the world) got its original name from two of its main seasonings: *vinho* or wine (actually wine vinegar) and *alhos* or garlic. This dish has now been thoroughly Indianized with the use of enormous amounts of dried red chilies brought, ironically enough, from the New World, as well as cumin, ginger and peppercorns.

A word about the chilies. The red ones that are used in Goa are Kashmiri chilies known more for the color they impart than their heat. I use a combination of ordinary red chilies and paprika to achieve the same effect.

A *vindalho* is made by Goan families on festive occasions – birthdays, weddings and even at Christmas. The dish, an unusual combination of a curry and a preserve, can be made up to a week in advance and often is. The vinegar acts as a preservative, making it an ideal party dish. Goans do take the precaution of bringing it to a boil once a day in the earthen vessel used for cooking. We in the West can also make it a few days in advance but I would keep it, well covered, in the refrigerator.

It is generally served with the local "red" rice, plain white rice or a basmati rice pilaf. A simple salad of tomatoes, lettuce and cucumber, dressed with lemon juice and salt, may be served on the side.

2¼ lb (1 kg) boneless pork from the shoulder, cut into 2 inch (5 cm) cubes
1½ teaspoons salt
6 tablespoons red wine vinegar

FOR THE SPICE PASTE:
4–10 dried hot red chilies
1 tablespoon bright red paprika
½ teaspoon cumin seeds

1 (2½ inch) (6 cm) cinnamon stick, broken up into smaller pieces
10–15 cloves
½ teaspoon black peppercorns

5–6 cardamom pods
10–12 garlic cloves, peeled
1 (1 inch) (2.5 cm) piece
  fresh ginger root, peeled
  and coarsely chopped
½ teaspoon ground
  turmeric

YOU ALSO NEED:
3 tablespoons vegetable oil
3–4 garlic cloves, peeled
  and lightly crushed
3 medium-sized onions,
  peeled and finely sliced

2 large tomatoes, chopped
6 fresh hot green chilies,
  sliced lengthwise in half
1 teaspoon sugar

Sprinkle the pork with 1 teaspoon of the salt. Add 3 tablespoons of the vinegar. Rub in well and set aside for 2–3 hours.

Make the spice paste: combine the red chilies, paprika, cumin seeds, cinnamon, cloves, peppercorns and cardamom pods in a clean coffee grinder and grind as finely as possible. Put the 10–12 garlic cloves and the ginger in the container of an electric blender along with 2 tablespoons of the vinegar and the turmeric. Blend well. Add the dry ground spices to the garlic mixture and blend again to mix. Rub the pork cubes with half of the spice paste, cover and refrigerate overnight. Cover and refrigerate the remaining spice paste.

Heat the 3 tablespoons oil in a wide, preferably non-stick pan over medium-high heat. When hot, put in the 3–4 garlic cloves. Stir and fry until they begin to pick up a little color. Put in the onions and continue to fry until browned. Now add the tomatoes and 3 of the green chilies. Stir for a minute. Add the remaining spice paste, the sugar and the remaining 1 tablespoon vinegar. Stir and fry until the paste begins to brown a little. Now add the marinated meat and all the spice paste clinging to it. Turn the heat to medium-low and cook, stirring, until the pork begins to exude its own liquid. Add 1¼ cups water and the remaining salt and bring to a boil. Cover, turn the heat to low and simmer gently until the meat is tender and the sauce has thickened somewhat, about 40 minutes.

If necessary, raise the heat to reduce the sauce to a medium-thick consistency towards the end. Add the remaining 3 green chilies and stir once.

S E R V E S   4 – 6

Sophie Gonsalves' Sorpatel
PORK COOKED WITH VINEGAR AND SPICES

A FAVORITE PARTY DISH, this is frequently cooked at Christmas-time and eaten with *sannas*, the spongy, crumpet-like breads on page 127. They are perfect for picking up the small-diced meat and soaking up the red-red sauce. *Sorpatel* is traditionally made up of various pig parts, including the tail and ears, but these days many families just use shoulder meat and liver. That is what I have done here. *Sorpatel*, rather like *vindalho*, is often made a few days ahead. The vinegar preserves it and the waiting period helps flavors to ripen.

∞

1½ lb (675 g) boneless, lean pork shoulder, cut into ½ inch (1 cm) cubes
8 oz (225 g) pork liver, cut into ½ inch (1 cm) cubes
4 tablespoons vegetable oil

FOR THE SPICE PASTE:
1 teaspoon cumin seeds
1 teaspoon black peppercorns

2 (1½ inch) (4 cm) cinnamon sticks, broken up
10 cloves
½ nutmeg
5–6 dried hot red chilies
1 teaspoon ground turmeric
1 tablespoon bright red paprika
⅔ cup cider vinegar

YOU ALSO NEED:
1 medium-large onion, peeled and sliced into fine half-rings
6–7 garlic cloves, peeled and finely chopped
1 (1 inch) (2 cm) piece fresh ginger root, peeled and very finely chopped
3 fresh hot green chilies, slit lengthwise into 3–4 pieces
1½ teaspoons salt or to taste

∞

Put the cubed pork shoulder and liver into 2 separate pans. Add enough water to each pan to just cover the meats. Place over medium-high heat and bring both pans to the boil. Turn the heat down to low, cover both pans and simmer gently for 20 minutes until the meats are cooked through. Drain, saving the stock from the shoulder, and allow to cool separately.

Put half of the liver into an electric blender. Blend briefly until it forms a paste.

When the shoulder meat and remaining liver are cool, heat 1 tablespoon of the oil in a non-stick frying pan over medium-high heat. When hot, add the cooled shoulder meat and liver. Toss and fry until lightly browned. Remove with a slotted spoon and set aside.

Put the cumin seeds, peppercorns, cinnamon, cloves, nutmeg and red chilies for the spice paste into a clean coffee grinder and grind to a fine powder. Empty into a small bowl. Add the turmeric, paprika and vinegar. Mix well and set aside.

Heat the remaining 3 tablespoons oil in a large, wide, preferably non-stick pan over medium-high heat. When hot, add the onions. Stir and fry until well browned. Add the garlic and ginger. Stir and fry for 2 minutes. Add the green chilies and the spice paste. Stir and fry until the spice paste browns a little. Put in the browned shoulder meat and liver cubes. Stir and toss until they are well coated with the spice paste. Add 2¼ cups of the stock, the salt and the liver paste. Stir and bring to a boil. Turn the heat to low, cover and simmer gently for about 30 minutes, or until the meat is very tender, adding more stock or water if necessary. Allow to cool. Empty into a bowl, cover and refrigerate overnight to let the flavor develop. Re-heat gently before serving.

SERVES 4

Jude Sequeira's Xacuti
CHICKEN WITH A ROASTED COCONUT SAUCE

THERE ARE PROBABLY AS many recipes for this as there are Goan homes. Here is a fairly traditional Catholic one. *Xacuti* (pronounced "sha-koo-tee") may be made out of rabbit, field heron, lamb or even with vegetables. What distinguishes a *xacuti* from other dishes is that all the seasonings in it are roasted before they are ground to a paste. It is supposed to be so spicy that it exorcizes all sniffles and coughs in the rainy monsoon season when farmers spend long hours knee-deep in the paddy fields. (For more on *xacuti*, see page 97.)

Today, many small neighborhood stalls serve it to truck-drivers and passers-by, in small saucers. Traditionally it is eaten with local breads such as the butterfly-shaped Goan bread *poee* (see page 128) or the bun-like *pao* or with rice. You may serve this chicken *xacuti* with a pilaf, plain rice or even a crusty bread. A salad or any Goan vegetable may be served on the side.

If you wish to substitute unsweetened, dried coconut for fresh coconut use 1¼ cups. Roast it in the same way as the fresh coconut, then soak it in ¾ cup water for 1 hour. Process the coconut and water together.

FOR THE SPICE PASTE:

2 cups freshly grated coconut (page 265)

½ teaspoon ground turmeric

5–6 dried hot red chilies

4 tablespoons coriander seeds

1 teaspoon cumin seeds

1 teaspoon fennel seeds

½ teaspoon black peppercorns

5–6 cardamom pods

½ teaspoon cloves

2 star anise

1 (2 inch) (5 cm) cinnamon stick, broken

A curl of mace

⅓ nutmeg

2 tablespoons white poppy seeds

1 tablespoon vegetable oil

1 medium-sized onion, peeled and cut into fine half-rings

1 (2 inch) (5 cm) piece fresh ginger root, peeled and thinly sliced

6–7 garlic cloves, peeled and coarsely chopped

YOU ALSO NEED:

3 lb (1.5 kg) chicken pieces, cut into small serving pieces (whole breasts into 6 and whole legs into 4 parts)

1½ teaspoons salt

2 tablespoons lemon juice

4 tablespoons vegetable oil

2 medium-sized onions, peeled and finely sliced into half-rings

About 15–20 fresh curry leaves (optional)

Make the spice paste: heat a cast-iron frying pan over medium-high heat. When hot, put in the coconut. Stir and roast until it is medium-brown. Add the turmeric and stir once or twice. Remove and set aside. Put the chilies, coriander seeds, cumin seeds, fennel seeds, peppercorns, cardamom pods, cloves, star anise, cinnamon, mace and nutmeg into the same hot pan. Stir until the spices are almost roasted. Add the poppy seeds. Keep roasting until the spices are lightly browned. Remove all the spices and let them cool slightly. Put the spices into a clean coffee grinder, in several batches if necessary, and grind to a fine powder.

Put the 1 tablespoon oil into the same pan and heat over medium-high heat. When hot, put in the onion, ginger and garlic. Sauté until medium-brown. Remove.

Put the coconut, ground spices and onion mixture in an electric blender. Add 1½ cups water or more and blend to a paste, in more than one batch, if needed.

Put the chicken pieces in a single layer on a large plate. Sprinkle on both sides with ¾ teaspoon of the salt and the lemon juice. Rub this in. Set aside for 20 minutes.

Heat the 4 tablespoons oil in a wide, preferably non-stick pan over medium-high heat. When hot, put in the sliced onions. Stir and fry until browned. Put in the spice paste. Stir and cook for 2–3 minutes. Put in the chicken and all accumulated juices as well as the remaining salt and 1¼ cups water. Stir and bring to a simmer. Cover, turn the heat to low and cook for about 25 minutes or until the chicken is tender. Add the curry leaves, if using, and stir them in.

SERVES 6

Maria Fernanda Sousa's Carangrejo Recheado
STUFFED CRAB

RECHEADO IS THE PORTUGUESE word for "stuffed" and these are whole crabs stuffed with what would be a very mild Mediterranean stuffing were it not for the use of hot green chilies. Serve with a simple green salad. On Goa's many beaches the stuffed crab often comes with chips but that, I suspect, is a more recent addition. Smaller-sized crabs make an excellent first course.

2 large crabs and their cooked meat

4 tablespoons olive oil

2 medium-sized onions, finely chopped

4 garlic cloves, peeled and finely chopped

2 medium-sized tomatoes, cut into small dice

2–3 fresh hot green chilies, finely chopped

4 tablespoons finely chopped, fresh green cilantro

2 tablespoons lemon juice

¾ teaspoon salt or to taste

Freshly ground black pepper

About 6 tablespoons dried breadcrumbs

Pre-heat the oven to 350°F (180°C).

Open up the crabs by pulling off their lower shells. Remove all the crabmeat, break it up into small lumps and save. Save the back, it will be used for serving.

Heat 3 tablespoons of the oil in a frying pan over medium-high heat. When hot, put in the onions and garlic. Stir and fry until they turn golden. Put in the tomatoes. Stir and fry until the tomatoes are soft. Add the chilies. Stir once or twice. Now put in the cilantro, crab meat, lemon juice and salt (put ½ teaspoon first, mix and taste) and pepper. Turn off the heat and mix well.

Spoon the crab meat into the two crab backs. Spread the breadcrumbs over the top, dribble over the remaining 1 tablespoon olive oil and bake in the oven for 10–15 minutes until heated through. Brown the top quickly under the broiler.

S E R V E S   2

Jude Sequeira's
"RECHAD" SPICE PASTE

EVERY HOUSEHOLD IN GOA, however humble, has a big jar of what is called *rechad masala* sitting in the kitchen. It looks very red, the color coming from the generous use of Kashmiri chili which has some of the same properties as the paprika pepper – it releases a lot of bright red dye. The other spices in the paste, all of which are ground in vinegar, include cumin, cinnamon and black pepper. Vinegar helps it to last.

The name of the paste comes, of course, from the Portuguese "*recheado,*" meaning "stuff," and while the paste is mainly used to stuff local fish, it is also used to curry squid and other creatures of the sea.

Here is a recipe for the paste. What is not used should be put in a jar, covered and refrigerated. It will keep for months.

---

1 oz (30 g) dried hot red chilies (about 45)
½ teaspoon cumin seeds
1 (1 inch) (2.5 cm) cinnamon stick, broken up
1 teaspoon cardamom pods
1 teaspoon cloves
1 tablespoon black peppercorns

2 tablespoons bright red paprika
1 tablespoon vegetable oil
1 small onion, peeled and coarsely chopped
½ head garlic, peeled and coarsely chopped

2 (2½ inch) (6 cm) pieces fresh ginger root, peeled and coarsely chopped
1 teaspoon salt
½ cup cider vinegar

Put the chilies, cumin seeds, cinnamon, cardamom pods, cloves and peppercorns into a clean coffee grinder and grind them to a powder. Put into the container of an electric blender. Add the paprika. Heat the oil in a small frying pan over medium-high heat. When hot, put in the onion, garlic and ginger. Cook, stirring, until the onion has softened a bit. Empty the contents of the pan into the electric blender. Add the salt and vinegar. Blend thoroughly.

MAKES ABOUT ½ CUP

Pomfret "Rechad"
STUFFED POMFRET

THE BEST FISH TO stuff with the *"Rechad"* Spice Paste (opposite) is the Indian pomfret. It is flat and meaty with very white flesh. Two large pockets are cut into it with a sharp knife that slides along both sides of the backbone. The stuffing is shoved inside and then the fish is sautéed. A light weight is sometimes put on top of the fish so that it does not open up. Other fish such as red snapper or sole may be used. Mackerel is also good; because of its shape it is better to make several diagonal slits across its sides rather than pockets, and use those for the stuffing.

Serve with boiled potatoes and a salad or with any vegetables of your choice.

---

4 (12 oz) (340 g) sole, red snapper or mackerel, cleaned

4 tablespoons lime or lemon juice
1 teaspoon salt
About 3 tablespoons *"Rechad"* Spice Paste (opposite)

About 4 tablespoons vegetable oil
4 lemon quarters, to serve

Pre-heat the oven to 350°F (180°C).

Make 2 deep slits on either side of the backbone of each fish. Rub each fish, inside and out, first with 1 tablespoon of the lime or lemon juice and then with ¼ teaspoon of the salt. Set aside for 10 minutes. Using about 2 teaspoons of the *"rechad"* paste for each fish, stuff the pockets, making sure you get deep inside the fish. (You could use more paste if you like.)

Alternatively, if you are using mackerel, instead of making deep pockets make 3 deep slashes diagonally across the body and stuff these with the paste.

Heat the oil in a large, preferably non-stick frying pan over medium-low heat. When hot, put in as many fish as the pan will hold in one layer and fry gently for about 5 minutes on each side. As the fish get fried, put them in a big baking sheet in a single layer. When all the fish are done, put them in the oven and bake for 10 minutes. Serve with lemon quarters.

S E R V E S   4

Maria Fernanda Sousa's Guisado de Peixe
FISH ON A BED OF POTATOES, ONIONS AND TOMATOES

THIS IS ANOTHER VERY Portuguese dish, enlivened with green chilies. Serve with a green salad. Mrs Sousa adds her precious wine at the end, but I have taken the liberty of putting it in a little earlier.

∾

4 tablespoons virgin olive oil

3 medium-sized onions, cut into fine half-rings

3 medium-sized tomatoes, cut into small dice

5 garlic cloves, finely chopped

Salt

A generous pinch of sugar

1 teaspoon black peppercorns

4 small-medium potatoes, peeled and cut into ½ inch (1 cm) thick slices

3 thinnish 6 oz (175 g) swordfish steaks

Freshly ground black pepper

⅔ cup dry white wine or dry vermouth

1–2 fresh hot green chilies, split into halves

∾

Heat the oil in a large, preferably non-stick frying pan over medium-high heat. When hot, put in the onions. Stir and fry until golden. Add the tomatoes, garlic, ¾ teaspoon salt, sugar and peppercorns. Stir and fry until the tomatoes are soft. Put in the potatoes. Stir gently a few times. Cover and cook gently over low heat, shaking occasionally, until the potatoes are almost tender.

Meanwhile, sprinkle the fish steaks lightly with salt and pepper on both sides and set aside.

When the potatoes are almost done, pour the wine or vermouth over them. Stir gently and cook for a minute. With a spoon, remove a little of the soft onion-garlic-tomato mixture. Then lay the fish steaks over the potatoes in a single layer. Spoon some of the onion-garlic-tomato mixture over them. Lay the green chilies over the top, cover and cook for 5–10 minutes or until the fish is just cooked through and the potatoes are tender.

S E R V E S   3

Chicken with a Roasted Coconut Sauce (page 105), Potatoes with Mustard Seeds (page 118) and Goan Bread (page 128).

Jude Sequeira's Squid Ambot Tik
S O U R   A N D   S P I C Y   S Q U I D

SQUID IS FOUND IN abundance in the waters of the Arabian Sea. The locals enjoy it but almost none is sent inland to the heart of the nation which, more is the pity, has not yet developed a taste for this excellent seafood. What the locals do not want is shipped to Japan.

There are many ways of cooking squid here, but perhaps the best is *ambot tik*, a sour and hot dish using what is locally called "*Rechad*" Spice Paste (page 108), a red spice paste that is found sitting promisingly in every kitchen, ensconced in a large jar.

Ambot tik is generally served with the Goan, half-milled "red" rice, but it could also be served with plain rice enriched perhaps by a dollop of butter. A salad and some vegetables on the side would be ideal.

❧

3 tablespoons vegetable oil

2 medium-sized onions, peeled and cut into fine half-rings

3 garlic cloves, peeled and finely chopped

1 medium-sized tomato, finely chopped

2–6 fresh hot green chilies, sliced lengthwise into 3–4 strips each

2 tablespoons "*Rechad*" Spice Paste (page 108)

1 lb (450 g) cleaned squid (page 285), opened up and cut crosswise into ¼ inch (5 mm) wide strips

4 pieces of *kokum* (page 272) or 1 tablespoon tamarind paste (page 278) or 1½ tablespoons lemon juice

½–¾ teaspoon salt or to taste

❧

Heat the oil in a frying pan over medium-high heat. When hot, add the onions. Stir and fry until golden. Add the garlic. Continue frying until the onions pick up brown edges. Add the tomatoes and chilies. Stir and fry until the tomatoes are soft and pulpy. Add the "*Rechad*" Spice Paste. Stir and cook for a minute. Then add 2 cups water. Bring to a boil. Lower the heat and simmer gently until the liquid is reduced by half. Now add the squid, the *kokum* or tamarind paste or lemon juice and the salt. Stir to mix. Cook, stirring, over medium-low heat until the squid has turned white, about 2–4 minutes.

S E R V E S   4

Jude Sequeira's Prawns Caldin
COCONUT AND GREEN CHILI PRAWNS (SHRIMP)

A SLIGHTLY SWEET (from the coconut milk) and slightly sour (from the tamarind) dish, this is generally eaten with the local "red" rice which helps to soak up the excellent and generous sauce. In the West, it would be best served with any plain white rice – basmati or another long-grain variety. Red Spinach (page 119) or a salad may be served on the side.

1 (14 fl oz) (397 g) can coconut milk
5–10 fresh hot green chilies, coarsely sliced
1 teaspoon ground turmeric
2 tablespoons finely chopped, fresh cilantro
1 teaspoon freshly ground black pepper
3 tablespoons ground coriander
1½ teaspoons ground cumin
2 tablespoons white poppy seeds
4 tablespoons vegetable oil
2 medium-sized onions, peeled and sliced into fine half-rings
2 garlic cloves, peeled and cut into fine slivers
1 (½ inch) (1 cm) piece of fresh ginger root, peeled and cut into fine slices and then into fine slivers
1 tablespoon tamarind paste (page 278)
1 teaspoon salt
2 lb (900g) uncooked, unpeeled, medium-sized headless prawns (shrimp)

Open the coconut can without shaking it. Remove the cream at the top. Save it. Now add enough water to the can to fill it to the top again. Put this thin coconut milk into a bowl.

Put the chilies, turmeric, fresh cilantro, pepper, ground coriander and ground cumin into the container of an electric blender along with 4 tablespoons of the thin coconut milk. Blend. Pour this spice mixture into the bowl with the thin coconut milk.

Put the poppy seeds into a clean coffee grinder and grind as finely as possible. Add to the thin coconut milk.

Heat the oil in a deep frying pan over medium-high heat. When hot, put in the onions, garlic and ginger. Stir and fry until they brown at the edges. Now pour in the seasoned thin coconut milk and add the tamarind, salt and ½ cup water. Cover and simmer gently for 10 minutes. Add the prawns (shrimp) and the reserved thick coconut cream. Mix well and bring to a simmer. As soon as the prawns (shrimp) turn opaque all the way through, they are done.

SERVES 6

Sophie Gonsalves' Samar Codi

PRAWN (SHRIMP) CURRY

When I arrive in Goa, the first dish I order is this simple prawn (shrimp) curry! It uses no oil as nothing in it requires frying or sautéeing. In many ways, it is the humblest of curries and may be made with very cheap fish cut into chunks, fish steaks or fillet pieces.

I like it made with juicy prawns (shrimp), fresh from the sea. With a spicy, red, coconutty sauce flowing over a bed of white, pearly rice – what else can one want? I rarely order this dish in the hotel that I stay in. I find a small beach shack covered with palm thatching, generally owned by real fishermen, and order it there. All I need with it is a cold glass of beer.

If you buy unpeeled, headless prawns (shrimp) you will need 1½ lb (675 g). Peel and devein them (page 285), then wash them and pat them dry.

∾

1 teaspoon cayenne pepper
1 tablespoon bright red
  paprika
½ teaspoon ground turmeric
4 garlic cloves, peeled and
  crushed to a pulp
1 (1 inch) (2.5 cm) piece of
  fresh ginger root, peeled
  and grated to a pulp

2 tablespoons coriander
  seeds
1 teaspoon cumin seeds
1 (14 oz) (397 g) can
  coconut milk, well stirred
¾ teaspoon salt or to taste

3 pieces of *kokum* (page
  272) or 1 tablespoon
  tamarind paste (page 278)
1 lb (450 g) peeled and
  deveined, medium-sized
  uncooked prawns
  (shrimps)

∾

In a bowl, combine 1¼ cups water with the cayenne pepper, paprika, turmeric, garlic and ginger root. Mix well. Grind the coriander seeds and cumin seeds in a clean coffee grinder and add to mixture.

Put the spice mixture into a pan and bring to a simmer. Turn the heat to medium-low and simmer for 10 minutes. The sauce should reduce and thicken. Add the coconut milk, salt, *kokum* or tamarind paste and bring to a simmer. Add the prawns (shrimp) and simmer, stirring now and then, until they turn opaque and are just cooked through.

Pork with Vinegar and Garlic (page 102) and
Okra with Dried Prawns/Shrimp (page 116).

S E R V E S   4

E N T R É E

Rita Themudo's Bhindi Bhaji
OKRA WITH DRIED PRAWNS (SHRIMP)

DRIED PRAWNS (SHRIMP) ARE required here. Those used in Goa are very tiny and flat. I tend to get the larger, pinkish ones sold by most Chinese grocers, and then grind them in a clean coffee grinder to get a powder which works quite beautifully with okra. Serve this dish with any Indian meal.

1 lb (450 g) okra

3 tablespoons vegetable oil

1 teaspoon cumin seeds

1 medium-sized onion, finely chopped

4 garlic cloves, finely chopped

2 large tomatoes, finely chopped

1 teaspoon ground cumin

1 teaspoon ground coriander

½ teaspoon ground turmeric

½ teaspoon cayenne pepper or to taste

¾–1 teaspoon salt or to taste

2 tablespoons dried prawns (shrimp), see above

Wipe the okra pods with a damp cloth. Cut them crosswise into ½ inch (1 cm) wide segments.

Heat the oil in a large, preferably non-stick frying pan over medium-high heat. When hot, put in the cumin seeds. Let them sizzle for a few seconds. Now put in the onion and garlic. Stir and fry until they start to brown. Put in the okra. Stir and fry until lightly browned. Add the tomatoes. Stir and cook until the tomatoes are soft. Add the ground cumin, coriander, turmeric, cayenne pepper and salt.

Stir to mix and toss for a minute. Add about ⅔ cup water and bring to a simmer. Cover, turn the heat to low and cook for 15–20 minutes, stirring now and then, until the okra is tender.

Meanwhile, rinse the prawns (shrimp) and pat them dry. Put them into a clean coffee grinder and grind to a powder. When the okra is tender add the prawn (shrimp) powder and stir it in.

SERVES 3 – 4

Jude Sequeira's Cashew Nut Bhaji
Ⓥ CASHEW NUTS WITH COCONUT

CASHEW NUTS ARE GROWN all over the southwest coast of India. They are harvested in winter, roasted lightly to rid them of their reddish-brown skins and then eaten out of hand or used in hundreds of cakes, puddings and *halvas*. The Hindus of Goa also serve them as a vegetable. Indian breads are the traditional accompaniment to this *bhaji*. It is best to use fresh coconut in this dish.

~

1 lb (450 g) (3 cups) raw cashew nuts

2 tablespoons vegetable oil

1 teaspoon brown mustard seeds

1 teaspoon cumin seeds

1 teaspoon *urad dal* (page 261)

2–3 dried hot red chilies, broken up

1½ teaspoons salt

½ teaspoon ground turmeric

1 cup freshly grated coconut (page 265)

2 fresh hot green chilies, slit lengthwise

1 teaspoon Goan five-spice mix (page 101)

1 tablespoon chopped, fresh cilantro

~

Soak the cashew nuts in water to cover for 8 hours or overnight. Drain.

Heat the oil in a large frying pan over medium-high heat. When hot, put in the mustard seeds. As soon as they start to pop, a matter of seconds, add the cumin, *urad dal* and red chilies. Stir and fry for a few seconds until the *dal* turns reddish and the chilies darken. Add the cashew nuts and salt. Stir for a minute.

Add the turmeric. Stir once and add ⅓ cup water. Cover and turn the heat to low. Simmer gently for 10 minutes. Remove the cover and add the coconut, green chilies and five-spice mix.

Mix well, sprinkle with the fresh cilantro and serve.

SERVES 4 – 6

Sookhi Bhaji
Ⓥ POTATOES WITH MUSTARD SEEDS

A HINDU DISH, THIS is served with the Goan bread "*pao*," or with fluffy *pooris* at most neighborhood stalls. It is generally ladled out into small saucers which serve as plates. You just dip your bread into it and eat. A popular place to find this combination of "*bhaji-pao*" is in the heart of Mapusa market at Café Corner, where local vendors, itinerant tribespeople and tourists all seem to want to come and eat. The place is jammed – and with good reason. The price is good (very cheap) and the taste of the food quite excellent.

Sookhi bhaji is eaten for breakfast, for lunch and even at teatime! In fact, a cup of steaming milky tea tastes particularly good with it.

❧

3 tablespoons vegetable oil
1 teaspoon cumin seeds
1 teaspoon brown mustard seeds
1 medium-sized onion, peeled and finely chopped
2–4 fresh hot green chilies, split into halves lengthwise
4 small-medium waxy potatoes, boiled, peeled and cut into ½ inch (1 cm) dice
1 teaspoon ground cumin
1 teaspoon ground coriander
½ teaspoon ground turmeric
1 teaspoon salt
¼ teaspoon cayenne pepper
1 tablespoon finely chopped, fresh cilantro

❧

Heat the oil in a wide pan over medium-high heat. When hot, put in the cumin seeds and mustard seeds. As soon as the mustard seeds begin to pop, a matter of a few seconds, put in the onion and chilies. Turn the heat to medium. Stir and cook until the onion is quite soft but not brown. Put in the potatoes, ground cumin, coriander, turmeric, salt and cayenne pepper. Stir gently once or twice.

Add ⅔ cup water and cook over medium-low heat for 8–10 minutes, stirring now and then, until all the spices have been absorbed by the potatoes. There should be just a hint of sauce at the bottom of the pan. Sprinkle the fresh cilantro over the top, stir it in and serve.

SERVES 4

Rita Themudo's Tamari Bhaji
Ⓥ RED SPINACH

THIS IS NORMALLY MADE with the heart-shaped "red spinach" leaves that are sold fresh in many of the "China Towns" of the West. Trim away the tough roots and stalks and coarsely slice the leaves. I have used green spinach as that is what is most easily available. Serve with any Indian meal.

If you wish to substitute unsweetened dried coconut for fresh coconut use 2 tablespoons. Just soak it in 4 tablespoons warm water and leave for 1 hour, then proceed with the recipe.

❧

2 lb (900 g) washed, trimmed spinach
3 tablespoons vegetable oil
2 medium-sized onions, cut into fine half-rings

2–3 fresh hot green chilies, cut into fine slivers
2 pieces of *kokum* (page 272) or 1 teaspoon tamarind paste (page 278) or 1 tablespoon lemon juice

¾–1 teaspoon salt
4 tablespoons freshly grated coconut (page 265)

❧

Cut the spinach leaves into thin strips.

Heat the oil in a wok or large, wide pan over medium-high heat. When hot, put in the onions. Stir and fry until they turn slightly brown. Put in the spinach, chilies and *kokum* or tamarind paste or lemon juice. Stir and fry briskly until the spinach has completely wilted and cooked through. Add the salt and mix. Put in the coconut and stir once (The *kokum* is not usually eaten.)

S E R V E S   4

Sophie Gonsalves' Osanay Samaray
ⓥ BEANS WITH ROASTED SPICES

OSANAY ARE SPECIAL BEANS, pinkish-green in color, that look like small kidney beans. When cooked with roasted spices the Goan way, they become rich and meaty. The best substitute is black-eyed beans, though pinto beans may also be used.

The souring is traditionally provided by the dried pit of an unripe green mango, a seasoning that is very common in Goa, especially for dried beans. What a creative way to use up what most of us just throw away! Not being able to procure this sour, dried pit easily, I have used lemon juice instead.

This dish may be eaten with the Goan bread "*poee*" (page 128) or with any crusty French or Italian bread. It is also excellent with *chapatis* or pita bread or even with rice. It may be served as part of a Goan or a general Indian meal.

If you wish to substitute unsweetened dried coconut for fresh coconut use 1¼ cups. Roast it first following the directions for fresh coconut, then soak in 1 cup warm water for 1 hour. Grind the liquid and coconut together.

∾

2½ cups black-eyed beans or Goan *osanay* beans
2–2¼ teaspoons salt

FOR THE SPICE PASTE:
About 2 cups finely grated fresh coconut (page 265)
1 tablespoon vegetable oil
4 garlic cloves

1 (1 inch) (2.5 cm) piece of fresh ginger root, peeled and thinly sliced
2 fresh hot green chilies, coarsely sliced
4–6 dried hot red chilies
1 teaspoon cumin seeds
2 teaspoons coriander seeds
2 cloves

2 star anise
1 tablespoon white poppy seeds

YOU ALSO NEED:
4 tablespoons vegetable oil
2 medium-sized onions, finely sliced
1–2 tablespoons lemon juice

∾

Pick over the beans and wash and drain them. Soak overnight in plenty of water. Drain. Cover with water by 2–3 inches (5–7.5 cm) and bring to the boil. Cook for 30 minutes or until the beans are just tender, adding about 1½ teaspoons salt during the last 5 minutes of cooking. Drain, saving the bean water, and set aside.

Make the spice paste: put the coconut in a cast-iron frying pan over medium-high heat. Stir and roast until lightly brown. Remove the coconut and put it into the container of an electric blender. Put the 1 tablespoon oil into a small frying pan and heat over medium-high heat. When hot, put in the garlic, ginger and green chilies. Stir and fry until lightly browned. Remove and put with the coconut in the electric blender. Add about 1 cup water or more as needed, and blend to a smooth purée. You may need to do this in more than one batch.

Now put the red chilies, cumin seeds, coriander seeds, cloves and star anise into the small frying pan and set over medium-high heat. Stir until very lightly roasted. Put in the poppy seeds, and roast for another minute. Remove and allow to cool. Grind just these dry spices in a clean coffee grinder. Combine with the coconut mixture. Mix and set aside.

Heat the 4 tablespoons oil in a large, wide pan over medium-high heat. When hot, put in the sliced onions. Stir and fry until lightly browned. Put in the spice paste. Stir and fry for 1 minute. Put in the beans and 4½ cups water (use up the bean water adding water to make up the necessary quantity). Bring to a simmer. Cook over low heat for 15–20 minutes, stirring gently now and then. Stir in the lemon juice. Check the salt, adding another ½–¾ teaspoon as needed.

S E R V E S   6 – 8

Sannas
Ⓥ STEAMED RICE "CRUMPETS"

SANNAS ARE CRUMPET-LIKE, steamed breads about 3–4 inches (7.5–10 cm) across and about ½ inch (1 cm) high, that are made with a batter of soaked, ground rice and finely ground coconut. The rice is the partially milled "red" rice that grows in most paddy fields here and the coconut is, of course, fresh, straight off the palm. The liquid in the batter is toddy, a sap taken from palms, that bubbles and ferments within a few hours of leaving the tree. It allows the batter to flow but acts as the yeast. Once the batter is made, it is allowed to rise before it is poured into molds and steamed into *sannas*.

Not being able to get many of the ingredients, I have used substitutes – a mixture of ordinary yeast, rice flour, all-purpose flour and dried coconut. To steam the *sannas*, you may use *idli* molds, sold by many Indian grocers, or you may pour the batter into medium-sized saucers or use large 3 inch (7.5 cm) custard cups. For general steaming instructions, see page 287. *Sannas* are traditionally eaten with Pork with Vinegar and Spices (page 104), but they may be served with any curry. Their pliable, spongy texture is ideal for soaking up hot and spicy meat sauces.

---

1 teaspoon sugar
2 teaspoons dried yeast
½ cup unsweetened dried
  coconut

1½ cups rice flour
4 teaspoons all-purpose
  flour
4 teaspoons sugar
½ teaspoon salt

A little vegetable oil for
  greasing

Let the sugar dissolve in 2 tablespoons warm water. Then sprinkle over the dried yeast. Set aside to allow the yeast to activate and froth.

Put the coconut into a clean coffee grinder and grind until fine. Empty into the container of an electric blender. Add the rice flour, all-purpose flour, sugar, salt and 1¼ cups warm water. Blend until you have a smooth paste. You may need to scrape down with a rubber spatula a few times. Add the yeast mixture and blend well. The batter should have the consistency of thick heavy cream. Pour into a bowl, cover with a cloth and leave in a warm place for about 15 minutes or until the batter has doubled in size.

Coconut Pancakes (page 131).

Grease ramekins, saucers or *idli* molds. Ladle in enough batter to come three-quarters of the way up the sides. If you are going to use large custard cups, grease them and fill only half way up the sides. Leave for another 10 minutes to rise again.

Meanwhile, prepare your steaming equipment. Half-fill the lower part with water and bring it to a boil. Rest the steaming tray on top. Place the ramekins, saucers or molds in the steaming tray – you may be able to fit in more than one layer. Cover and steam for 15 minutes. Repeat if necessary to use up all the batter. Allow to cool slightly before gently easing the *sannas* out by running a knife around the sides.

SERVES 4 – 6

Poee
Ⓥ GOAN BREAD

POEE IS SOMEWHAT LIKE pita bread only it is butterfly-shaped and very spongy inside, full of large, airy holes. It can be bought in most Goan markets but it is best to go straight to the local baker and buy it just as it comes out of the oven.

There is one such bakery, with a huge beehive oven made of clay, glass pieces and salt, in the tiny town of Parra. Large, wooden paddles push dough in and pull breads out. Breads line the room. Huge blobs of very soft dough rise in another room. The smell is heavenly.

"Poees" can be eaten with all Goan and many other Indian meals.

1 teaspoon sugar	**3½ cups all-purpose flour,**	**A pinch of salt**
1 teaspoon dried yeast	**plus extra flour for dusting**	

Let the sugar dissolve in ½ cup warm water. Then sprinkle over the dried yeast. Mix until smooth. Set aside for 10 minutes until the yeast is frothy.

Place the flour and salt in a large bowl. Pour in the yeast mixture and 1½ cups water. Mix well, using your hands or a fork. When all the liquid has been incorporated into the flour, turn the dough out onto a well-floured board (it will be very soft) and knead well for 5 minutes, dusting with flour frequently to prevent it from sticking to the surface. When it has become smooth and elastic, place it in a bowl and cover with a clean cloth. Put the bowl in a warm place for about an hour, or until the dough has doubled in size.

Pre-heat the oven to 425°F (220°C).

Turn the dough out and knead briefly again on a well-floured board. Cut into 6 equal pieces and knead these into slightly flattened rounds (see *figure 1*). Slash each over the top in the center with a sharp knife or blade (see *figure 2*) and spread out both to the right and left, as if you were opening a book (see *figure 3*). Place the buns on a greased baking sheet and allow to rise for at least 30 minutes – they should now look like fat butterflies (see *figure 4*).

Sprinkle the breads with flour and place them in the oven for 15–20 minutes, until they are golden-brown.

M A K E S   6   B R E A D S

figure 1

figure 2

figure 3

figure 4

Sophie Gonsalves' Chutney
ⓥ GOAN COCONUT CHUTNEY

A SWEET, SOUR AND hot chutney that is mellow and pungent at the same time, this may be served with all Goan meals, indeed, with all Indian meals. It also makes a superb dip (just thin it out with a little water), and is quite delicious spread out on bread and eaten as a sandwich.

If you wish to substitute unsweetened, dried coconut for fresh coconut use 1 cup plus 1 tablespoon. Soak it in ¾ cup warm water for 30 minutes, then blend using the soaking water. You may also use ⅓ cup coconut cream mixed with 3 tablespoons warm water. The texture of the chutney will be different, but it will still be good.

---

1 cup freshly grated coconut (page 265 and above)

3 cups fresh cilantro, chopped

1 small onion or 2 shallots, peeled and coarsely chopped

1 (1 inch) (2.5 cm) piece fresh ginger root, peeled and coarsely chopped

2 garlic cloves, peeled and coarsely chopped

2 fresh hot green chilies, coarsely chopped

2 tablespoons lemon juice

1 teaspoon coriander seeds

2 cloves

1 (½ inch)(1 cm) piece of cinnamon stick

1 teaspoon salt

1 teaspoon sugar

Put the coconut, cilantro, onion or shallot, ginger, garlic, chilies and lemon juice in a food processor. Blend, adding 4 or more tablespoons water as needed to get a thick, coarse paste. You may, if you wish, put this mixture into the container of an electric blender in several batches to get a much finer paste, adding a little water as needed.

Put the coriander seeds, cloves and cinnamon into a clean coffee grinder and grind them to a fine powder. Mix the powder with the coconut mixture. Add the salt and sugar. Stir to mix and taste for the blend of sweet and sour. Cover and refrigerate until needed.

The chutney lasts 24–36 hours. It may also be frozen.

SERVES 6 – 8

Alebele
Ⓥ COCONUT PANCAKES

THIS DESSERT COMBINES THE crêpe of the Western world with a delicious cardamom-flavored coconut-cashew filling which could only come out of the tropical East.

Only fresh coconut should be used for the filling.

❧

FOR THE BATTER:
1 scant cup all-purpose
   flour
A pinch of salt
1 large egg plus 1 egg yolk
1¼ cups milk
1 tablespoon melted butter
¼ teaspoon ground
   cardamom

FOR THE FILLING:
1½ cups freshly grated
   coconut (page 265)
¾ cup chopped, roasted,
   unsalted cashews
8 tablespoons dark brown
   sugar
¼ teaspoon ground
   cardamom

2 tablespoons golden raisins

YOU ALSO NEED:
3–4 tablespoons vegetable
   oil
1 juicy lemon

❧

Put all the ingredients for the batter in the container of an electric blender. Blend until smooth. Set aside for at least 30 minutes. Empty into a bowl. Have ready a ladle that will pick up about 4–5 tablespoons of batter.

Combine all the ingredients for the filling. Set aside.

Brush a 7 inch (18 cm) crêpe pan or a non-stick frying pan with a little oil and set over medium heat. When smoking hot, pour in 4–5 tablespoons of the batter. Quickly tilt the pan in all directions so that the batter flows to the ends and forms a thin film. (Any extra batter may be poured back into the bowl.)

Cook the pancake for a few minutes until the bottom has some brown spots and the edges can be lifted. Turn the pancake over with a spatula and cook for another minute. Remove and put on a plate. Start to make the second pancake as you made the first. As it cooks, put 2–3 tablespoons of filling on the first pancake, squeeze a generous amount of lemon juice over that and roll it up. Keep it in a covered dish. Make all the pancakes this way, keeping them in a single layer. When they are all made, you could re-heat them briefly in a warming oven.

S E R V E S   6

Bebinca
ⓥ PANCAKE CAKE

THIS IS THE FESTIVE cake Goans make for Christmas. Come December even the humblest of housewives sets about the task of making her *bebinca*. First one pancake is made. Then, batter for the second is poured over it and cooked from the top. Then comes the batter for the third and then the fourth . . . and so on until she ends up with a caramelized confection that tastes like a rich, dense fruit cake. For anyone who wants high cakes of many layers, it can take all day. This particular cake has only 5–6 layers. A *bebinca* can be made several days in advance. Store, covered, in a cool spot.

---

1 generous cup brown sugar
5 cardamom pods, crushed
1 generous cup all-purpose flour

5 egg yolks
1 cup coconut milk, well stirred from a can or thick fresh milk (page 266)

½ tablespoon *ghee* (page 271) or melted butter

Make a syrup by putting the sugar and the crushed cardamom pods in a small pan and adding 1 cup water. Heat gently until all the sugar has dissolved and then allow to cool. Strain to remove the cardamom pods (it is fine if a few traces remain).

Combine the flour, egg yolks, coconut milk and cooled syrup in a medium-sized bowl. Beat well to make a smooth batter. Set aside to rest for 30 minutes.

Turn the broiler to high. Take an 8 inch (20 cm) crêpe pan or sturdy non-stick frying pan and set it over medium-high heat. Pour in the *ghee* or butter. When hot, ladle in ½ cup of the batter, making sure that it spreads to the edges by tilting the pan in all directions. Cook over medium heat until the bottom is golden. Place the pan under the broiler and allow the pancake to turn golden-brown on the top. You may need to adjust your broiler by turning the heat down slightly. The pancake should not burn. Now ladle a further ½ cup batter over the first pancake, spread it around and place under the broiler until the second layer, too, is golden-brown. Continue this way until all the batter is used up. Allow the *bebinca* to cool overnight before turning it out of the pan.

Cut into thin wedges when serving.

S E R V E S   6 – 8

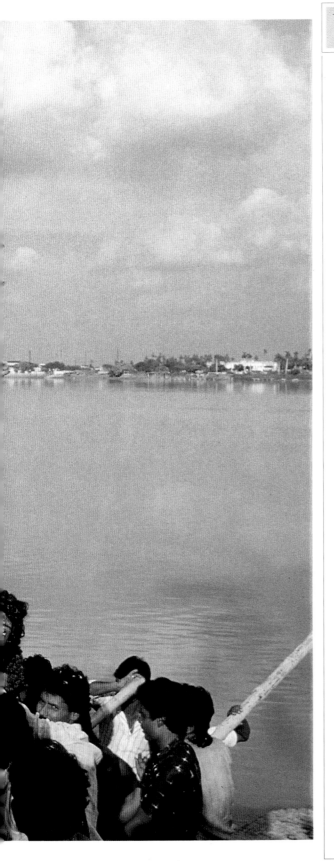

WEST BENGAL

THE BABY, HIS EYES lined with kohl, sits on his mother's lap, staring with surprise and some apprehension at all the fussing adults. He is six months old and the ceremony of *annaprasan* will mark one of his first rites of passage – the gentle leap from a liquid diet to the eating of solids, which, in West Bengal, consist mainly of rice, fish and vegetables.

Two families, his mother's and his father's, have braved the capital city's chaotic traffic to get here – and Calcutta's traffic is truly chaotic! There are double-decker buses, rusted through and through, that tilt wildly as they career along, slow-moving, exhaust-spewing trucks piled high with green coconuts, rickshaws carrying demure nymphet students who hold up umbrellas against the sun (or rain) and trams from which people jump on and off in a speeded-up game of musical chairs. Waves of bicycles keep ringing their shrill bells hoping, vainly, that something, any-thing, in front of them will move and wooden bullock carts tote – would you believe it – freshly printed books. And, of course, there are cars upon cars. Some are spit-and-polished, chauffeur-driven, with lethargic, fashionable, be-pearled ladies sitting at the back on their way to "the Club" (whichever hard-to-get into, high-priced, exclusive club they – really their husbands – have managed to get into).

Other cars, barely held together with tape, string and plastic, are driven by harassed, bespectacled intellectuals on their way to lowly jobs on some Bengali newspaper.

The families have also braved Calcutta's weather, which Mark Twain described as hot and humid enough "to make a door knob mushy," weather which once inspired very rich Bengalis to build flat, all-marble beds on which they could roll whenever they needed to cool themselves. Only these (and not the more conventional four-poster, mattressed beds, even those with fans) provided a cool enough surface.

West Bengal sits just above the Bay of Bengal in eastern India and its main river, the mighty Ganges, breaks up here into dozens of rivers and rivulets before it flows into the sea. These encourage the proliferation of many kinds of edible fish. They also make the air so moisture-laden that every form of greenery from bananas, jackfruit and gourds to eggplants, marrows, flat beans and rice, grows with pleasing generosity.

A *thali* is placed in front of the six-month-old baby who, if he is going to be anything like Calcutta's other ten million inhabitants, will grow to love his idiosyncratic capital city with a justifiable passion, traffic and weather notwithstanding. In the *thali* there is rice (the grain or *anna* in the name of the ceremony) in two forms: plain rice with peas and *payesh*, a sweet rice

pudding. The baby is given a spoon of *payesh*. He likes it and opens his mouth for more. He will eat rice every day of his life as it is the premier grain that lies at the heart of Bengali cuisine. With it, as he grows older, he will have some of the other dishes that are also on the *thali*.

There is a fish head, fried to a crisp with an initial rubbing of salt and turmeric, there is a dish of green plantains and yet another of potatoes cooked with *kalonji*. There is *moong dal* that has been roasted and then cooked with spinach and there is *shukto*, a very Bengali vegetable stew. The staple starter at lunchtime, *shukto* is pale in color, lightly bitter in flavor (this bitterness can come from bitter greens or any bitter vegetable), thickened with powdered ginger and ground mustard seeds and spiced with the traditional regional mixture, *panch phoran*, a five-spice combination which contains fennel seeds, cumin seeds, *radhuni* (somewhat like a celery seed, this has now given way to mustard seeds), fenugreek seeds and *kalonji*.

Most elements of Bengali cuisine are represented in these dishes. There is the use of *panch phoran*, which originated in the region; the fennel it contains gives food a sweet, anise-like accent while the *kalonji* gives it a deeper peppery quality.

Then there is the use of mustard oil, now as synonymous with Bengali food as olive oil is with the cuisine of the Mediterranean. Deep yellow in color, it is pungent when it leaves the bottle but turns disarm-

Previous page: An effigy of the Hindu goddess Durga is thrown into the Ganges in West Bengal.

ingly sweet when heated. It is used in both its forms: pungent and sweet. At times fish – such as prawns (shrimp) or the shad-like *hilsa* – are rubbed with a thin paste of ground mustard seeds, ground turmeric, salt, chilies and the pungent mustard oil, then steamed until cooked (*chingri* or *elish bhapey*). Mashed potatoes are enjoyed with a simple dressing of the pungent oil, salt and chopped green chilies (*alu bharta*). Both these dishes are spectacular.

When a milder form of mustard oil is required it is first set to heat until it is almost smoking. Its sharp fumes rise into the air, swirl around the kitchen for a bit and vanish. The oil turns sweet, while retaining its mustardy smell and taste. It can now be used to cook any vegetable or fish. It is much milder this way.

There is also the use of bitter vegetables which, although not unique to Bengal, has been refined here to become an essential taste in the daily diet. Eggplants may be cooked with bitter *neem* leaves (*neem begun*) and the *shukto* mentioned earlier often contains a little bitter gourd or some bitter leaves of a small local gourd (*patol*). The blending of the bitter with the other ingredients is done with the same care a clever European baker shows in adding just the right number of bitter almonds to an almond cake. Many bitter greens in India come with ancient reputations. They have, we are told, cleansing, healing properties and can, with judicious use, counteract intestinal mucus, keep smallpox at bay and

even prevent cancer. Children resist the taste in their early years but soon succumb.

Crushed mustard seeds also have their own special bitterness. When used with care they add a most inviting pungency to many Bengali sauces. Bengalis sometimes grind together both the Indian brown and the European yellow mustard seeds for the same dish. This is an effort to tame the sharpness of the first with some of the mellowness of the second. I have seen Bengalis add a chili or a little salt when they are grinding the mustard seeds. "It keeps the bitterness under control," they explain knowingly.

There are beans in one of the *batis* (small bowls, the same as North Indian *katoris*) on the *thali*. Although they are an essential part of the Bengali diet today, this was not always the case. Bengalis, like their neighbors to the east, the Burmese, Thais and Malays, thrived mostly on rice, fish and vegetables. It was the vegetarian movements coming out of the Indian heartland that prompted the addition of split peas to the local diet (not that the Bengalis gave up their fish!). But here, too, the Bengalis have put a unique twist to the taste. They often roast the split peas before they cook them, giving them a special nutty flavor and use *kalonji* or *panch phoran* for their final seasoning (*tarka* or *phoran*, as they say here). This makes the split peas taste unlike anything else in the rest of India.

And then there is the fish. The auspicious fish head, sitting straight up in the *thali*, stares at the baby and the baby, unfazed, stares back at it. Fish and rice will be there to mark many more rites of passage in his life. They will be there when, as a teenager, a holy thread is placed across his chest (only if he is of the high brahmin caste, of course); when he marries, his wife will hold a live fish as she is welcomed into his house; and at his death, balls of cooked rice and fish will be offered to his deceased ancestors.

As the baby grows older, he may find tiny prawns (shrimps) in his vegetables and his split peas may be cooked with a fish head or with large fish bones (rather like a pea soup is cooked with a ham bone in the West). His fish may be fried (*bhaja*), steamed with ground mustard seeds and coconut (*bhapey*), cooked in yogurt (*dohi machh*), cooked with tamarind (*tetul ilish*) wrapped inside banana leaves and smoked (*paturi*) or, for everyday lunches, cooked in mustard oil with a simple sauce (*jhol*) of coriander, cumin, turmeric, cayenne pepper and whole green chilies. Rice – reliable, amenable rice – will always be the accompaniment.

Strangely enough, none of the fish the growing child eats will come from the sea. Some may come from brackish estuary waters and some (such as the mackerel-like *hilsa* or *elish*) will be fish that spend part of their time in the sea but come inland to spawn, but most will be from the rivers, lakes, tanks and ponds that pit the land. Why this is, is hard to know. When asked the question, Bengalis always get a look on

their faces which seems to say, "Isn't the answer obvious?" When pressed further, they manage, "But freshwater fish is so much sweeter." The Bay of Bengal is a wild body of water, throwing up mad typhoons at short notice. Could some ancient fear of the sea be the reason?

To see the fish and how it is bought, dressed and sold, I decide to visit the Manik Tala market in north Calcutta. This is the older part of town.

Palaces, dozens of them, many built by wealthy Indian feudal lords who made their fortunes in opium, jute and indigo during the British Raj, lie crumbling – vast Palladian monuments scattered about like so much decaying rubble. It is easy to see why Calcutta was known as the "City of Palaces" in the eighteenth and nineteenth centuries. By now the humid weather and pigeons, acting as the greatest of levellers, have gnawed many of the buildings to the bone. But their skeletons, fleshed out here and there by memories of past glory, still stand. And people still live in them.

I decide to visit one such palace, now owned by several members of a prominent West Bengal family. Their last name is Basu. The octogenarian patriarch studied at Oxford University. Much of the furniture is made of finely carved mahogany. The chandeliers and lamps are made with European glass. It is that sort of family.

A street scene in Calcutta, West Bengal.

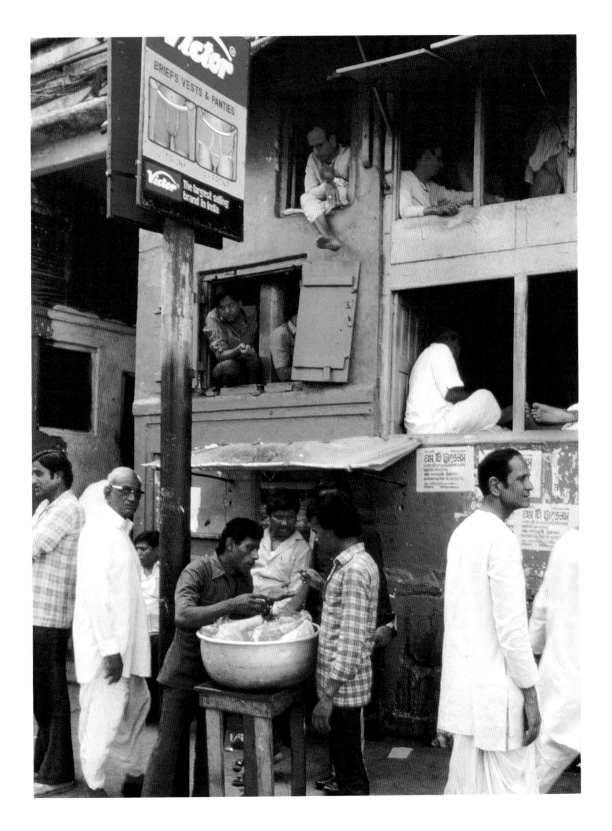

Smoke, followed by the heavenly smell of food being cooked by loving hands, seems to be coming from . . . a corridor? The dusty ruin looks like a set from one of Satyajit Ray's films about Bengali aristocracy. Little boys are playing cricket in one of the larger courtyards.

Two retainers seem to have pitched their "tent" in a corridor already blackened with smoke and are cooking their dinner over a charcoal grill. "What are you making?" I yell at them – they are old and do not hear too well. *"Mangshor jhol"* one answers as he stirs the pot, a simple stew of goat meat and potatoes cooked in mustard oil with lots of black pepper, cumin, coriander, green chilies and a touch of sugar.

Goat meat is well liked and eaten by many Hindu Bengalis. Indeed, the patron goddess of the city, Kali, the one with a black face and sticking out tongue, has a temple dedicated to her in south Calcutta where goats are sacrificed on a daily basis. Some of her devotees make do with offerings of red hibiscus garlands (red being the color of the blood she likes) but others, with more money or deeper anxieties, offer live goats. The animals are led to a marble enclosure, their necks are stretched over a kind of guillotine, the all-important wish of the devotee whispered into the goat's ear and the creature is then swiftly dispatched, carrying the message straight to the goddess Kali. The meat, now considered holy food, is then cooked and served.

There are other meat-eaters. In 1690 Muslims, with a diet similar to that found in the rest of North India, ruled Bengal. Those local people they converted to Islam continued to eat the traditional Hindu diet of rice, fish and vegetables but added to it meat *pullaos* (pilafs), lamb and goat cooked with plenty of onions and garlic, and chickens cooked slowly with cinnamon and cloves. By the twentieth century, they had evolved unique dishes like the *rezala* (lamb cooked in milk and yogurt). Cubes of lamb are first marinated in milk, yogurt, ginger, garlic, cardamom, cloves and nutmeg. The meat is then removed and lightly browned. The marinade goes back in and the meat stews gently. A few red and green chilies are thrown in and a few drops of aromatic *kewra* (screwpine essence). This exquisite dish is then ready to be eaten with flat yeast breads such as the *naan*.

At the Basu palace, I taste some of the retainers' dinner, enjoy its spicy simplicity and jot down the recipe. I am really looking for Mrs. Sonali Basu who is to take me to the fish market. She is not in the main palace but in a more modern structure on her husband's share of the family property.

The daughter of a film director and herself once an actress, Sonali informs me that it is too late to go to the fish market – we really needed to have left around dawn – but will I not stay and have some *jalkhabar* with her.

Bengalis tend to have five meals a day. There is breakfast which could consist of puffed rice eaten either wet with milk and liquid palm jaggery or dryish in combination with green chilies, coconut, onion and a little mustard oil. Then there is a mid-morning snack. This is followed by lunch which, if it is formal, would have several courses, all served with rice. It would probably start with the bitter *shukto*, then go on to a split pea dish with some fried vegetable fritters (such as *alu bhaja* made with potato slices and a chick-pea flour batter) on the side. Then a vegetable dish would be served, followed by a fish and vegetable combination. Next, a dish using small fish would appear, then one using large fish. This would be followed by meat or chicken (perhaps a chicken cooked with mustard seeds or fresh cilantro), then a sweet chutney course and finally the dessert, generally made with milk or yogurt. After a siesta, another snack appears. Then there is dinner which would consist perhaps of white flour breads (*loochis*), a marrow dish, a bean, a green vegetable and a chicken or meat dish. There would invariably be some sweetmeats as Bengalis cannot seem to live without them.

It is the mid-morning and late afternoon snacks that are known as *jalkhabar*. They could comprise a simple cold coffee served with a *singhara* (a kind of *samosa* – savory pastry – filled with ground meat or potatoes and peas) but Sonali's *jalkhabar* threatens to be much more generous. She wants to make a whole meal of it. Even as I demur, she brings me *begun bhaja* eggplant slices dipped in batter and fried, *koraishuti*

kachori (a deep-fried, puffed-up bread stuffed with green peas), some *alu dum* (small new potatoes cooked with cumin, cardamom, cinnamon, ginger and tomatoes), a cup of steaming milky tea ("Would you prefer a cold Coca-Cola? Or Limca?") and then, to end, she offers *mishti doi*, a marvellous, creamy yogurt made with sweetened milk ("We always get ours from the same shop in north Calcutta"). I am told to come back early the next day if I want to go to the fish market.

I arrive at 6:30 a.m. The market, entered through a covered alley, is already in full swing. Men carrying cloth bags crowd around every shop. It is an accepted tradition that heads of households, always male, do the morning shopping.

I have never before seen such large quantities of such fresh fish, eyes gleaming, gills all red, skins shimmering. The silvery *hilsa*, with hints of gold, could have come straight from a jeweler. The striped tiger prawns are equally attractive and even more pricey. Many small fish such as the *koi* or climbing perch are sold live. Bengalis will not buy them any other way. They hop around on the scales.

It is here that I can watch how the fish is cut. Bengalis are as idiosyncratic about dismembering their fish as they are about everything else. First of all, traditionally, no knife is used. Instead, there is a *bonti*. A plank of wood, held down by the squatting fishmonger's foot, has attached to it, like the prow of a haughty boat, a large lethal

Whether Hindu, Christian or Muslim, all Bengalis seem to be agreed on one thing. They love sweets. Today, a sweet shop like Chhappan Bhog (this translates as "56 offerings") carries at least a few dozen varieties of *sandesh* alone. This sweetmeat is made with a very fresh cheese (*chhana*) that is squeezed of all whey, kneaded into a dough and then pressed into a mold. *Sandesh* is probably *chhana* in its simplest, purest form. Bengalis love it but are very fussy about where they buy it.

Chhappan Bhog can sell them *sandesh* made with strawberries (very modern), *sandesh* made with saffron (very traditional and expensive), *sandesh* "sandwiches" filled with reduced milk (very popular), pistachio *sandesh* and many others.

Once the cheese "dough" is made, the magician sweet maker transform it into all manner of other sweetmeats as well. It can be rolled into balls and boiled in syrup until it puffs up and becomes spongy (*rossogolla*); it can be shaped into diamonds, boiled in syrup and then "iced" with dollops of reduced milk (*chum chum*); mixed with reduced milk, rice flour and rose attar then fried and put into syrup, it becomes Lady Kenny (named after Lady Canning, the wife of a nineteenth-century governor-general of India).

With Calcutta's heavy and torpor-inducing air that moves listlessly around decaying buildings, a never-ending Metro construction project that not only snarls traffic but is known to swallow up whole buildings and permanent settlements of discontented refugees, a first-time visitor to the city might well think that it would be nothing short of madness to live here. But after a brief stay, even the first-time visitor is infected by its intellectual passions, its eccentric brown Englishmen, its quirky publishers, gallery owners, film directors and actors. And the first-time visitor falls deeply in love with its bitter-sweet foods. Then the first-time visitor begins to think, "How can I extend my stay?"

Sonali Basu's Begun Bhaja
ⓥ DEEP-FRIED EGGPLANTS IN BATTER

CRISP FRITTERS AND SOFT, malleable rice are often offered as one of the first courses at formal meals in Bengal. The fritters may be made out of potato skins or eggplants or whatever else happens to be in season. I find that the fritters, served by themselves, are also quite perfect with tea and with drinks. White poppy seeds are frequently substituted for *kalonji*.

❧

FOR THE BATTER:
1½ cups chick-pea flour, sifted
1 teaspoon cayenne pepper
1 teaspoon salt
A pinch of ground turmeric
½ teaspoon baking soda

YOU ALSO NEED:
Oil for deep-frying
12 oz (350 g) eggplants, cut into ½ × ½ × 3 inch (1 × 1 × 7.5 cm) fingers; use any slim variety or the large purple ones

Salt
Freshly ground black pepper
1¼ teaspoon *kalonji* (page 272)

❧

Put the ingredients for the batter into a bowl. Mix well. Slowly add 1¼ cups water, whisking constantly to produce a smooth, thick batter. You may leave the batter this consistency – many people prefer a thick coating – or you could thin it further by adding up to ½ cup water.

Heat the oil for deep-frying in a wok or deep frying pan over medium heat. The oil is sufficiently hot when a cube of bread sizzles nicely and turns golden.

Meanwhile, put the pieces of eggplant onto a plate in a single layer. Sprinkle each piece with a little salt and pepper on all sides. When the oil is hot, use one hand to dip the eggplants into the batter, only as many pieces as the wok or pan will hold in a single layer. Shake off the excess batter, sprinkle some *kalonji* over the top with the fingers of your second, clean hand, and put straight into the hot oil. Deep-fry for 5–7 minutes, turning the fritters halfway through. They should turn golden and crisp. Remove with a slotted spoon and drain on paper towels. You may need to do the frying in several batches. Serve immediately. (Any remaining batter can be refrigerated and kept for 2 days.)

SERVES 4–6

Christine Ward's Masala Steak
SPICY STEAK

HERE IS AN ANGLO-INDIAN speciality. Even though it is called "Masala Steak," it really contains no steaks as we know them in the West. Rather, it consists of flat, rectangular pieces of meat (lamb or beef), much smaller and thinner than official steaks, cooked with very Indian seasonings. Traditionally it is served with bread or *chapatis*. I also love it with Stir-Fried Rice with Split Peas (see page 166) or with a crusty French or Italian loaf. Serve a green salad on the side.

FOR THE PASTE:
1 (3 inch) (7.5 cm) piece fresh ginger root, peeled and roughly chopped
7–8 garlic cloves, peeled and chopped
1 medium-sized onion, finely chopped

FOR THE SPICE POWDER:
1 tablespoon ground coriander
1 tablespoon cumin seeds
1 tablespoon brown mustard seeds
½ teaspoon ground turmeric
1 teaspoon cayenne pepper

YOU ALSO NEED:
3 tablespoons vegetable oil
2¼ lb (1 kg) boneless lamb, cut into 3 × 1 × ¼ inch (7.5 cm × 2.5cm × 5 mm) pieces
2 medium-sized red onions, cut into thin rings
2 medium-sized potatoes, peeled and cut into ¼ inch (5 mm) thick rounds
1¾–2 teaspoons salt

Put the ginger, garlic and onion for the spice paste into the container of an electric blender along with ½ cup water. Blend to a fine paste. You may need to push the mixture down with a spatula from time to time to achieve this. Set aside.

Put the ingredients for the spice powder into a clean coffee grinder. Grind to a fine powder. Set aside.

Heat the oil in a large, wide, preferably non-stick pan or wok over high heat. When hot, put in the lamb. Stir and fry for 10–15 minutes or until the lamb pieces brown. Reduce the heat to medium and add the ginger-and-garlic paste and the spice powder. Stir once or twice to mix well. Add 2 cups water and bring to the boil. Cover, turn the heat to low and cook for 45 minutes. Add the onion rings, potato slices and salt to taste. Stir to mix. Cover and cook for a further 15–20 minutes, until the potatoes are cooked and the sauce is thick enough to just coat the lamb.

SERVES 4–6

Mrs Dasgupta's Rezala
LAMB COOKED IN MILK AND YOGURT

REZALA, WHICH CAN BE made with both lamb and chicken, is a specialty of the Muslims of Bengal. It is eaten at celebratory meals. It is almost always made with rather fatty rib chops. I prefer to use boned lamb shoulder.

When the dish has almost finished cooking, many Muslim families add a sprinkling of *kewra* water. This has a marvellously flowery aroma. Most serious Indian grocers sell it. Use rose water or orange blossom water as substitutes. Serve with *naans*, *chapatis*, *pita* breads or any rice dish of your choice.

❧

FOR THE MARINADE:
1 (3 inch) (7.5 cm) piece fresh ginger root, peeled and finely chopped
8–9 garlic cloves, peeled and coarsely chopped
1½ cups rich yogurt, lightly beaten
1 cup milk
3–4 bay leaves

8–10 cardamom pods
8–10 cloves
1 teaspoon ground mace
½ teaspoon ground nutmeg

YOU ALSO NEED:
2¼ lb (1 kg) boned lamb from the shoulder
1 tablespoon vegetable oil
3 tablespoons *ghee* (page 271) or vegetable oil

1½–1¾ teaspoons salt
½ teaspoon sugar
10 fresh hot green chilies, each with a small slit at one end
6–8 dried hot red chilies, soaked in warm water for 10 minutes
1 teaspoon *kewra* water (page 272)

❧

Make the marinade: put the ginger and garlic into the container of an electric blender. Add 4 tablespoons water. Blend to a fine, frothy paste. Put the paste into a large bowl. Add the remaining marinating ingredients and mix well. Add the lamb. Leave to stand unrefrigerated for 3–4 hours. (You may marinate the meat overnight. Cover and refrigerate and bring to room temperature before cooking.)

Remove the meat from the marinade and put the marinade to one side.

Heat the oil and *ghee* in a large, wide, preferably non-stick pan or wok over high heat. When hot, add the lamb, salt and sugar. Stir and fry for 8–10 minutes until the meat is lightly browned. Reduce the heat to very low. Add the marinade. Cover and cook for 1 hour or until the meat is tender. Add the green and red chilies. Cook for a further 5–10 minutes. Add the *kewra* water, stir and serve.

S E R V E S   4

Rakhi Dasgupta's Murgi Dhuniya Patta Diya
CHICKEN IN FRESH CILANTRO

A WONDERFUL CHICKEN DISH to serve with rice. You may use the more traditional thick coconut milk (see page 266) instead of cream.

❧

FOR THE MARINADE:
4 cloves
4 cardamom pods
2–3 bay leaves
1 (1 inch) (2.5 cm) cinnamon stick
2 tablespoons ground coriander
A pinch of salt

1 cup plain yogurt, lightly beaten
1 (2¼ lb) (1 kg) chicken, skinned and cut into 3 inch (7.5 cm) pieces

YOU ALSO NEED:
5 tablespoons mustard oil or any other vegetable oil
A pinch of ground *asafetida*

2½ cups fresh cilantro, finely chopped, plus extra for garnishing
1½ teaspoons salt
1 teaspoon sugar
6–8 fresh hot green chilies, split into halves
⅔ cup whipping cream

❧

Put the cloves, cardamom pods, bay leaves, cinnamon and ground coriander for the marinade into a clean coffee grinder. Grind to a fine powder. Empty the ground spices into a bowl. Add the salt and yogurt. Stir to mix. Add the chicken. Mix well to coat all the chicken pieces. Refrigerate and leave to marinate for 1–2 hours (overnight will not hurt). Take the chicken pieces out of the marinade and put the marinade to one side.

Heat the oil in a large, wide, preferably non-stick pan or wok over medium heat. When hot, add the *asafetida*. Let it sizzle for 4–5 seconds. Turn the heat to high and immediately add the chicken. Stir and fry for 15 minutes until the

chicken is browned. Add the marinade, 2½ cups fresh cilantro, salt and sugar. Stir and fry over medium heat for a further 5–10 minutes until the chicken is almost tender. Add the chilies. Stir and fry for 2–3 minutes until the chilies soften. Add the cream. Stir to mix. Reduce the heat to low and allow to simmer for a further 5–8 minutes or until the sauce is thick. It should coat the chicken pieces and leave a little extra at the bottom of the pan.

Serve garnished with the remaining fresh cilantro.

SERVES   4 – 6

Christine Ward's
COUNTRY CAPTAIN

I HAVE YET TO find two explanations for the name of this dish that agree! But there it is, an Anglo-Indian name, however obscure, for an Anglo-Indian dish that may well have originated in Calcutta. It is delicious and easy to prepare, tending to disappear as soon as it is made! Serve with plain rice or with Stir-Fried Rice with Split Peas (page 166) and Stewed Tomato Relish (page 168).

FOR THE PASTE:
1 (3 inch) (7.5 cm) piece of fresh ginger root, peeled and finely chopped
5 garlic cloves, peeled and coarsely chopped
1 small red onion, roughly chopped

YOU ALSO NEED:
2 tablespoons vegetable oil
1 medium-large red onion, finely sliced
1 (2¼ lb) (1 kg) chicken, skinned and cut into 2 inch (5 cm) pieces
1 teaspoon cayenne pepper
1¼–1½ teaspoons salt
¼ teaspoon sugar

1–2 tablespoons white wine vinegar
2 large, ripe tomatoes, chopped into 1 inch (2.5 cm) pieces
5–6 fresh hot green chilies, each with a small slit at one end
2 green bell peppers, cored, seeded and finely sliced

Put the ginger, garlic and onion for the paste into the container of an electric blender. Add ½ cup water. Blend to a fine paste. You may need to push the mixture down with a spatula from time to time to achieve this.

Heat the oil in a large, wide, preferably non-stick pan or wok over high heat. When hot, add half the sliced onion. Stir and fry for 2–3 minutes until the onion begins to soften. Add the chicken. Stir and fry for 8–10 minutes until browned. Reduce the heat to medium and add the paste from the blender, and the cayenne

pepper, salt, sugar and vinegar to taste. Stir and fry for a further 10–15 minutes until the chicken is tender. The spicy sauce should be thick enough to coat the chicken pieces. Add the tomatoes, remaining onion, chilies and peppers.

Stir and fry for 3–4 minutes so that the flavors blend but the peppers remain green and crisp.

SERVES 4

Sorse Murgi
CHICKEN WITH MUSTARD SEEDS

ANOTHER, VERY MUSTARDY, VERY typically Bengali creation to be eaten with plain rice.

1¼–1½ teaspoons salt
1 teaspoon ground turmeric
1 (2¼ lb) (1 kg) chicken,
  cut into serving pieces
  (each leg into drumstick
  and thigh and the breast
  into 6 pieces)

1 tablespoon brown
  mustard seeds
4–5 fresh hot green chilies,
  roughly chopped

4½ tablespoons mustard oil
  or any other vegetable oil
3 tablespoons chopped,
  fresh cilantro

Rub 1 teaspoon of the salt and ½ teaspoon of the turmeric over the chicken.

Put the mustard seeds into a clean coffee grinder. Grind to a fine powder.

Put the ground mustard seeds, chilies and ¼ teaspoon of the turmeric into the container of an electric blender. Add 4 tablespoons water. Blend to a smooth paste. Set the paste aside.

Heat 3 tablespoons of the oil in a large, wide, preferably non-stick pan or wok over high heat. When hot, add the chicken. Stir and fry for 12–15 minutes until golden. Remove from the pan.

Add the remaining oil to the pan. When hot add the mustard-and-chili paste and turn the heat to low. Stir and fry for 3–4 minutes until the oil bubbles at the surface. Add the chicken and the remaining salt and turmeric. Stir to mix. Add 1¼ cups water. Bring to the boil over medium heat. Cover and cook for 10–15 minutes or until the chicken is tender and the sauce has reduced to just coat the pieces.

Sprinkle the fresh cilantro over the top before serving.

SERVES 4

Country Captain (page 149) with Stir-fried Rice with Split Peas (page 166) and Stewed Tomato Relish (page 168).

Rakhi Dasgupta's Tetul Ilish

TAMARIND FISH

HILSA, A BEAUTIFUL SILVERY fish, is found in the estuaries of Bengal's rivers where it comes in from the sea to spawn. It is much loved. As it is very expensive, it is almost revered and reserved for special occasions. Shad, if available, makes a good substitute and so does salmon.

∾

1 lb (450 g) *hilsa* or salmon steaks, 1 inch (2.5 cm) thick

¾ teaspoon ground turmeric

¾–1 teaspoon salt

½ cup mustard oil or any other vegetable oil

3 tablespoons thick tamarind paste (page 278)

½ teaspoon cayenne pepper

½ teaspoon sugar

½ teaspoon brown mustard seeds

∾

Rub ½ teaspoon of the turmeric and ½ teaspoon of the salt over the fish steaks. Set aside for 10 minutes.

Heat the oil in a large, wide, preferably non-stick frying pan over medium-high heat. When hot, put in the fish. Fry each side for 2–3 minutes until golden. Remove the fish from the pan using a slotted spoon, leaving the oil behind. Set aside.

Meanwhile, put the tamarind paste, cayenne pepper, sugar, remaining salt, remaining turmeric and 1 cup water into a bowl. Mix well.

Take 2 tablespoons of the oil used for frying the fish and heat in a clean, large frying pan over medium-high heat. When hot, put in the mustard seeds. As soon as they pop, a matter of seconds, add the tamarind mixture. Bring to the boil over medium-high heat. Turn the heat to low and allow to simmer for 10–12 minutes, stirring regularly, until the oil bubbles at the surface and the sauce becomes very thick. Return the fish to the pan. Continue to simmer for 5–8 minutes, turning the fish pieces once very gently during this time. The sauce should just coat the fish.

SERVES 4

Yogurt Fish (page 152) and Cooling Mango Chutney (page 169).

Alu Tikki
Ⓥ STUFFED POTATO PATTIES

WITHIN BENGAL THERE IS a vegetarian tradition where no garlic and onions are used and certain vegetables and beans are forbidden. Such food is supposed to be eaten by widows. While many women have followed these rules, they have created from this adversity some of Bengal's most delicious dishes. This is one of them. Serve with a salad or as part of an Indian meal.

4 small-medium peeled potatoes
1¼ teaspoons salt
1 teaspoon black peppercorns
¼ teaspoon fennel seeds
1 (1 inch) (2.5 cm) piece fresh ginger root, peeled and finely chopped

5–6 fresh hot green chilies, finely chopped
About 5 tablespoons vegetable oil
½ cup shelled peas (frozen peas, defrosted well, may be used)
⅓ cup grated carrot

½–¾ cup pumpkin or squash, peeled and cut into ½ inch (1 cm) dice
½–¾ cup cauliflower, cut into ½ inch (1 cm) pieces
½ teaspoon sugar
1 cup all-purpose flour

Boil the potatoes until cooked. Mash well with ¾ teaspoon of the salt.

Put the peppercorns and fennel seeds into a clean coffee grinder. Grind to a fine powder.

Put the ginger, chilies and the ground black pepper mixture into the container of an electric blender. Add ½ cup water. Blend to a fine paste.

Heat 1 tablespoon of the oil in a small pan over medium heat. When hot, add the vegetables, spice paste, remaining salt and the sugar. Stir and fry for 6–8 minutes over medium-low heat until the vegetables are tender. Add a sprinkling of water, if needed, to prevent them sticking. Remove from the heat.

Put the mashed potatoes and cooked vegetables into a bowl. Mix well. Divide the mixture into 1½ inch (4 cm) balls. With lightly floured hands flatten each ball to roughly 3 inch (7.5 cm) rounds. Coat with the flour.

Heat 3 tablespoons of the oil in a large, wide frying pan over medium heat. When hot, put in as many of the potato patties as the pan will hold easily in a single layer. Fry for 2–3 minutes on each side until golden and hot in the center. Make all the patties this way, adding more oil as needed. Serve immediately.

MAKES 10–12 PATTIES

Sonali Basu's Alu Dum
Ⓥ WHOLE POTATOES WITH TOMATOES

A SIMPLE, EVERYDAY DISH, eaten both as a snack with Deep-Fried Stuffed Breads (page 167) and as part of a regular lunch, this is made with small, whole potatoes. New potatoes about ¾ inch (2 cm) in diameter are ideal. Larger ones may be cut to size. This recipe belongs to the Ghoti tradition of West Bengal.

2 teaspoons mustard oil or any other vegetable oil
¼ teaspoon cumin seeds
3–4 cardamom pods
1 (1 inch) (2.5 cm) cinnamon stick
1 bay leaf

8–9 small new potatoes, boiled, peeled and left whole
1 (1 inch) (2.5 cm) piece fresh ginger root, peeled and very finely grated to a pulp

2 large tomatoes, roughly chopped
½–¾ teaspoon salt
1 teaspoon sugar
2 tablespoons finely chopped, fresh cilantro

Heat the oil in a small, preferably non-stick pan over medium heat. When hot, add the cumin, cardamom pods, cinnamon and bay leaf. Stir and fry for 10–20 seconds or until the spices just turn color. Add the boiled potatoes. Stir to mix. Add the ginger, tomatoes, salt, sugar and 1 tablespoon water. Reduce the heat to low, cover and cook for 8–10 minutes, shaking the pan occasionally to prevent the potatoes from sticking.

Remove from the heat and garnish with the cilantro.

SERVES 2–4

Prawns (Shrimp) Steamed with Mustard Seeds and Coconut (page 158).

Maya's Phulkopir Posto
Ⓥ CAULIFLOWER ENCRUSTED WITH POPPY SEEDS

EAT THIS WITH DEEP-FRIED Stuffed Breads (page 167) as a snack or at lunchtime, or with any Indian meal. When cooking this dish, remember to dry up all the sauce. You may need to adjust your heat to achieve this.

FOR THE SPICE PASTE:
**3 dried hot red chilies,
 roughly broken**
**5 tablespoons white poppy
 seeds**

YOU ALSO NEED:
½ teaspoon ground turmeric

1 teaspoon salt
1 teaspoon sugar
**1 medium-sized cauliflower,
 cut into 1½–2 inch
 (4–5 cm) wide florets with
 minimal stalk (net weight
 1 lb/450 g)**

**7 tablespoons mustard oil
 or any other vegetable oil**
**½ teaspoon *kalonji*
 (page 272)**
2 bay leaves
3–4 dried hot red chilies

Put the chilies and poppy seeds for the spice paste into a clean coffee grinder. Grind to a fine powder. Put the powder into a small bowl. Add 6 tablespoons water. Mix well. Set aside.

Rub the turmeric, ½ teaspoon of the salt and ½ teaspoon of the sugar over the cauliflower florets. Set aside.

Heat 4 tablespoons of the oil in a large, wide, preferably non-stick frying pan or wok over medium-high heat. When hot, add the cauliflower. Stir and fry for 4–5 minutes until the cauliflower just starts to brown. Remove the florets from the pan with a slotted spoon, leaving as much oil behind as possible. Gently shake the florets in paper towels to remove the excess oil. Set aside.

Add the remaining oil to the pan and set over medium heat. When hot, add the *kalonji*, bay leaves and chilies. Stir once or twice. Quickly add the spice paste. Stir and fry for 2–3 minutes or until the mixture turns a reddish-brown color. Add the cauliflower and the remaining salt and sugar. Stir gently to coat the cauliflower with the spices. Add ⅔ cup water. Stir to mix and bring to the boil. Cover, reduce the heat and allow to simmer gently for 10–12 minutes. Stir occasionally to prevent sticking, adding a sprinkling of water when necessary. The sauce should be absorbed and the florets should remain slightly crunchy and be evenly coated with the spices.

SERVES 4–6

Sonali Basu's Tak Dal
Ⓥ SWEET AND SOUR RED LENTILS

THE GHOTI COMMUNITY OF West Bengal uses a fair amount of sugar in its food. Many of its dishes, such as this *dal*, are sweet and sour. The sourness may be provided by thin slices of raw green mangoes in season or tamarind. Eat this with plain rice and a selection of vegetables and fish.

1¼ cups red lentils
¼ teaspoon ground
   turmeric
2 tablespoons mustard or
   any other vegetable oil

½ teaspoon brown mustard
   seeds
½ teaspoon *panch phoran*
   (page 275)
4 hot dried red chilies
1 bay leaf

1¼–1½ teaspoons salt
2 tablespoons thick
   tamarind paste (page 278)
   or to taste
1 tablespoon sugar or to
   taste

Wash the lentils in several changes of water until the water runs clear. Put them in a medium-sized pan with the turmeric and mix. Cover with 4½ cups water. Bring the lentils to the boil over medium-high heat. Reduce the heat to low, cover partially and simmer for 40 minutes or until the lentils are tender. Stir now and then during the last 10 minutes. When the lentils are cooked, mash with a spoon to a pulp-like consistency.

Heat the oil in a large, wide, preferably non-stick pan or wok over medium-high heat. When hot, add the mustard seeds. As soon as they pop, a matter of seconds, add the *panch phoran*, chilies and bay leaf. Stir and fry for 5–6 seconds or until the chilies darken in color. Add the cooked lentils, ⅔ cup water and the salt. Stir to mix. Add the tamarind paste, a little at a time to get the sourness you desire. Add just enough sugar to balance the sourness. Bring to the boil. Turn the heat to low and simmer for 8–10 minutes. The finished *dal* should have the consistency of a thick purée.

S E R V E S   4

Christine Ward's Bhuna Khichuri
ⓥ STIR-FRIED RICE WITH SPLIT PEAS

KHICHURI, A NOURISHING MIXTURE of rice and split peas, is one of India's oldest dishes, recorded in ancient texts. The Anglo-Indians have also adopted it and this is their version. It may be served with Spicy Steak (page 146), Country Captain (page 149) or with any combination of meat and vegetarian dishes.

❧

½ cup plus 1 tablespoon *moong dal* (page 260)
2 cups basmati rice or any long-grain rice
3 tablespoons *ghee* (page 271) or vegetable oil

2 bay leaves
2 cloves
3 cardamom pods
1 (1 inch) (2.5 cm) cinnamon stick

1 medium-sized red onion, finely sliced
1 teaspoon salt

❧

Wash the *moong dal* in several changes of water until the water runs clear. Soak in water to cover by roughly 4 inches (10 cm) for 3–4 hours. Drain.

Wash the rice in several changes of water until the water runs clear. Soak in water to cover by roughly 2 inches (5 cm) for 30 minutes. Drain.

Heat the *ghee* in a heavy, medium-sized pan over medium-high heat. When hot, add the bay leaves, cloves, cardamom pods and cinnamon. Stir for a few seconds, until the bay leaves turn color. Add the onion. Stir and fry over medium heat for 4–5 minutes until the onion is nicely browned. Add the rice, *moong dal* and salt. Stir and fry gently for 1–2 minutes.

Add 2⅔ cups water. Bring to the boil over high heat. Cover tightly, reduce the heat to very low and allow to cook for 20–25 minutes or until the rice is tender.

Stir gently before serving.

SERVES 4–6

Sonali Basu's Koraishuti Kachori
Ⓥ DEEP-FRIED STUFFED BREADS

BENGALIS LIKE THEIR DEEP-FRIED breads made out of white flour. While other northerners eat *pooris* made out of whole wheat flour, Bengalis make very similar breads that they call *loochis* out of plain white flour. Sometimes, these *loochis* are stuffed with crushed peas. They are then called *koraishuti kachori* and are eaten at breakfast or as a mid-morning snack with a vegetable such as Whole Potatoes with Tomatoes (page 162). There are many recipes for both dishes. I like this version of the bread.

❧

FOR THE STUFFING:
1 cup shelled green peas
  (frozen, defrosted peas
  may be used)
1 (¾ inch) (2 cm) piece
  fresh ginger root, peeled
  and finely sliced
2 fresh hot green chilies,
  roughly chopped

1½ teaspoons sugar
1 teaspoon salt
4 tablespoons vegetable oil
1 teaspoon *ghee* (page 271)
  or vegetable oil
1½ tablespoons all-purpose
  flour
1 tablespoon cumin seeds
1 bay leaf

FOR THE DOUGH:
2 scant cups all-purpose
  flour, plus extra for rolling
½ tablespoon vegetable oil
½ teaspoon salt
½ teaspoon sugar
A pinch of *kalonji* (page 272)
Oil for deep-frying

❧

Make the stuffing: put the peas, ginger, chilies, sugar and salt into the container of an electric blender. Add 3 tablespoons water. Blend to a purée.

Heat the 4 tablespoons oil and the *ghee* in a large, wide, preferably non-stick pan or wok over medium heat. When hot, add the puréed peas. Stir and fry for 6–8 minutes. Add the 1½ tablespoons flour. Stir and fry for 2 minutes and remove from the heat.

Set a small pan over low heat. When hot, dry roast the cumin seeds and bay leaf for 2 minutes until the cumin seeds turn golden.

Remove from the heat. Put the roasted cumin and bay leaves into a clean coffee grinder. Grind to a fine powder. Add the ground bay leaves and cumin to the puréed peas. Stir to mix. Set aside to cool.

Make the dough: put the flour, oil, salt, sugar, *kalonji* and ⅔ cup water into a bowl. Mix and knead, using your hands, for about 5 minutes to make a smooth dough. Divide the dough into 15 equal-sized balls. Flatten each ball to a 2 inch (5 cm) round. Put 1 teaspoon of the pea purée into the center of each round. Close the dough around the pea mixture and squeeze the edges to seal the opening well, so that no pea purée will escape. On a lightly floured surface, roll the stuffed dough balls to 5 inch (13 cm) circles.

Meanwhile, heat the oil for deep-frying in a wok or frying pan over medium heat. Let the oil get really hot. Drop in one of the breads carefully, making sure that it does not double over. It should start sizzling immediately. Baste the bread with quick motions, pushing it gently into the oil. It should puff up in seconds. Turn it over and cook for another 30 seconds. Remove with a slotted spoon. Make all the breads this way. Either eat them immediately or stack them on a plate and keep them covered with an inverted plate.

MAKES 15

Christine Ward's Tomato Bharta
Ⓥ STEWED TOMATO RELISH

THIS IS REALLY A kind of tomato salad that is made with very lightly cooked tomatoes. Like a Mexican *salsa* or a North Indian onion and tomato relish, it may be eaten with all Indian meals.

To peel the tomatoes, bring 3 cups water to a rolling boil in a pan over high heat. Meanwhile, score the skin of each tomato with a cross at the bottom end. Put the tomatoes into the pan of water for 10 seconds. Remove from the water with a slotted spoon. The skins will be easy to peel.

❧

4 large, red ripe tomatoes, peeled and roughly chopped
1 medium-sized red onion, finely chopped

3 fresh hot green chilies, finely chopped
1 tablespoon finely chopped, fresh cilantro

¼ teaspoon salt
¼ teaspoon sugar

❧

Put the tomatoes into a small, preferably non-stick pan. Stew over medium-low heat for 4–5 minutes, stirring continuously, until a bit soft. Mash lightly with a spoon. Remove from heat. Add the onion, chilies, cilantro, salt and sugar. Stir to mix. Check the seasoning.

Cool. The relish will keep for 3–4 days in a clean air-tight jar in the refrigerator.

MAKES 1¼ CUPS

Mrs Dasgupta's Aam Jhol
Ⓥ COOLING MANGO CHUTNEY

A CROSS BETWEEN A drink and a chutney, this is served in bowls at the end of
a meal in the summer months when green, unripe mangoes are in season.
   Unripe, green mangoes can be bought from Indian grocers. Ask for green
pickling mangoes.

❧

**1 lb (450 g) green, unripe
  mangoes, unpeeled
1 teaspoon vegetable oil**

**A generous pinch of *panch
  phoran* (page 275)**

**1½ tablespoons sugar
½ teaspoon salt**

❧

Cut 2 thick slices, as close to the pit as
possible, off the 2 flatter sides of each mango.
Now cut the side slices off as well. Discard
the pit. Without peeling, cut the slices, crosswise, at ¾ inch (2 cm) intervals into thick slices.

Heat the oil in a large, wide, preferably non-
stick pan or wok over medium heat. When hot,
add the *panch phoran*. Stir for a few seconds.
Add the mangoes. Stir once or twice. Add
1¼ cups water and the sugar and salt. Bring to
the boil. Reduce the heat to medium and
simmer gently for 4–6 minutes until the
mangoes are tender, but not pulp-like. Remove
from the heat. Serve chilled. The chutney will
keep for 48 hours.

M A K E S   3   C U P S
A N D   S E R V E S   4 – 6

Bhapa Doi
Ⓥ STEAMED YOGURT

ONE OF THE SIMPLEST of Bengali sweets, this is really a yogurt enriched with
raisins and almonds. Serve it at the end of a meal. It is cool and refreshing.

❧

1 cup canned sweetened condensed milk
1 cup plain yogurt

2 tablespoons brown sugar
2 tablespoons raisins, soaked in hot water for 40 minutes and drained

2 tablespoons sliced almonds

Pre-heat the oven to 300°F (150°C).

Put the sweetened condensed milk and yogurt into a medium-sized bowl. Beat to mix well using a fork. Pour the beaten mixture into a 2-cup ovenproof mold or suitable serving dish. Put the dish into a large, deep baking pan. Put enough water into the baking pan to cover the bottom by 2–3 inches (5–7.5 cm).

Put the baking pan into the pre-heated oven. Bake for 40–45 minutes or until the steamed yogurt has just set but has not browned. Sprinkle the top with the sugar, raisins and almonds. Bake for another 3–5 minutes until the sugar caramelizes. Serve hot or chilled.

S E R V E S   4

Rakhi Dasgupta's Aam Kheer

ⓥ MANGO PUDDING

A DELIGHTFUL DESSERT, PERFECT after a spicy meal.

---

5 cups milk
1 cup sugar
½ cup canned sweetened condensed milk

4 medium-sized ripe mangoes, peeled and with their pits removed, cut into ½ inch (1 cm) cubes

---

Bring the milk to the boil in a thick-bottomed pan over medium-high heat. As soon as it starts to bubble up, turn the heat down a bit to medium. Cook for 30 minutes, stirring regularly. The quantity of milk should reduce by half. Add the sugar. Stir and boil for a further 5 minutes. Add the sweetened condensed milk. Stir and boil for 3–4 minutes. Remove the pan from the heat. Leave to cool. Add the mangoes. Stir to mix. Serve chilled.

Pancakes in Syrup (page 172).

S E R V E S   6

Sunlay Basu's Malpua
ⓥ PANCAKES IN SYRUP

PANCAKES PROBABLY ORIGINATED IN India which has had sugar and wheat flour since ancient times. The *malpua* is one of our oldest sweet pancakes. It is best to use the semolina (*sooji*) that is sold by Indian grocers and not the supermarket semolina used for puddings.

---

2 teaspoons fennel seeds
1 generous cup all-purpose flour

⅓ cup plus 1 tablespoon semolina (page 277)
1 cup plus 2 tablespoons milk

1⅓ cups sugar
1¼ cups oil for deep-frying

Put the fennel seeds into a clean coffee grinder. Grind to a fine powder.

Put the flour, semolina, ground fennel seeds and milk into a medium-sized bowl. Whisk to a smooth batter.

Meanwhile, put the sugar and 1 cup water into a heavy-bottomed pan. Boil over medium-high heat, stirring continuously, for 4–5 minutes. The syrup will thicken so that it forms a single thread when a little is dropped from a spoon into a cup of cold water.

Heat the oil for deep-frying in a wok over medium heat. The oil is sufficiently hot when a cube of bread sizzles nicely and turns golden.

Using a ladle, pour roughly 4 tablespoons batter into the hot oil. Allow the batter to sink to the bottom. It will form a circular shape. When it rises to the surface, turn it over and cook for 1–2 minutes until golden. Remove the pancake with a slotted spoon and place it on a large plate.

Repeat the process with the remaining batter, arranging the pancakes in a single layer on a large plate or 2 large plates. Pour the syrup over them. Leave to soak for 1–2 minutes or longer. Serve at room temperature or warmed.

SERVES 4–6

Sandesh
ⓥ FRESH CHEESE SWEETS

THIS IS A VERY basic Bengali sweet, much loved by all and generally bought from sweet-sellers who specialize in it. It is sometimes made with sugar and sometimes with palm jaggery sugar (page 272). These days it comes in many flavors, including fresh strawberry! Milk is first curdled into soft curds. These are hung up to drip. The resulting *chhana* is then kneaded, cooked with sugar and finally pressed into pretty molds shaped like leaves or diamonds.

❧

8¾ cups whole milk	2 tablespoons lemon juice 1⅔ cups sugar	2 tablespoons *ghee* (page 271)

❧

At least 9 hours before serving, bring the milk to a boil. Add the lemon juice and stir. Turn off the heat and leave the milk to curdle. Put a sieve over a large bowl. Line the sieve with a doubled-up piece of cheesecloth, large enough to tie into a bundle later. Empty the curdled milk – the curds and whey – into the sieve. Let the whey drain into the bowl. You will not need it. Tie the 4 corners of the cheesecloth in such a way that you form a bundle that can be suspended over a sink or bowl. Leave to hang for 7–8 hours until the curds drain and acquire the texture of cottage cheese.

Put the sugar and drained milk on a large plate or chopping board. Mix and knead, using the heels of your hands, for 10–15 minutes. This will break down the lumps and the mixture will become smooth and moist.

Heat a large, wide, preferably non-stick pan or wok over low heat. When hot, add the sugar and milk mixture. Stir and fry for 10–12 minutes. The mixture will cling to the side and have a consistency similar to that of porridge. Spoon the mixture into a lightly greased baking sheet. Spread it out and leave it to cool.

Using a pastry brush, lightly grease 16 confectioners' sweet molds or cookie-cutters with the *ghee*. Put a little of the mixture, enough to just fill, into each of the molds or with the cookie cutters just press down firmly. Leave to set in the refrigerator for 15–20 minutes. Remove the sweets from the molds.

The sweets will keep for up to 2 days in the refrigerator.

M A K E S   1 6   S W E E T S

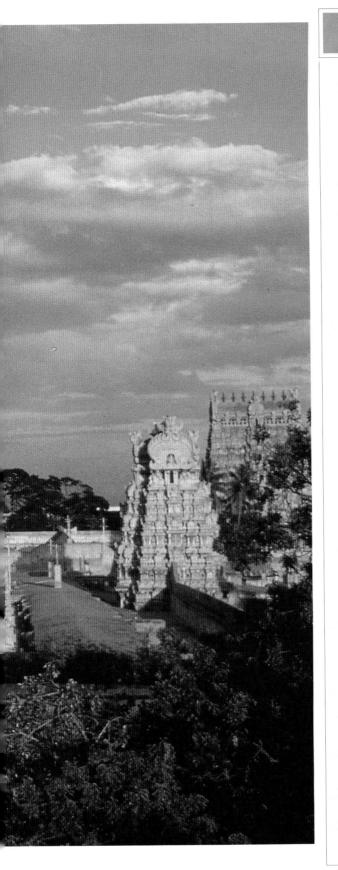

TAMIL NADU

WESTERNERS WHO COME TO Madras, Tamil Nadu's capital city, expecting its cuisine to be a living endorsement of "Madras" curry powder, will be in for a surprise. Curry powders are indeed manufactured here, mixed in huge machines that look and sound like cement mixers, but they are strictly for export. Not an ounce is for home consumption. It never has been, even though some families have, over several generations, become wealthy on its sale to foreign nations.

The superb foods of southern India are little known in the Western world and nor are its true seasonings, which are quite different from those used in northern India. The highly aromatic mixture of roasted coriander seeds, roasted red chilies and roasted fenugreek, the startling use of *urad dal*, a bean, as a spice, and its combination with fresh curry leaves and mustard seeds to perk up the simplest of vegetables, the use of fennel seeds in the cooking of meats, the use of fresh coconut to give body and a slight sweetness to sauces and the use of yogurt, almost as a dressing, for steamed vegetables and rice salads is all very, very southern.

South Indian traders, with easy access to the sea, have carried their foods to the East with more ease than they have to the West. Since ancient times they have had businesses in Singapore, Malaysia and the ports along the South China Sea. Here their foods still flourish as they do at home:

∾

crisp pancakes (*dosas*) sometimes 2 feet (60 centimeters) in diameter, that come all rolled up like precious parchment; fluffy *idlis*, steamed rice cakes whose delicacy is compared to jasmine flowers and whose name can be expressed in the elegant hand gestures of classical South Indian dance; spicy semolina "polenta" dotted with cut vegetables; young shark's meat that is shredded, sautéed with ginger, shallots and green chilies; soupy *rasams* made with crabs; lamb cooked with fennel seeds and coconut; chicken sautéed with poppy seeds and peppercorns – these are just some of the glories of Tamil Nadu's kitchens.

While meat, poultry and seafood are all eaten, what lies at the very heart of the cuisine of Tamil Nadu are beans and rice. Especially rice.

In a small village west of Madras city, on the way to the ancient temples and rich silks of Kanchipuram, is a long, modest shed. It has been here since the 1930s, performing a crucial function. Using techniques as old as those used to make the rich, gold-threaded silks farther along the road, the men and women inside prepare "boiled" rice. No, this is not rice that is ready to eat. It is par-boiled or "converted" rice that is crucial to the diet of Tamil Nadu (and, indeed, much of the south) where many people, perhaps as many as one-third of its population, are vegetarian.

Previous page: Hindu temples in Madurai, Tamil Nadu.

When ordinary rice is husked and hulled, it loses a great many of its nutrients. However, if it is par-boiled before it is milled, the B vitamins in the bran and germ get pushed into the grain itself. How this was known 2000 years ago is anybody's guess, but known it was and this ancient treatment of rice, which prevents diseases like beri-beri that plague other rice-eating nations, continues to this day. The methods that are used to par-boil the rice do not seem to have changed much.

The British, under the protection of the East India Company, may have settled here in 1639, building forts, churches and later colleges along the beautiful marina in Madras and the French and the Portuguese may have tried to wrest power, authority and converts from them, but even while the European powers ruled, none of them had any effect on the basic diet of the local people. Rice, mainly "boiled" rice, remained at its core.

Behind the shed is a large open yard where stalks of rice, hand-cut with a scythe and already dried, are brought in for threshing. Women pass sheaves to the men and the men, in a continuous, fluid motion, hit the sheaves hard against tilted stones. Rice grains come spilling out.

These grains are soaked for a day in outdoor tanks after which they are dropped into a huge, smoke-blackened vat with a few inches of boiling water at the bottom. Once the water comes to a boil again, the actual cooking – steaming really – takes less than 5 minutes. The rice, now smelling like wet, sweet hay, is emptied out on to the ground with buckets. Steam rises as it starts to cool. Two men, one pulling and the other pushing a stubby wooden rake, quickly spread it out. It must dry for 4–5 hours. It is then gathered into heaps, covered with sacks and allowed to "ripen." This "ripening" is essential or the grains will break during the milling. Many simple tests are done. A little rice is removed, rubbed between the palms to remove the husks and then, if the grains remain whole, heads are shaken in approval. The rice is considered ready. Only then, after some more drying, can it be milled, the only part of the process that is now done mechanically.

This par-boiling goes on in every single rice-growing village and in many private homes as well. Rice, both par-boiled and "raw," is at the heart of every single meal and of every course in every single meal. All else is built up around it.

The gods eat it. At exactly 12 noon in the Varadharaja temple at Kanchipuram, a curtain is pulled in front of the diamond- and gold-encrusted statues of Vishnu and his consort, Lakshmi. It is time for their lunch and they must be allowed to enjoy it in privacy. What they delight in most, it seems, is the Kanchipuram *idli*, a steamed, cylinder-shaped savory cake made from a batter of rice and *urad dal* that has been flavored with cumin, peppercorns, ginger and *asafetida*. Nearby, Lord Shiva and Parvati have their own Ekambareeshwara

temple built around an ancient, 3500-year-old (so it is believed) mango tree where, according to legend, they married. The tree bears sweet, sour and bitter mangoes. Shaved pilgrims come here, sacrificing their "earthly beauty," their hair, to a greater cause. The gods can give them something in return. A child perhaps, if that is what they desire. Shiva and Parvati also dine in privacy. The curtains are drawn and they enjoy hot and tart tamarind rice or sweet "Pongal" rice, newly harvested grains cooked with cashew nuts and jaggery, a form of raw lump cane sugar.

The Western nutritionists who suggest to us that grains and beans form the major part of our meals should come here to see how it is done. They should, perhaps, visit the family of Mrs. A. Santha Ramanujam in Madras.

Shoes are left at the door of this simple, first floor apartment. This is a traditional Ayengar family of the upper Brahmin caste, worshippers of Lord Vishnu. Mornings begin with ablutions and prayers. Sacred designs with rice flour are drawn on a part of the floor. "If she is very good and has done all her homework, I let her make the designs," a daughter-in-law says of her 10-year-old child. Tradition is being passed on from mother to daughter with gentle enticements. The designs are made not only because they are sacred but because they will provide food for ants and squirrels.

The women of the house have risen at dawn to prepare both breakfast and lunch.

The cooking begins at 6 a.m. when the day is still cool and is finished by 7:30 a.m. First, there are coffee beans to be roasted. People tend not to ask for just "coffee" when they are buying but rather a specific bean or a chosen combination of beans, all of which grow in the state. This family likes Peaberry beans which sit in a jar, grayish-green and rather sad. They are thrown into a heated, cast-iron wok and roasted slowly. As they are tossed – the process takes 20 minutes – the beans begin to come to life and the come-and-get-it aroma of coffee starts spreading through the house. As soon as they turn brown, a tiny amount of sugar is thrown into the wok. This caramelizes around the beans adding both flavor and color. The beans are removed, ground and put through a filter. The coffee is strong but it is drunk with at least an equal amount of hot milk and some sugar.

This is very much a coffee-drinking area. Coffee beans were first introduced to India's west coast by early Arab traders. From here, they filtered inland. In those days, many families in the Nilgiri Hills (in western Tamil Nadu) had a couple of coffee trees in their kitchen gardens, enough for their own needs. It was the British who later built large plantations and turned the growing of coffee into a business. It was on some of these large estates, in sprawling bungalows built for bored coffee-planters, that many of the British "curries" were created, hybrid mixtures of East and West, the kind that contained apples, the kind that are now found only in the Western world. Such creations could be a wonderful subject for a future book. They do not quite belong here.

Some sons of the Ramanujam household drink quick cups of coffee and dash off to their offices on motor-cycles and scooters, the wind in their faces ameliorating the effects of the heat and Madras traffic. One son opts for a glass of butter-milk (*neer mor*), actually thinned out yogurt, flavored with crushed ginger, green chilies, fresh cilantro, curry leaves, ground fenugreek, *asafetida* and, for good measure, a few rose petals – a heavenly concoction.

Now the women in their cool saris and the children all ribboned and ready for school, sit down to the serious business of a substantial breakfast. The ceiling fan is turned on in the dining-room. Birds chirp loudly in the shady trees outside.

Look at their many choices. They could have *idi appam,* a total delight that is almost unknown in the West or, for that matter, in North India. First you make fresh rice noodles. With the right tools, it is a breeze. Rice has already been washed and dried at home and then sent off to the mill to be ground. This special flour is mixed with boiling water to make a dough with the texture of play dough. Balls of it are put into a wooden press and the press held over an oiled saucer. As you press, thin noodles

Rice growing by the side of a dam in Tamil Nadu.

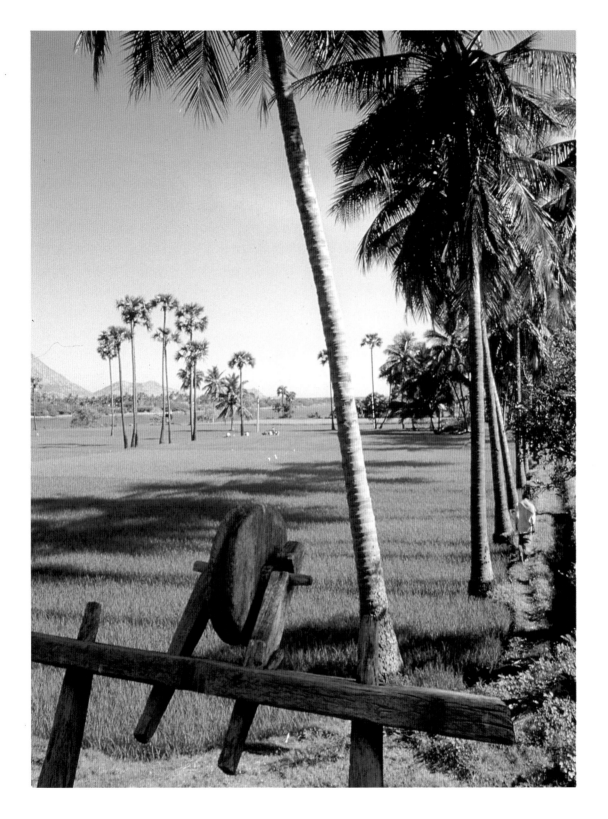

ooze out. If you move the press in a circular motion, you get a small nest of noodles. Several saucers are filled this way. All are stacked in a steamer and steamed for 5–7 minutes. ("Each plate is only 1 calorie," the youngest daughter-in-law says brightly.) You add to the calories somewhat by eating these noodles with freshly squeezed, cardamom-flavored coconut milk or with *ghee* that has been perked up with mustard seeds, *urad dal*, curry leaves and dried red chilies, traditional Tamilian seasonings.

I have already mentioned these seasonings. South Indian cuisine is the only one I know where hulled beans and split peas are used as spices might be. Oil is heated and a mixture of whole spices and split peas are thrown in. As they are stirred around, the split peas become red and give the oil a very pleasant nutty flavor and aroma. The flavored oil, in turn, completely changes the taste of any food that it touches.

Back to the breakfast. The noodles are one choice. You could have *rava khichri*, a spicy semolina "polenta" chockful of fresh vegetables, or one of the two dishes for which the south is justly famous – the *idli* or the *dosa*.

Both are made out of rice and *urad dal* batters. The two main ingredients, the rice and the split peas, are soaked and ground separately and then combined and left overnight to bubble, ferment and turn into light, frothy batter. With tropical temperatures set permanently at "balmy," much of the state uses the climate as a God-given

cooking tool. Fermentation takes place easily, tenderizing foods, making them more digestible and cutting down on cooking time. Once the protein-rich batter is ready, it can be poured into a stack of steaming trays with round depressions to make the flying-saucer-shaped, everyday *idlis*; or it can be fermented a bit more and made into the lightest of pancakes, *dosas*, golden-red on one side, pale cream on the other. Both may be eaten with *sambar*, a split pea stew which is varied daily with the addition of, say, caramelized shallots or tomatoes or okra or eggplant poached in tamarind juice. The *dosa* itself can be varied endlessly. Add tomatoes, onions and green chilies to it and it turns into an *utthappam*. Roll it around spicy potatoes and it becomes a *masala dosa*.

The biggest meal of the day in the Ramanujam household is not breakfast but lunch. All the sons come home for it. This is a rice meal. Every course is eaten with "boiled" (converted) rice, which is cooked just a bit softer than rice is in the North. The grains are white, short, fat and plump. "We like to mash the other foods into the rice," the young daughter-in-law with jasmine in her hair explains.

But first of all, a sweet is placed on the plate. This could be a square of a slightly crispy, chick-pea flour brittle (*Mysore pak*) or a *halva* made with semolina. Then you are served plain rice and vegetables – cabbage and carrots stir-fried with mustard seeds and curry leaves (*mutta kose kilangu*) or mixed vegetables dressed with a stunning sauce of ground coconut and green chilies (*kurma*) or eggplants or okra or marrow or green plantains, whatever is in season. Then comes *sambar*, the split pea stew. More rice is put on the plate, this to be eaten with *rasam*, a very thin split pea broth. A variety of possible flavorings may be added to it such as black pepper – making it the very health-giving "pepper-water" (*milagu tanni*), which Anglo-Indians turned into their mulligatawny soup – tomatoes and even garlic, supposed to be perfect for those who have over-indulged. The final course, considered the cleansing one, is yogurt, rice and pickles, all mixed and eaten together. (Whenever I see Tamils doing this, I think of their similarity to the Japanese, who like to end meals with rice, pickles and tea.) Sometimes the yogurt and rice are combined in a salad (*bhakala bhat*), with bits of green mango, cucumber, ginger, green chilies and even grapes added to it.

Dinner, like breakfast, is light. "We generally do not eat rice for dinner," Mrs Ramanujam explains. Instead, the easy-to-digest fermented foods such as the *idlis* and *dosas* are preferred. With the batter already made in the morning and sitting in a bowl, they take just a few minutes to prepare.

For those who do not like to cook or are too busy, there are vast, fast food restaurants serving the very dishes that vegetarians eat at home. The Hotel Saravana Bhavan in Madras is one such place. It is a sea of people. Each day 4000 customers are served. The kitchen produces 5000 *dosas*. The staff of 300 works in two shifts that go from six in the morning to ten at night.

The work is carried on with great speed. A folded banana leaf is placed before the diner plus a tumbler of water. The leaf is your plate. You unfold it, and sprinkle water on it. It is now considered washed.

Next comes the food. A round metal plate, a *thali*, holds the rice and a set of metal bowls. In the bowls are all the vegetables, *sambars*, *rasams* and freshly made chutneys. On top of all, covering the first layer and forming the basis of a second layer, is a large poppadom. On top of that is the dessert, generally a squiggly, orange *jahangiri* (similar to the northern *jalebi*) all filled with oozing syrup. This is a fast food joint and you are supposed to undo the layers and arrange the food on the banana leaf yourself. Fresh rice appears just when you are eating what seems to be the last mouthful. When you finish, you fold up your banana leaf again. It is picked up by a wandering youth and dropped into a pail. You get up. The next diner is hovering and immediately sits down in your place. A fresh banana leaf appears. Hotel Saravana Bhavan has nine branches and they all do a roaring business in the city.

What if you wish to eat at home but do not want to make, say, the scrumptious coconut rice from scratch? A shop near the Mylapore temple sells all the spice mixtures needed to make coconut rice, tamarind rice, lime rice and all manner of crisp nibbles which Tamils like to mix in with their rice – giant poppadums the size of elephant feet as well as dozens of varieties of pickles. If you wait a while, a new vending machine is also on its way, already working feverishly in test kitchens. It will cook and serve 50 *dosas* in 75 seconds and also pour out the *sambar* – and coconut chutney! Life in Madras, for those with power or money, is on the fast track!

Not everyone in the state is vegetarian and many will never get on the fast track. Thousands of betel-nut-chewing fishermen with gleaming black skin and worn teeth go out to sea daily with the tide. Their simple catamarans, consisting of seven to eight carved, tapering logs tied up with rope, look exactly the same as they do in seventeenth-century prints and paintings. They can be seen on the waters off South Beach Road where the British built the grand Fort St George and St Mary's Church (Robert Clive and Elihu Yale both married here and went on to amass great wealth). The fishermen live on their humble catches – sometimes a single crab poached in spiced-up tamarind juice or a baby shark boiled up with salt and chilies, all to be eaten with rice.

Not far from them live some other non-vegetarians with fuller coffers. Just look at the Chettiars of the formerly royal state of Chettinad who eat, with great enjoyment, some of the most exquisite meat, chicken and fish dishes in the region. It is worth visiting one of their major residences in Madras.

In the choicest of locations, just where the Adyar River meets the Bay of Bengal, is a large palace. Its many acres double as a bird sanctuary. It once belonged to Rajah Sir Annamalai Chettiar. His descendants live there now, two of them served by 127 servants.

The spacious rooms are lined with Italian marble floors. The high ceilings and doors are carved from solid Burma teak, acquired in Burma, along with vast fortunes, when the Chettiar men went to work there in the last several centuries. (The women always stayed in India.) No one is allowed to forget what they were born to do. Their motto, "Strive, save and serve," is everywhere.

What they mainly strove to do was make money. The Chettiars, a trading community, were always money-lenders and bankers. Today, they are major industrialists as well. They are canny, not only at making money but at keeping it in the family. Marriage takes place between first cousins, ensuring that the bride's dowry of diamonds, rubies and sapphires, of dozens and dozens of rich silk saris, of rooms filled with silver utensils and cut glass and carpets, never travels too far from home!

In a palace lined with photographs of racing horses and garlanded portraits of sober-faced forebears, Rajah Sir Annamalai Chettiar's descendants enjoy meals served by discreet family retainers on silver *thalis*

Put the fennel seeds and poppy seeds into a clean coffee grinder and grind until you have a fine powder. Empty into a bowl. Add the coriander, cayenne pepper, paprika and turmeric. Mix and set aside.

In the container of an electric blender combine the garlic, ginger and coconut. Add 1 cup water. Blend until you have a smooth paste, scraping down with a rubber spatula when necessary. This is the spice paste.

Heat the 6 tablespoons oil in a heavy, well-seasoned wok or a large, wide, preferably non-stick pan over medium-high heat. When hot, put in the ¼ teaspoon fennel seeds, bay leaves, cardamom pods and cinnamon. Stir once or twice and put in the curry leaves, if using. Stir once and put in the onions. Stir and fry until the onions soften a bit and begin to turn brown at the edges. Put in the tomatoes. Stir and fry until the tomatoes soften. Now put in the coconut spice paste, spice powder and salt. Stir and fry for 5–6 minutes, sprinkling in a little water if it seems to stick. Put in the lamb. Stir and cook for 2–3 minutes. Now add 3¾ cups water. Bring to the boil. Cover, turn the heat down to a simmer and cook for 60–70 minutes or until the lamb is tender. If the sauce is too watery, turn the heat up and reduce it to the consistency of thick cream soup.

Sprinkle the fresh cilantro on the top before serving.

S E R V E S   4 – 6

Eraichi Porial
LAMB PEPPER-FRY

THIS FRAGRANT MEAT DISH can be served with any plain or seasoned rice. If you wish to substitute unsweetened, dried coconut for fresh coconut use ⅔ cup. Just cover with warm water and leave for 1 hour then proceed with the recipe.

~

FOR THE DRY SPICE MIXTURE:

1 tablespoon coriander seeds

1 teaspoon black peppercorns

1 tablespoon fennel seeds

5 dried hot red chilies

FOR THE SPICE PASTE:

2 tablespoons vegetable oil

2 medium-sized onions, peeled and chopped

6 garlic cloves, peeled and chopped

1 (½ inch) (1 cm) piece fresh ginger root, peeled and chopped

4–5 fresh hot green chilies, coarsely chopped

1 cup freshly grated coconut (page 265)

YOU ALSO NEED:

4 tablespoons vegetable oil

1 (1 inch) (2.5 cm) cinnamon stick

1 large onion, sliced into very fine half-rings

2 lb (900 g) boned lamb from the shoulder, cut into 1 inch (2.5 cm) cubes

2 large tomatoes, chopped

1½ teaspoons salt

~

Set a small, frying pan over medium heat. When hot, put in all the ingredients for the dry spice mixture. Stir and fry for 2–3 minutes or until they turn a few shades darker and smell roasted. Cool a bit and then grind in a clean coffee grinder.

Heat the 2 tablespoons oil for the spice paste in a large, preferably non-stick, frying pan over medium-high heat. When hot, put in the onions, garlic, ginger and green chilies. Stir and fry until the onions brown a bit. Put in the coconut. Continue to stir and fry until the coconut browns as well. Empty the contents of this pan into the container of a food processor. Add ½ cup water and blend to a paste. Set aside.

Heat the 4 tablespoons oil in a large, preferably non-stick pan over medium-high heat. When hot, put in the cinnamon. Stir once and put in the large onion sliced into half-rings. Stir and fry until the onion is browned. Add the meat. Stir and fry for 10 minutes. Add the tomatoes, the dry spice mixture, the spice paste and the salt. Stir and cook for 5 minutes. Add 2 cups water and bring to the boil. Cover, turn the heat down to low and simmer gently for 60–70 minutes or until the lamb is tender. Uncover and boil away most of the liquid over high heat. The sauce should cling to the meat.

SERVES 6

From the home of A. C. Muthiah: Koli Milagu Masala
CHETTINAD PEPPER CHICKEN

ANOTHER EXQUISITE DISH FROM the Chettiar community, this is generally served with plain rice. It may also be served with Rice and Split Pea Pancakes (page 205) and Savory Rice Cakes (page 204), even Savory Rice Breads (page 39), but in that case it is a good idea to keep the sauce a bit thinner so it can be sopped up.

What gives the dish a very special southern flavor is the use of fennel seeds, curry leaves and, of course, the bean, *urad dal*. This is definitely a dish you will want to make very frequently.

5 tablespoons oil

FOR THE SPICE PASTE:
1½ tablespoons cumin seeds
8–10 dried hot red chilies, broken into halves
3 tablespoons coriander seeds
1½ teaspoons fennel seeds
1½ teaspoons black peppercorns
1½ teaspoons white poppy seeds
5 garlic cloves, peeled and roughly chopped

1 (1½ inch) (4 cm) piece fresh ginger root, peeled and roughly chopped
½ teaspoon ground turmeric
1½ –2 teaspoons salt

YOU ALSO NEED:
3 bay leaves
5 cardamom pods
1 (1 inch) (2.5 cm) cinnamon stick, broken
1 teaspoon fennel seeds
3 cloves
1½ teaspoons *urad dal* (page 261)

15–20 fresh curry leaves (optional)
2 medium-sized onions, peeled and finely chopped
1 large tomato, chopped
1 (2¼ lb) (1 kg) chicken, skinned and cut into smallish serving pieces (breast halves into 3 and legs into drumsticks and thighs)

Make the spice paste: in a small frying pan, heat 1 tablespoon of the oil over medium-high heat. When hot add the cumin seeds, chilies, coriander seeds, fennel seeds, black peppercorns and poppy seeds. Stir and fry briefly until lightly roasted. Now, put these into a clean coffee grinder and grind to a powder. Empty into the container of an electric blender. Put the garlic, ginger, turmeric and salt into the blender as well, along with 6–8 tablespoons water. Process until you have a fine paste, pushing down with a rubber spatula if needed. Set aside.

Heat the remaining 4 tablespoons oil in a

large saucepan over medium-high heat. When hot, add the bay leaves, cardamom pods, cinnamon, fennel seeds, cloves and *urad dal*. Stir and fry briefly until the *urad dal* turns red, then add the curry leaves, if using. Stir once or twice and add the onions. Fry the onions until they are soft and just lightly colored. Now add the spice paste. Continue to stir and fry for about 4–6 minutes, adding a little water to prevent sticking. Add the tomato. Stir and fry for a further 3–4 minutes.

Add the chicken pieces to the onion and spice mixture. Stir until they are well coated, then add 2½ cups water, just enough to cover. Bring to the boil. Turn the heat to low, cover and simmer until the chicken is almost cooked, about 20–25 minutes.

Using a slotted spoon, remove the chicken pieces. Turn the heat up to medium-high, and reduce the sauce until very thick. This should take about 6–8 minutes. Replace the chicken, fold gently into the sauce and cook for a further 5 minutes before serving.

S E R V E S   4 – 6

Lamb in a Fennel-flavored Coconut Sauce (page 186).

From the Dakshin restaurant at the Park Sheraton: Koli Uppakari
GINGER CHICKEN WITH MUSTARD SEEDS

THIS CHETTIAR RECIPE, FROM chef Praveen Anand, is easy to prepare and utterly scrumptious. It does require a marination period. Overnight is ideal but 3–4 hours will do. After marinating in ginger juice, the chicken pieces are stir-fried in a wok with very South Indian seasonings such as mustard seeds, *urad dal* and fennel seeds. When it is ready, the chicken turns reddish-brown on the outside, is encrusted with spices and is meltingly tender inside.

In the south it is eaten with rice but you may serve this with any Indian bread. You may use any chicken pieces for this dish, though the thigh is ideal. Since the pieces need to be small each thigh should be cut into two pieces. It is best if you ask the butcher to do this. If you wish to do it yourself, use a sharp, heavy cleaver, aim well at the center of the thigh bone and hit hard once.

1¼ lb (550 g) skinned chicken thighs, each cut into 2 pieces

¼ teaspoon ground turmeric

1¼–1½ teaspoons salt

1 (3 inch) (7.5 cm) piece fresh ginger root, peeled

4–5 tablespoons vegetable oil

4–5 dried hot red chilies, each broken into 2–3 pieces

¾ teaspoon brown mustard seeds

¾ teaspoon *urad dal* (page 261)

½ teaspoon fennel seeds

2 small cinnamon sticks

5–6 garlic cloves, peeled and finely chopped

1 medium-sized onion, peeled and sliced into fine half-rings

2 medium-sized tomatoes, peeled and chopped

½ teaspoon cayenne pepper

Lots of freshly ground black pepper

Wedges of tomatoes, and chopped fresh cilantro for sprinkling over the top (optional)

Put the chicken pieces into a bowl. Add the turmeric and 1 teaspoon of the salt. Now, either grate the ginger on the finest part of the grater or else chop it finely and put it into the container of an electric blender along with 1 tablespoon water and blend to a paste. Using your hand, squeeze the juice from the ginger over the chicken. (Discard the pulp.) Mix the chicken with the ginger juice. Cover the chicken and refrigerate for 3–4 hours or overnight.

Heat the oil in a wok or a large, preferably

non-stick frying pan over medium-high heat. When hot, put in the red chilies, mustard seeds, *urad dal*, fennel seeds and cinnamon. Stir for a few seconds or until the chilies turn dark and the mustard seeds pop. Now put in the garlic. Stir once or twice. Put in the onion. Stir and sauté until the onion is soft and just starting to turn brown. Put in the tomatoes. Stir and fry for 2–3 minutes or until the tomatoes are soft. Now put in the chicken with its marinade juices, cayenne pepper and the remaining salt. Stir and fry on high heat until the chicken has browned. This will take about 6 minutes. Cover, turn the heat to low and cook for another 10–12 minutes, stirring now and then until the chicken is done. Remove the cover and sprinkle in lots of freshly ground black pepper. If there is any liquid left in the pan, turn the heat up and dry it off before serving.

Sprinkle the fresh cilantro over the top and serve with the tomato wedges if you wish.

SERVES 3 – 4

From the home of A. C. Muthiah: Koli Kurma
EGGS IN CHILI-COCONUT SAUCE

A CHETTIAR DISH WITH a sauce to swoon over, this can also be made with chicken or even small, halved, slightly sautéed eggplants. If you wish to substitute unsweetened dried coconut for fresh coconut use ⅔ cup. Just cover with warm water and leave for 1 hour, then proceed with the recipe.

FOR THE SPICE PASTE:
6 raw cashew nuts, split into halves lengthwise
2 tablespoons fennel seeds
2 teaspoons roasted *chana dal* (page 260)
5–8 fresh hot green chilies, coarsely sliced
4 garlic cloves, peeled

1 (2 inch) (5 cm) piece fresh ginger root, peeled and coarsely chopped
1 cup freshly grated coconut (page 265)

YOU ALSO NEED:
4 tablespoons vegetable oil or *ghee* (page 271)
2 bay leaves

2 (1 inch) (2.5 cm) cinnamon sticks
5 cardamom pods
1 fresh hot green chili, cut into 3 segments
2 medium-sized onions, peeled and finely chopped
1¼–1½ teaspoons salt
6–8 hard-boiled eggs
2 tablespoons chopped, fresh cilantro

Make the spice paste: put the cashew nuts, fennel seeds and roasted *chana dal* into a clean coffee grinder and grind finely. Empty the contents of the coffee grinder into the container of an electric blender. Add the chilies, garlic, ginger, coconut and ½ cup water. Grind to a paste.

Heat the 4 tablespoons oil in a large, wide, preferably non-stick pan over medium-high heat. When hot, put in the bay leaves, cinnamon and cardamom pods. Stir and fry for 10 seconds. Put in the green chili. Stir and fry until it softens. Add the onions. Stir and fry

until they begin to soften. Add the spice paste. Stir and fry for 2–3 minutes. Add the salt and 1 cup water. Bring to the boil. Reduce the heat to medium-low and simmer for 7–8 minutes.

Meanwhile, make a 2 inch (5 cm) incision arching over the top of each egg only as deep as its yolk. Do the same around the tip of each egg but at a right angle to the top incision. When the sauce has finished cooking, drop in the eggs and bring to the boil. Turn off the heat. Let the eggs sit for at least 2 hours before serving. Sprinkle the fresh cilantro over the top.

SERVES 3–4

From the home of A. C. Muthiah: Meen Varuval
SPICY PAN-FRIED FISH STEAKS CHETTINAD

KINGFISH STEAKS ARE ENCRUSTED with simple spices – coriander and chilies mixed into a paste with salt and lime juice – and then quickly pan-fried. Nothing could be simpler or better. It helps if the coriander seeds are freshly ground and sifted as they have a wonderful aroma. A fresh packet of ground coriander from your Indian grocer will also be very good.

You may serve this as part of a rice-based meal, as they do in Chettiar homes, or you may serve it Western style, with plain boiled potatoes and a vegetable or a salad. You might like to try it with Potatoes with Mustard Seeds and Onions (page 200) and a green salad. In spite of the rather large quantity of cayenne pepper, this dish has medium heat.

Kingfish is commonly used for this dish. You could also use swordfish (Mahi Mahi) steaks or mackerel steaks cut at a diagonal. (The steaks look much larger this way. They are traditionally cut from between the tail and the stomach.)

2½ tablespoons ground coriander
2½ tablespoons cayenne pepper
½ teaspoon ground turmeric
1 teaspoon ground cumin

2 teaspoons salt
5–6 teaspoons lime juice or lemon juice
4 (½ inch) (1 cm) thick kingfish, swordfish or mackerel steaks

About 3 tablespoons vegetable oil
Extra lime or lemon wedges for serving

Combine the coriander, cayenne pepper, turmeric, cumin, salt and lime or lemon juice on a large plate and mix. Add about 6 table-spoons water to make a thick paste. Taste for balance of sour and salt. The paste should be fairly salty at this stage. Rub the fish steaks on both sides with the paste and set aside for 15 minutes. (You could marinate them for up to 3 hours. Refrigerate in that case.)

Rub the bottom of a heavy frying pan with a little of the oil and set over medium-high heat. When hot, put in as many steaks as the pan will hold in a single layer. Cook the steaks for about 6–8 minutes on each side, or until they are nicely browned and just cooked through. Do all steaks this way, adding more oil as needed.

Serve with the lime or lemon wedges.

SERVES 4

ENTRÉE

From the home of A. C. Muthiah: Sora Puttu
SHARK WITH SPICES AND FRESH CILANTRO

THIS RECIPE COMES FROM the kitchen of a princely Chettiar home. The flaked flesh of baby sharks can be cooked so that it remains moist but it can also be stirred and stirred until the flakes turn crisp. This recipe is the second version. Generally, it is mixed with plain rice and eaten with a *sambar* (see Split Peas with Shallots, page 202). If you cannot get shark, use fresh tuna or swordfish.

If you wish to substitute unsweetened, dried coconut for fresh coconut use ⅔ cup. Barely cover with warm water and leave for 1 hour. Squeeze dry and proceed with the recipe.

---

1 lb (450 g) shark, tuna or swordfish, the younger the better, cut into thick steaks
2 teaspoons salt
1 teaspoon ground turmeric
5 tablespoons vegetable oil
1 (1 inch) (2.5 cm) cinnamon stick, broken
8–10 shallots, finely chopped

½ teaspoon fennel seeds
1 (1½ inch) (4 cm) piece fresh ginger root, finely chopped or grated
4–5 fresh hot green chilies, cut into fine half-rounds
5 garlic cloves, finely chopped

20 fresh curry leaves (optional)
1 cup freshly grated coconut (page 265)
2 tablespoons chopped, fresh cilantro, plus extra for garnishing
2 teaspoons lemon juice

Put the shark, 1 teaspoon of the salt and the turmeric in a large saucepan with 4½ cups water. Bring to the boil over medium heat. Reduce the heat to a gentle simmer. Cook for 15–20 minutes until the shark is tender. Drain and allow to cool. Remove the skin and cartilage of the shark and flake. Put in a large bowl and set aside.

Heat the oil in a large frying pan over medium-high heat. When hot, add the cinnamon, shallots and fennel seeds. Stir and fry for 4–5 minutes or until the shallots are golden. Add the ginger, chilies and garlic. Stir and fry until lightly browned and softened. Add the remaining salt and the flaked shark. Stir and fry briskly for 10–15 minutes.

Add the curry leaves, if using, coconut and 2 tablespoons cilantro. Cook until dry. Just before serving, add the lemon juice. Serve hot, garnished with the remaining cilantro.

S E R V E S   4 – 6

Mrs A. Santha Ramanujam's Mutta Kose Kilangu
Ⓥ STIR-FRIED CABBAGE AND CARROTS

STRANGELY ENOUGH, WHEN TAMILS speaking English refer to a curry they mean a dry dish, totally devoid of any sauce. This is one such "curry." You could cook the cabbage plain, or with carrots as I have done here, or with the addition of shelled peas. A similar dish can be made out of green beans, boiled beets and the pear-shaped green vegetable called "chow chow" and known more correctly as the chayote or sayote squash.

If you wish to substitute unsweetened, dried coconut for fresh coconut use 5 tablespoons. Barely cover with warm water and soak for 1 hour, then proceed with the recipe.

This dish may be served with all Indian meals.

❧

3 tablespoons vegetable oil
1½ teaspoons *chana dal* (page 260)
1½ teaspoons *urad dal* (page 261)
1 teaspoon mustard seeds

20 fresh curry leaves (optional)
2–4 fresh hot green chilies, cut into long slivers
3 cups finely shredded cabbage

2 medium-sized carrots, coarsely grated
¾–1 teaspoon salt
½ cup freshly grated coconut (page 265)

❧

Heat the oil in a large frying pan over medium-high heat. When hot, add the *chana dal, urad dal* and mustard seeds. Stir and fry until the mustard seeds pop and the *dals* turn reddish, a matter of seconds. Add the curry leaves, if using. Stir for a few seconds. Add the chilies and stir once. Now add the cabbage and carrots. Stir once to mix. Add the salt and mix

again. Cover, turn the heat to low and cook for 5–6 minutes or until the cabbage is wilted and just tender.

Remove the cover. Add the coconut and mix it in with the cabbage, stirring vigorously for a minute or so.

SERVES 4

Shoba Ramji's Vendaka Pakoda
ⓥ DEEP-FRIED OKRA IN BATTER

CRISP, DEEP-FRIED CLUMPS OF sliced okra in batter are often served as part of a meal. Crunchy foods are enjoyed here with the blander rice. I like to serve them with drinks or with tea. The rice flour in the batter keeps them very crisp.

❧

8 oz (225 g) fresh okra
¾ cup chick-pea flour
1½ tablespoons cream of
  rice cereal

1 tablespoon cayenne
  pepper
1¼ teaspoons salt
1 teaspoon ground turmeric

1 tablespoon vegetable oil
  plus extra vegetable oil for
  deep-frying
¼ teaspoon *ajwain* seeds
  (page 259) (optional)

❧

Gently wipe the okra with a lightly dampened cloth and cut into ½ inch (1 cm) thick rounds. Set aside.

Sift the chick-pea flour, rice flour, cayenne pepper, salt and turmeric into a medium-sized bowl. Rub in the 1 tablespoon oil to get a coarse breadcrumb consistency. Add the *ajwain* seeds, if using, and mix them in. Add about ½ cup water, a little at a time, to make a paste about the consistency of thick, heavy cream. Make sure there are no lumps.

Heat the oil in a deep frying pan or wok over medium-low heat. When it is hot enough for a cube of bread to sizzle nicely and turn golden-brown, fold the okra gently into the batter. With a tablespoon take small dollops of the okra and batter and gently drop into the oil. Fry, turning now and then, until the fritters are crisp and golden. This will take about 6–7 minutes.

Serve immediately.

S E R V E S   4

Chettinad Pepper Chicken (page 189).

Shoba Ramji's Urala Kilangu
POTATOES WITH MUSTARD SEEDS AND ONIONS

EACH HOUSEHOLD IN TAMIL Nadu – indeed in all of India – must have several dozen potato recipes, each one better than the next. This particular dish has onions and tomatoes in it. Serve it with any Indian meal. I even love to serve it with a leg of lamb or with broiled sausages.

ᘒ

3–4 tablespoons vegetable oil

1 teaspoon brown mustard seeds

2 tablespoons *urad dal* (page 261)

2–3 dried hot red chilies, broken into halves

20–25 fresh curry leaves (optional)

2 medium-sized onions, peeled, quartered and finely sliced

1–1¼ teaspoons salt

½ teaspoon ground turmeric

¼–½ teaspoon cayenne pepper

1 lb (450 g) potatoes, peeled and cut into ½ inch (1 cm) dice

1 medium-sized tomato, chopped

A pinch of ground *asafetida*

ᘒ

Heat the oil in a well-seasoned wok or a large, preferably non-stick frying pan over medium-high heat. When hot, put in the mustard seeds, *urad dal* and chilies. Stir until the mustard seeds pop and the *dal* turns red, a matter of seconds. Put in the curry leaves, if using. Stir once or twice. Now put in the onions. Stir and fry until the onions just begin to turn brown at the edges. Put in the salt, turmeric and cayenne pepper. Stir for 5 seconds. Add the potatoes. Stir and fry for a minute. Add the tomato and *asafetida*. Stir and fry for a minute. Now put in about 1 cup plus 2 tablespoons water and bring to a boil. Cover, turn the heat to medium and cook fairly vigorously for about 10 minutes or until the potatoes are just tender and the water is absorbed. You may have to adjust the heat. Remove the cover. Stir and fry the potatoes on medium-low heat for 4-5 minutes to get a rich reddish-yellow color.

S E R V E S   6

Mrs A. Santha Ramanujam's Kurma
Ⓥ MIXED VEGETABLE CURRY

NOTHING COULD BE SIMPLER or, for that matter, more delicious. Vegetables, whatever happens to be in season, are lightly par-boiled or steamed and then "dressed" with a ground paste of fresh coconut, poppy seeds and green chilies. The "dressing" is not just poured over the top. Instead, it is cooked briefly with the vegetables so that it is absorbed by them. This is best with plain rice. You could serve it as part of a larger meal with Ginger Chicken with Mustard Seeds (page 192) and a relish, such as Sweet Beet Chutney (page 209).

If you wish to substitute unsweetened, dried coconut for fresh coconut use 5 tablespoons. Barely cover with warm water and leave for 1 hour, then proceed with the recipe.

❧

½ medium-sized eggplant, cut into ¾ × ½ inch (2 × 1 cm) sticks

2 small carrots, peeled and cut into ¾ × ½ inch (2 × 1 cm) sticks

1 cup peas

4 oz (100 g) French green beans, cut into 1 inch (2.5 cm) pieces

1 medium-sized potato, peeled and cut into ¾ × ½ inch (2 × 1 cm) sticks

½ cup freshly grated coconut (page 265)

4 fresh hot green chilies

2 tablespoons white poppy seeds

1¼ teaspoons salt

3 medium-sized tomatoes, roughly chopped

1 tablespoon plain yogurt

1 teaspoon *garam masala* (page 270)

2 tablespoons chopped, fresh cilantro

❧

Place the eggplant, carrots, peas, French green beans and potato in a medium-sized saucepan. Add 1 cup water. Bring to the boil. Cover, turn the heat to medium and cook for 4 minutes or until the vegetables are just tender.

Meanwhile put the coconut, chilies, poppy seeds and salt in the container of an electric blender. Add ⅔ cup water and grind to a fine paste. Set aside.

When the vegetables are cooked, add the spice paste and another ⅔ cup water. Stir and simmer gently for 5 minutes. Now add the tomatoes, the yogurt and the *garam masala*. Stir gently to mix well. Bring to the boil and simmer gently for 2–3 minutes. Turn into a serving dish and garnish with the fresh cilantro.

S E R V E S   4 – 6

Mrs A. Santha Ramanujam's Vengayam Sambar

ⓥ SPLIT PEAS WITH SHALLOTS

Sambar AND RICE ARE the meat and potatoes of Tamil Nadu. Plain *toovar dal* is first boiled. It is then made deliciously sour with tamarind paste and exquisitely spicy with the addition of a special *sambar* powder that contains a mixture of roasted spices (page 276). This basic *sambar* can be varied daily with the addition of different vegetables. One of my favorites is shallot *sambar*. The shallots are lightly sautéed before being added to the *sambar*, giving them a sweet, glazed quality. Pickling onions may be substituted.

Serve with plain rice or Savory Rice Cakes (page 204) or Rice and Split Pea Pancakes (page 205).

❧

**¾ cup *toovar dal*
(page 261), picked over
and washed in several
changes of water**

3 tablespoons vegetable oil

**1 fresh hot green chili, split
in half lengthwise**

**12–14 even-sized shallots,
peeled**

**2 tablespoons tamarind
paste (page 278)**

**2–2½ tablespoons *sambar*
powder (page 276)**

1½ teaspoons salt

½ teaspoon ground turmeric

**½ teaspoon brown mustard
seeds**

**15–20 fresh curry leaves
(optional)**

**1 tablespoon finely chopped,
fresh cilantro**

❧

Place the *toovar dal* in a medium-sized saucepan with 2½ cups water. Bring to the boil. Cover partially, turn the heat to low, and simmer for 45 minutes – 1 hour or until the *dal* is tender. When cooked, stir with a spoon to mash up the *dal*.

Heat 2 tablespoons of the oil in a medium-sized frying pan over medium-high heat. When hot, put in the chili. Stir for a few seconds until the chili softens. Add the shallots. Stir and fry until the shallots are very lightly browned. Turn the heat down and cook until the shallots soften and cook through.

Add the tamarind paste, *sambar* powder,

salt, turmeric and 2 cups water to the saucepan of *toovar dal*. Also add the contents of the frying pan. Mix and bring to a simmer. Simmer gently, uncovered, for 10 minutes, stirring now and then.

Meanwhile, heat the remaining 1 tablespoon oil in a small saucepan or small frying pan over medium-high heat. When hot add the mustard seeds. As soon as the mustard seeds pop, a matter of seconds, throw in the curry leaves, if using. Stir once and quickly pour over the *sambar*. Sprinkle the fresh cilantro over the top.

SERVES 4

Mrs A. Santha Ramanujam's Tengai Sadam
ⓥ COCONUT RICE

THIS IS AN EXCELLENT RICE dish, perked up with lightly roasted coconut and a very South Indian spice combination that includes split peas, chilies and mustard seeds. Eat as part of any meal, northern or southern. If you are stir-frying fresh prawns (shrimp) or scallops, serve this on the side.

If you wish to substitute unsweetened, dried coconut for fresh coconut use 1¼ cups. Barely cover with warm water and leave for 1 hour. Squeeze dry and proceed with the recipe.

❧

2 cups long-grain rice
3 tablespoons coconut oil
  or any other vegetable oil
7 dried hot red chilies,
  broken into ½ inch
  (1 cm) pieces

1½ teaspoons *chana dal*
  (page 260)
1½ teaspoons *urad dal*
  (page 261)
1 teaspoon brown mustard
  seeds
10–15 curry leaves
  (optional)

1 teaspoon salt
¼ teaspoon ground
  asafetida
1¾ cups freshly grated
  coconut (page 265)
2 tablespoons chopped,
  fresh cilantro

❧

Wash the rice in several changes of water, until the water runs clear. Cover well with water and soak for 30 minutes. Drain. Put the rice in a saucepan and cover with 2⅔ cups water. Bring to the boil. Cover tightly, turn the heat to very low and cook gently for 25 minutes.

Meanwhile, heat the oil in a medium-sized saucepan or wok over medium-high heat. When hot, add the chilies, *chana dal*, *urad dal* and mustard seeds. Stir and fry until the chilies darken and the *dals* turn reddish. Now add the curry leaves, if using, salt, *asafetida* and, finally, the coconut.

Stir and fry over high heat for a minute or so, then turn the heat down and cook gently until the coconut is a light reddish-brown and quite crisp. Turn the mixture out onto a large wide dish (such as a *thali*, page 283), spread out and allow to cool.

When the rice is cooked, take it out of the pan and spread it evenly over the coconut mixture. As soon as it is cool enough to handle mix the two together, preferably using your hands or otherwise a spoon. Garnish with the fresh cilantro and serve.

S E R V E S   4

Mrs A. Santha Ramanujam's Idlis
ⓥ SAVORY RICE CAKES

THESE STEAMED CAKES ARE eaten rather as rice might be, with beans and vegetables. Because they are light, they are a very popular breakfast and snack food. Rice and *urad dal* are soaked and ground into a creamy paste. This batter is left to ferment overnight, by which time it increases in volume by about 1½ times. Now all airy and bubbly, it is poured into egg-poacher-type molds and quickly steamed. The *idlis* that come out of the steamer are fat in the middle and tapering at the ends. They may be eaten with Coconut Chutney (page 212) or with a *sambar* such as Split Peas with Shallots (page 202).

Idli steamers may be bought from many Indian grocers. They come in all sizes and basically consist of a central trunk on which several discs may be fitted at intervals. Each disc has several depressions for individual *idlis*. The discs are oiled lightly before batter is poured into them. The entire tree is then put inside a steaming vessel that has boiling water at the bottom. The vessel is covered and the *idlis* are allowed to steam for 15 minutes. If you cannot find these molds, you can improvise. Use a steaming tray (Chinese grocers sell them) that is about 6 inches (15 cm) in diameter. Put the tray inside a colander. Line the tray and sides of the colander with a double layer of wet cheesecloth. Pour a ½ inch (1 cm) thickness of batter into the cheesecloth, cover the colander and then fold the overhanging edges of cheesecloth over the lid. Set the colander over a pan of boiling water in such a way that the water stays below the level of the *idli*. You will end up with a large *idli* which you can cut into squares or diamonds.

---

2 cups long-grain rice, washed in several changes of water

1 cup *urad dal* (page 261), picked over and washed in several changes of water

1 teaspoon salt
About 3 tablespoons refined sesame seed oil or any other vegetable oil

---

Soak the rice and *urad dal* in separate bowls for 2 hours. Water should cover them by about 1 inch (2.5 cm). Drain. Put the *urad dal* into the container of an electric blender. Add ¾ cup water and blend until the mixture is smooth, pale, light and airy, almost like a meringue mixture. This will take 5–8 minutes. Empty into a large bowl. Put the drained rice into the container of the blender. Add 6 tablespoons water and blend until the rice turns into a fine but granular paste. Add to the bowl with the dal. Add the salt and mix gently.

Leave the batter to ferment for 12-15 hours in a warm place with a temperature that hovers around 80°F (27°C). The batter should ferment to 1½ times its original volume.

Prepare your steaming apparatus and bring the water to a rolling boil. Grease the *idli* molds with the oil and fill each with the batter. Remove the batter very carefully from its bowl to preserve its bubbly lightness. Cover the steaming vessel and steam for 15 minutes. Ease each *idli* out with the help of a knife and serve hot with its smoother side up.

MAKES
20-25 CAKES

Mrs A. Santha Ramanujam's Dosas
ⓥ RICE AND SPLIT PEA PANCAKES

THESE WONDERFULLY NUTRITIOUS PANCAKES can be eaten for breakfast, as a light lunch and for dinner. They may be eaten plain with Coconut Chutney (page 212) or else they may be folded over potatoes (see Potatoes with Mustard Seeds and Onions, page 200) to make what is called *masala dosas*.

The batter used here is exactly the same as that for the *idli* in the preceding recipe, only it is allowed to ferment longer. It should double in volume.

Ideally, *dosas* should be eaten as soon as they are made. If you wish to make them ahead of time, keep them covered with a second upturned plate as they are made, then wrap the stack of cooked pancakes in foil and place in a moderate oven 325°F (160°C) for 15 minutes to re-heat. They will not stay crisp but will be very good. Left-over batter may be refrigerated and used the following day.

Get everything ready to make your *dosas* before you start. You will need an 8 inch (20 cm) well-seasoned frying pan – a larger one will be just as good – with a spatula, nearby should be your batter and a ladle that can easily pick up ½ cup, a teaspoon for the oil, a rounded soup spoon for spreading the batter and a plate to put the cooked *dosas* on as they get made.

❧

Batter for Savory Rice Cakes (see preceding **recipe), made up to the point before fermenting** **About 1¼ cups vegetable oil**

Once the batter is made, cover it and leave it to ferment in a warm place for 24–26 hours. The batter should double in volume. Add 1 scant cup water to it and fold it in gently. Cover and leave in a warm place for another 1½ hours.

Put 1½ teaspoons of the oil in the frying pan and set over medium-low heat. When the oil is hot, pick up ½ cup of the batter and drop it in the center of the pan. Put the rounded bottom of the soup spoon very lightly in the center of the batter. Using a slow, gentle and continuously spiral motion, spread the batter outwards with the back of the spoon until you have a pancake 7 inches (18 cm) in diameter. Dribble ½ teaspoon of the oil over the pancake and another ½ teaspoon around its edges. Cover and cook for 1½–2 minutes or until the *dosa* turns reddish-brown. Turn the *dosa* over and cook it, uncovered, for another minute or until the second side develops reddish spots. Make all the *dosas* this way.

MAKES 15–16 PANCAKES

Mrs A. Santha Ramanujam's Bhakala Bhat
Ⓥ RICE WITH YOGURT

YOU COULD CALL THIS a salad. It is generally served at the end of a meal. Light and clean-tasting, it leaves the palate wonderfully refreshed.

2 cups long-grain rice
2–3 tablespoons milk
2 cups plus 2 tablespoons plain yogurt, beaten lightly
½ cup cucumber, seeded and cut into ¼ inch (5 mm) dice
⅓ cup green mango or green apple, cut into ¼ inch (5 mm) dice
½ cup seedless green grapes, halved if large
1 tablespoon *ghee* (page 271) or vegetable oil
½ teaspoon *urad dal* (page 261)
½ teaspoon brown mustard seeds
1 fresh hot green chili, sliced into fine rounds
1 (½ inch) (1 cm) piece fresh ginger root, peeled and very finely chopped
1½ teaspoons salt or to taste
1–2 tablespoons chopped, fresh cilantro

Rice and Split Pea Pancakes (page 205) with Coconut Chutney (page 212) and Split Peas with Shallots (page 202).

Shoba Ramji's Alimucha Oorga
Ⓥ LIME PICKLE

TAMILS LIKE TO END their meals with plain rice, yogurt and pickles. This is one of the many pickles they like to eat.

❧

4 limes, cut into ¾ inch
  (2 cm) pieces
1 teaspoon plus
  4 tablespoons oil
1½ teaspoons brown
  mustard seeds

½ teaspoon fenugreek seeds
15–20 curry leaves
  (optional)
½ cup lime juice

1 teaspoon ground turmeric
2 teaspoons cayenne pepper
½ teaspoon ground
  asafetida
1 tablespoon salt

❧

Put the limes in a small stainless steel pan with water to cover and bring to the boil. Boil vigorously for 1 minute. Discard the water and repeat the process once more. Put the limes in fresh water and boil again, this time for 20–25 minutes. The limes should become tender and discolor. Drain them and put them to one side.

Meanwhile, heat the 1 teaspoon oil in a frying pan over medium-high heat. When hot, put in ½ teaspoon of the mustard seeds and the fenugreek seeds. Stir and fry until the mustard seeds pop, a matter of seconds. Remove from the heat and put into the container of a clean mortar. Pound into a powder. Set aside.

Heat the 4 tablespoons oil in a medium-sized stainless steel pan over medium-high heat. When hot, add the remaining 1 teaspoon mustard seeds. As soon as they start to pop, a matter of seconds, add the curry leaves, if using. Stir once or twice. Remove the pan from the heat. Add the limes, lime juice, turmeric, cayenne pepper, *asafetida*, mustard powder and salt. Mix well.

When cool, put into a very clean glass jar or plastic container. Cover the pickle and leave, unrefrigerated, for at least a week before using. Refrigerate after 2 weeks.

This pickle will keep well for up to 1 year.

M A K E S   2½   C U P S

Mixed Vegetable Curry (page 201) and Deep-fried Okra in Batter (page 199).

Thengay Chutney
Ⓥ COCONUT CHUTNEY

THIS CHUTNEY GOES PARTICULARLY well with Rice and Split Pea Pancakes
(page 205) and Savory Rice Cakes (page 204) but it may be served with all
South Indian meals.

**1½ cups freshly grated
coconut (page 265) (no
substitutes here)**

**1 tablespoon tamarind paste
(page 278)**
2 teaspoons vegetable oil
**1 teaspoon brown mustard
seeds**

**1½ tablespoons *urad dal*
(page 261)**
1–2 dried hot red chilies
**A generous pinch of ground
*asafetida***
½ teaspoon salt

Put the coconut, tamarind paste and ⅔ cup
water into the container of an electric blender.
Blend as finely as possible. Leave in the
blender.

Heat the oil in a small frying pan over
medium-high heat. When hot, put in the
mustard seeds. As soon as the mustard seeds
pop, a matter of seconds, put in the *urad dal*.
Stir and roast until the *dal* just begins to pick
up a little color. Add the chilies. Continue to
roast until the *dal* turns reddish and the chilies

become dark. Add the *asafetida* and remove
from the heat to cool a bit.

Empty the cooled spices into a clean coffee
grinder and grind to a powder. Add this to the
coconut mixture with the salt and blend again,
thinning the chutney out with more water if
needed. It should have the consistency of a
thick batter. It will keep for 48 hours.

SERVES 6

Mrs A. Santha Ramanujam's Mysore Pak
ⓥ CHICK-PEA FLOUR BRITTLE

THESE RICH, BRITTLE SQUARES are generally offered in Tamil Nadu at the start of a meal. You may, of course, serve them with coffee at the very end.

My desserts often consist of individual plates of fruit. I like to put one or two small squares of *Mysore pak* on each plate for added interest and a new taste.

❧

1½ cups *ghee* (page 271), divided into 2 equal portions, plus a little extra for greasing

1 scant cup chick-pea flour, sifted

1¾ cups sugar

❧

Grease an 11 inch (28 cm) *thali* (see page 283) or a similar-sized baking sheet. (A smaller baking sheet will give you a thicker brittle.)

Heat one half-portion of the *ghee* in a large, preferably non-stick, pan over medium heat. When hot, add the sifted chick-pea flour. Stir and fry for about 3 minutes until it is a shade darker and is golden. (The raw taste should go away.) Remove the flour from the pan and set aside. Clean the pan.

Put the remaining *ghee* in a smaller pan and heat over medium-low heat. Keep hot over low heat. At the same time, put 1¼ cups water into the cleaned first pan and set it over a high heat. Bring to the boil. Add the sugar and cook over high heat until the syrup forms a single thread when a little is dropped from a spoon into a cup of cold water. This should take about 4–5 minutes. Stir the fried chick-pea flour and add. Stir continuously for about 6 minutes on high heat, adding small ladlefuls of the hot *ghee* and stirring them in.

Time this so that the last ladleful of *ghee* goes in just as the frothy, lava-like mixture is turning a rich caramel color.

Quickly pour this mixture into the greased *thali* or baking sheet, tilting and tapping the utensil gently so that the mixture is evenly thick all over. Using a wet knife cut into 1 inch (2.5 cm) squares but allow to cool completely in the *thali* or baking sheet before removing.

SERVES 8–10

PUNJAB

THERE IS NOTHING MORE important to a Punjabi man's diet than bread. He usually eats *rotis* (flat, round, wholewheat breads), which he embellishes with beans and vegetables, but when he is in the mood for something richer he opts for the flakier, wholewheat *paratha*, where each layer is separated with a generous layer of *ghee*. Indeed, in the towns and villages of this northwestern state, if a wife has a pot of rice on the stove many a husband walking into the home has been known to take a deep sniff and complain, *"Eh purabiya kithhon aa gaya?"* ("Did some easterner show up?") Rice may do for special occasions or for making rice pudding (*kheer*) but the only food that makes a Punjabi feel that he has eaten a proper meal is his bread.

There has been wheat in the Punjab as long as anyone can remember and the earth has been known to yield grains of wheat that are 7000 years old. There is also evidence of ancient fields where wheat was planted in neat rows. The Punjab, named after the five generous rivers that flowed through the undivided state before it was partitioned to become a part of both India and Pakistan, has always been a rich, fertile plain with wheat for breads, sugar cane for sugar and milk for the much beloved dairy products. It was the site of the thriving Indus Valley civilization in 2000 BC and today the section of the Punjab that has fallen to India's lot is its most prosperous state and its breadbasket.

As about 85 percent of the Punjab is under cultivation and 70 percent of its people work in agriculture, it is best to visit a village in its heartland in order to understand the rhythms of its daily life. Gandiwind is only about an hour and a half away from Amritsar.

It is the end of the monsoon season and a soft mist hangs over the still darkened fields. Electric lights – in the Punjab every village has electricity – begin to glow, one by one, in all the houses. It is only four o'clock but Tarlok Singh and his brothers are already up, tumblers of sweet, milky tea in hand.

The first task of the day is the milking. If you expect to see the hallowed Indian cow here, much prized by the Aryan ancestors of these turbaned Sikh villagers, you will be in for a surprise. Tethered in the walled courtyard of the enclosed family compound are a dozen water buffaloes, dark horns arcing over their heads, eyes in pleasant contemplation of the cud they are constantly chewing.

In a state where richness in foods is unabashedly desired and the dreaded Western "cholesterol" is considered but an invention of the effete, buffalo milk, with its 3 percent higher fat content, is thought to be far superior to that of the cow.

The milking is done by men who squat beside the buffalo and, with their powerful

Previous page: A Sikh priest in the Golden Temple in Amritsar, Punjab.

hands, squeeze the fresh milk rhythmically into a pail. The frothy milk will now have a short or long journey, depending upon what is to happen to it. Most of the milk is emptied into narrow-necked brass pots, tied to motorcycles and bicycles, covered with dampened burlap to protect it from the heat which is already building up and sent off to various markets in the neighboring towns and cities. The remainder is kept for home consumption.

Some of it is just boiled and used for tea or for drinking. A good amount is poured into a round-bottomed earthenware pot, covered with a well-perforated lid and placed in a *bhadoli*. This is a simple but unique contraption. It looks like a huge, deep earthen bowl lined with India's most old fashioned fuel – dried patties made with buffalo (or cow) dung. On top of the gently smoldering fuel goes the pot of milk. Here it sits for many hours, evaporating slowly, thick layers of clotted cream forming at the top. Many Punjabis living away from their villages dream of this thick, rich milk, this *kadiya hoya dudh* which smacks of home, of parents and comfort.

It is the walled family courtyard with the tethered water buffaloes that bustles with all this early morning activity. There is an indoor kitchen but much of the cutting, chopping and cooking seems to be done under the cool shade of the banyan tree which spreads its ample branches over half of the courtyard and certainly over the many outdoor stoves and ovens that work their magic from morning to night. On one ledge sits the *bhadoli*, the rich milk in it getting richer by the minute. Some of this milk will later be set into yogurt. Layers of thick cream will then be removed from the top of the yogurt pot and churned into white butter. A portion of the white butter will be saved to put on breads and vegetables, the rest will be cooked slowly until it turns into *ghee*. All of the buffalo milk, every last ounce of it, will, in some form or other, be used with the greatest of enjoyment. Buttermilk will be drunk at midday, yogurt will be eaten at breakfast, *ghee* will be used in the cooking at lunch, white butter will be put on the breads at night – and surely no member of the household will consider going to bed without a tall glass of hot milk? Does it not make everyone sleep better?

Breakfast is relatively simple but wholesome. First, *rotis* need to be made. A *tava* could be used and often is but today the family has decided on an oven – a special, very effective, Punjabi oven. A large clay vat that sits near the trunk of the banyan tree is lit with wood. This is the *tandoor*, now known throughout the world. When its walls are very hot, a dough is made of wholewheat flour and water. This is divided into balls. Using the palms of their hands, the women of the house flatten these balls into discs and slap them against the hot inside walls of the vat. Here the discs cook for a few minutes, puffing up

slightly as they do so. Then they are pulled out, smeared with white butter and eaten with fresh yogurt and pickles.

By this time farmhands are beginning to arrive. (The Singhs are prosperous farmers who can afford to hire help.) The water buffaloes need to be taken to the pond so that their dark sensitive skins may get a much-needed soaking, and work needs to be done to harvest the rice and cut the fodder for the animals. Oddly enough, in this land of wheat and sugar cane, the water table of the soil has been rising as more and more canals have been built to distribute the waters of the rivers. The soil can now grow rice. And so the farmers plant it. The fields – with the help of many fertilizers and new seeds – are in constant use. Plain rice is being harvested now. By November, basmati, the queen of rices with its aristocratic jade green leaves that stand out from the rest, will have ripened as well. It is always the last rice to ripen. But what else can you expect of the queen?

That will end the rice season. Mustard greens, peas and chick-peas will be next, only to be followed by the all-important wheat which will be ready to harvest by the time of the Baisakhi festival in April. Harvest-time may be hard and busy but it will also be gay with all the males collecting to dance the vigorous *bhangra*.

After the men leave for work in the fields the women start the preparation of lunch. It is a tradition in the Punjab that the women of the house cook not only for their men but for all the farmhands as well. The food is the same. What their husbands, brothers and sons eat, so will the field-workers.

The *loh* is lit up. Rather like a large *tava*, it is made out of cast-iron and tends to be slightly concave. The one here is about 5 feet (1.5 m) long and 4 feet (1.2 m) wide, and is raised off the ground by two walls of bricks about 1 foot (30 cm) high. It too is lit with wood, a mixture of brush and small branches. Three or four women in long shirts (*kameez*) and loose trousers that narrow at the ankles (*salwars*) and with their heads covered with long scarves (*chunnis*) sit on one side. They are going to make *parathas* today. One woman with spectacles makes the ball of dough. She then flattens it out with her hands, puts melted *ghee* on the disc and folds it in thirds twice until she has a square. She dips the square in flour and hands it to a second woman. The second woman rolls it out into a large *paratha* and slaps it on to the *loh*. A third woman turns it over every 30 seconds, brushing it with *ghee* when needed. As soon as it is done, she throws it into a basket and covers it with a cloth. Ten to fifteen *parathas* cook at the same time. It is very much an assembly line at work, only this work is being done at home.

As the *parathas* pile up in the basket, a man who is perhaps too old to work in the fields stands over a huge pot just a few feet away. He stirs the onions in it with a massive metal paddle. When they are lightly browned he puts in some garlic and ginger. He stirs some more. Now in go the turmeric, cayenne pepper, *garam masala*, tomatoes, green chilies and salt and then finally, potatoes and some water. These will all cook slowly over a wood fire. When they are done huge pails will be filled up and taken to the fields together with the baskets of bread. All work will stop as workers are handed two *parathas* each. Some potatoes are put on the top *paratha* which acts as a medieval trencher – plate and bread in one. Sometimes there is some raw onion which is smashed with a fist before it is eaten. For drinking, there is fresh water from the tube wells.

The women will eat the same food, though they may also draw on the many pickles sitting in neat jars. There is the sour lime pickle and what about grandmother's green mango pickle – or how about the cauliflower and carrot pickle left over from the winter?

Meanwhile, the children are all at the village school. The older ones are learning English but the little three-year-olds learn of an idyllic life by rote. They repeat these words, line by line:

There is water in the well
My mummy is a queen
My daddy is a king
I have fresh fruit to eat
My windows are made of silver
My doors are made of gold
I am dancing with joy

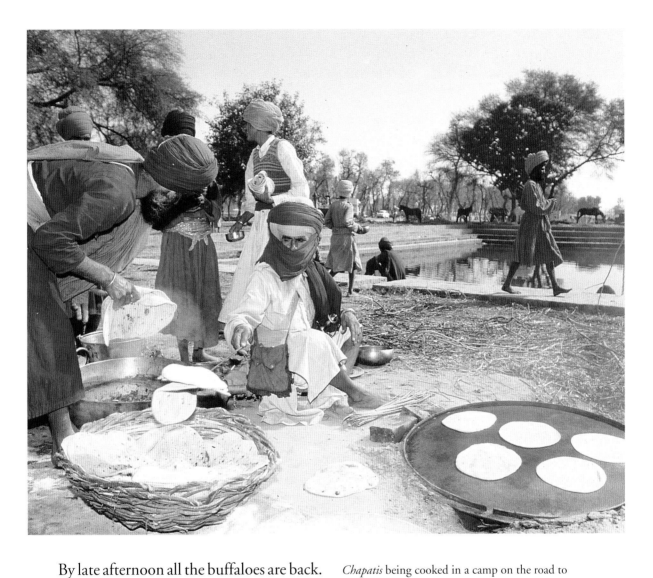

Chapatis being cooked in a camp on the road to Amritsar.

By late afternoon all the buffaloes are back. There is another milking in the evening. Again, the milk must be dealt with immediately. The men may now start drinking the local booze distilled from sugar cane juice or from oranges – which they have with yogurt or some radishes and salt.

Dinner, like lunch, is simple – and vegetarian. With the breads may be served whole beans: small black *ma di dal* (whole black *urad*) and kidney beans cooked to-gether slowly in the hot ashes of the *tandoor*. When they are tender onions, ginger and garlic are sautéed, some tomatoes are thrown in and this mixture is added to the pot of beans. Nothing more is needed for the dish other than a dollop of white butter! There may also be whole bitter melons stuffed with a paste of ground onions, dried pomegranate seeds, turmeric, cayenne pepper and salt and then sautéed gently until brown and slightly crisp on the outside. Or there may be *bharta*, for which whole eggplants are roasted in ashes and their pulp sautéed with onions, ginger, hot green chilies and tomatoes. Of course, there will be the glass of milk before retiring.

The motorcyclists who left Gandiwind with the narrow-necked brass pots may well roar into Amritsar, bearded and turbaned easy riders bearing milk. They may deliver their milk to Munim di Hatti. This café specializes in *lassi* (a yogurt drink) and in *paneer* (fresh cheese). One side window serves nothing but *lassis* to a waiting line of customers. Pramod Singh, the *lassi*-maker, uses a kidney-shaped disc to remove some thick yogurt from a deep metal dish. He puts it into a bowl. He adds more such scoops until the bowl is full. He empties all this into an electric mixer. Next he adds some sugar, cold milk and ice, mixes it all and then lets it pour out from a spigot into a tall glass. It is consumed just about as fast as it is made.

It is in the back of the café, in an open courtyard, that the yogurt and *paneer* are made. For the yogurt, the milk is first boiled in a huge pot then allowed to cool slightly in deep dishes. Diluted yogurt is added and the yogurt is left to set for 5 hours. Making the *paneer* is just as simple. Jugs of whey are added to the boiled milk to make it curdle. The curds are poured into a basket lined with cheesecloth. Once

the whey has drained away, the cheesecloth is lifted up, tied into a loose bundle and put under a weight for 5 minutes. The weight is removed and the very fresh *paneer*, still warm to the touch and now in the shape of a wheel, is ready to be cut to order and sold.

Since *paneer* is so easy to make, many people buy buffalo milk from the market and prepare the cheese at home. This is what Promila Kapoor does. When her husband returns from his work at the flour mill he owns, he likes to relax with a drink. To accompany it she sometimes buys crispy, flaky *mutthries* (savory crackers), all made with pure *ghee*, from the little lanes of the old city and sometimes she makes little snacks with *paneer*. For the second, she quickly boils up some milk in a pot, curdles it with lime juice and empties the contents of the pot into a strainer. The whey drains away. She pats the curds into the shape of a cake, lets the cake sit in the strainer for 5 minutes and then cuts this fresh cheese into slices. Next, she puts some chopped onions, tomatoes, ginger, green chilies and fresh cilantro into a bowl. To this she adds salt, pepper, cayenne pepper, lime juice and *chaat masala*, a spice mixture that contains *amchoor* (sour mango powder). She mixes all these ingredients and puts spoonfuls of the mixture on the cheese pieces. The snack is as refreshing as it is quick to prepare.

Paneer is used to make dozens of main dishes as well. To see them turned out in rapid succession, it is best to visit a *dhaba*.

A *dhaba* is a cheap, fast food joint and there is no better one to go to than one on the Grand Trunk Road near the small town of Kartarpur. The road has many *dhabas*. But there are *dhabas* and *dhabas*. Many develop reputations. Truck drivers whoosh to a stop at this one and jump out to have a quick, nourishing bite. The food here is good. Some of them may be driving all the way to Calcutta and who knows where the next good food stop might be!

There are some rough tables with benches or cots to sit on. A truck driver walks in. His order is taken: one *paneer bhurji* with three *rotis*. The "kitchen," all outdoors under a rough canopy, consists of an aisle between two simple, earthen counters. The man on the right counter cooks the breads while the man on the left one does the main dishes. "Three *rotis*," the man on the right is told. "One *paneer bhurji*," is barked at the man on the left. Both work fast. While breads get slapped on a *loh* on the right, a wok is heated on the left. Into the wok goes a little oil and some onions. They are quickly and noisily stirred about. In go some green chilies, ginger, tomato. They are stirred about. Now some *paneer*, made here earlier, is crumbled in. The scrambled-egg-like *paneer* dish is ready. For an order of *paneer* with tomatoes, lots more tomatoes are put in and the cheese is cut into larger cubes. A dollop of white butter is added as a bonus. If *paneer* with spinach is required, puréed spinach is added to the tomato mixture to be followed by the cubes of *paneer* and the dollop of butter. *Paneer* can even be made into fritters with a chick-pea flour batter.

Dhabas specialize in different foods. Some have *chana-bhatura* (spicy chick-peas served with deep-fried, puffed, slightly leavened breads). Others specialize in *tandoori* chicken or all manner of kebabs known as *tikkas*, or in batter-fried, crisp on the outside and meltingly tender inside Amritsari river fish.

Many Indian restaurants in the West serve Punjabi-style foods and as there is a preponderance of meat at these eating-places, it may be hard to believe that more than half the people of the Punjab are vegetarians, a percentage that can compare only with the state of Gujarat where more than 60 percent are vegetarians. Much of rural Punjab eats no meat at all. The cities, however, are a different story. An excellent creation made with lamb chops might feature in one house while another might serve a royal chicken, rich with cream and nuts. Nevertheless, some of the Punjab's most popular non-vegetarian dishes seem to be found in the *dhabas* that specialize in them.

Surjit's Chicken House is on Lawrence Road in Amritsar, a much sought after *dhaba* on a popular thoroughfare. An expensive car pulls up. A man alights and walks up to the front counter over which dozens of marinated chickens hang like red bunting. He orders two of them. At 100 Indian Rupees each, they are not such a bargain. He waits as Amarjit, the owner's young son, splits each chicken into four parts, skewers them and thrusts them into the single large *tandoor* in front of him. Every now and then he pulls the skewers up and bastes the chickens with *ghee*.

Meanwhile, the ladies in the expensive car are fanning themselves and looking impatient. The man returns to the car and makes reassuring noises. After about 20 minutes the chicken is done. It is pulled out of the *tandoor* and expertly chopped into smaller pieces which are put into a shallow bowl. A great deal of *chaat masala* is sprinkled over the top and the chicken tossed around with much acrobatic flair. It is now put into a piece of old newspaper and tied up with string. The man now has parcel A. Parcel B, which comes a bit later, consists of sliced radishes, some pieces of lime and a cilantro-spinach-green-chili chutney that is offered in tiny polythene bags. The man makes for the car, clutching his goodies. He and his male friends will eat the juicy, luscious chicken with cold glasses of beer. The women will have soft drinks.

While the origins of the freestanding, vat-like *tandoors* remain unclear, the fact that they have been around in the Punjab for centuries is not. They may even have developed here. If examined closely, they are seen to be primitive, yet most effective, ovens. Some are made right by the bus station in Amritsar.

A woman takes some good clay and kneads it with water until it is pliable. She adds some shredded coir rope to the clay "dough" and kneads some more. Then, free hand, she begins to form the sides of a vat. There is no bottom as the *tandoor* must stand on a clear, non-flammable surface – usually the earth. She only raises the sides to about 6–8 inches (15–20 cm) as they are wet and would collapse if she went higher. At this stage she also puts in an opening through which ashes can be cleared. This much of the *tandoor* must dry in the hot sun for at least half a day before she can proceed. She then builds up the vat bit by bit, doing its neck and top opening last. *Tandoors* are made in all sizes, from very small ones for single families to very large ones for restaurants. Once sold, the buyer needs to do more work on them. A paste of mustard oil, brown sugar, yogurt and ground spinach is rubbed generously on the inside to harden it up. Then, just before breads are cooked, salted water is sprinkled on the inside walls to make sure the flat breads adhere to them and do not fall into the fire below.

If *tandoori* foods are associated with the Punjab, so are corn breads and mustard greens. Corn probably came to India with the Portuguese. Nowhere did it find more welcoming a home than in the Punjab. The Punjabis honored it by using it for bread. They learned to make flat breads (*makki di roti*) by hand – a neat trick as the dough cracks easily. They also discovered that, as wine goes with cheese and champagne

A farmer in a mustard field in the Punjab.

with caviar, they had, growing in their own backyards, delicious mustard greens (*sarson da saag*) that would help make an equally immortal pairing. They learned to add a few green chilies to the greens and cook them very slowly, until even the stems were buttery-soft. They knew that they should then beat the greens into a thick purée and thicken it slightly with cornmeal flour, finally adding to it a sautéed mixture of onions, garlic, tomatoes and lots of ginger. And, of course, they knew that before a bowl of these mustard greens was put on the table a big piece of white butter just had to be floated over the top of them.

Nobody goes hungry in the Punjab. If nothing else, there is always free food at the Sikh *gurdwaras* (temples). On festival days it is considered an honor to eat there. At the Golden Temple in Amritsar the mass feedings seem almost miraculous. The many doors of the dining hall open in unison and people rush in, sitting down instantly in neat rows that face each other. When 3000 have been seated the doors close. The rest must wait for the next seating. Young boys, all volunteers, now put metal plates before each diner. More volunteers come in with baskets of *rotis*. Two are dropped on each plate. Next comes the beans, the *ma di dal*, which is ladled out from buckets. There are stewed chick-peas and some semolina *halva*. The volunteers keep moving. The turbans of the diners – reds, yellows, pinks and purples – nod and wave. There are chants and cries of *"Bolay so nihal, Sat Sri Akal"* ("Whoever takes the name of God will be in ecstasy"). Old toothless men break their bread up into small pieces which they mix with the beans, hoping to soften them. They must eat fast. A sitting lasts but half an hour. After the half-hour, doors open and everyone leaves. The doors close and the entire hall is swept from one end to the other by a row of women. Then the doors open again and the next batch of 3000 diners comes in. This goes on all day. Every last person who desires it is fed. Such is the tradition of the Punjab.

224

Promila Kapoor's Paneer Chat
Ⓥ SPICY FRESH CHEESE SNACK

THIS ABSOLUTELY DELIGHTFUL DISH may be served as a snack, as an accompaniment for drinks or as a first course at a more formal meal. The cheese (*paneer*) is very like the Italian mozzarella.

❧

FOR THE CHEESE:
7½ cups whole milk
About 3–4 tablespoons
  lemon juice

YOU ALSO NEED:
1 (1 inch) (2.5 cm) piece
  fresh ginger root, peeled
  and minced

4 tablespoons finely
  chopped onion
4 tablespoons finely
  chopped tomato
1–2 fresh hot green chilies,
  finely chopped
2 tablespoons finely
  chopped, fresh cilantro or
  mint or a mixture of the
  two

1 teaspoon salt
Freshly ground black
  pepper
½–1 teaspoon *chaat masala*
  (page 263)
2–3 tablespoons lemon
  juice

❧

Make the cheese: bring the milk to the boil in a heavy saucepan. As soon as it begins to froth, add 3 tablespoons of the lemon juice, stir it in and turn off the heat. The curds should separate from the whey – if they don't do so completely, bring the milk to the boil again and add another tablespoon or so of lemon juice. Stir and turn the heat off.

Line a strainer with a large, doubled-up piece of cheesecloth. Set the strainer over a large bowl. Pour the contents of the saucepan into the strainer. Let the whey drain away. Lift up the 4 corners of the cheesecloth. Using one of the corners tie up the cheese in the cheesecloth into a bundle. Put this bundle on a board set in the sink. Put a plate on the bundle.

Now put a weight – such as a medium-sized pan filled with water – on top of the plate. Remove the weight after 3–4 minutes. Untie the bundle. The cheese is ready. It can be refrigerated if necessary.

Combine in a bowl the ginger, onion, tomato, chilies, cilantro or mint, salt and black pepper, *chaat masala* and lemon juice. Toss. Taste for the balance of the seasonings.

Cut the cheese into ⅛ inch (3 mm) thick slices. Arrange the slices in a single layer on a serving dish or on several individual plates. Put a generous dollop of the onion-tomato mixture on top of each piece and serve immediately.

SERVES 4

Hoshiyar Singh at the Mohan International Hotel: Mutton Tikka
LAMB KEBAB

TINY KEBAB STALLS ARE scattered all over the city of Amritsar. People either eat the kebabs on the street or take them home for dinner or to accompany drinks. They can be rolled up in any Punjabi bread or eaten with a salad and rice.

¾ cup whole milk yogurt

6 tablespoons mustard oil or any other vegetable oil

1 (2 inch) (5 cm) piece fresh ginger root, peeled and grated to a pulp

2 garlic cloves, peeled and mashed to a pulp

1 tablespoon Punjabi *garam masala* (page 270)

1 teaspoon cayenne pepper

2 teaspoons Kashmiri chili powder (page 264)

2 teaspoons salt

2¼ lb (1 kg) lamb from the leg, cut into ¾ inch (2 cm) cubes

3 tablespoons *ghee* (page 271), melted unsalted butter or vegetable oil

1 teaspoon *chaat masala* (page 263)

3–4 tablespoons chopped, fresh cilantro

½ medium-sized red onion, cut into very fine rings

Lime wedges

Place a strainer in the sink and line it with cheesecloth. Empty the yogurt into it and let it sit for 10 minutes. Put the drained yogurt into a bowl and add the mustard oil, ginger, garlic, *garam masala*, cayenne pepper, chili powder and salt. Beat well with a whisk or eggbeater. Put in the cubes of meat and mix well. Cover and marinate overnight in the refrigerator.

Pre-heat the broiler. Lift the lamb pieces out of the marinade and divide equally between 4–6 skewers. Brush with the *ghee* or the butter or

oil and place under the broiler about 4–5 inches (10–13 cm) from the source of heat. Broil for 3–4 minutes on one side until lightly browned. Turn the pieces over and broil for another 3–4 minutes until the lamb is browned and just cooked through to your liking. Remove from the skewers and spread out on a serving plate. Sprinkle the *chaat masala*, fresh cilantro and onion rings over the top and serve with the lime wedges.

S E R V E S   6

Spicy Fresh Cheese Snack (page 225) and Mint and White Radish Chutney (page 251).

Kheema Cholay
GROUND LAMB WITH CHICK-PEAS

FOR A FAMILY DINNER or gathering of friends, I can imagine nothing better than this dish with a plate of Puffed Leavened Breads (page 249) or Flaky Breads (page 245), a yogurt relish, sliced raw onions and some pickles!

FOR THE CHICK-PEAS:
¾ cup dried chick-peas
1 bay leaf
¼ teaspoon ground
 asafetida
2 cloves
1 (½ inch) (1 cm)
 cinnamon stick
1 teaspoon salt
2 tablespoons vegetable oil
1 tablespoon peeled and
 finely grated fresh ginger
 root

1 tablespoon finely chopped
 garlic
½–1 teaspoon cayenne
 pepper

FOR THE GROUND MEAT:
4 tablespoons *ghee* (page
 271) or vegetable oil
1¾ lb (800 g) ground lamb
1 large onion, finely
 chopped
1 tablespoon peeled and
 finely grated fresh ginger
 root

1 tablespoon finely chopped
 garlic
1 tablespoon ground
 coriander
4 very finely chopped plum
 tomatoes
2–4 fresh hot green chilies,
 finely chopped
1½–2 teaspoons salt
2 teaspoons ground
 amchoor (page 259)
2–3 tablespoons coarsely
 chopped, fresh cilantro

Prepare the chick-peas: soak the chick-peas in water overnight. The water should cover them by 5 inches (13 cm). Drain. Put 5 cups water into a saucepan. Add the chick-peas, bay leaf, *asafetida*, cloves, cinnamon and 1 teaspoon salt. Bring to the boil. Cover, turn the heat to low and simmer gently for 2–3 hours or until the chick-peas are very tender. Drain, saving the liquid, and set aside.

Heat the oil for the chick-peas in a large wok or frying pan over medium-high heat. When hot, add the 1 tablespoon ginger and 1 table-

spoon garlic. Stir-fry for a minute. Add the drained chick-peas. Stir and cook for 2 minutes. Add ½ cup of the drained chick-pea liquid (or a mixture of water and chick-pea liquid) and the cayenne pepper and bring to the boil. Turn the heat to low and simmer gently for 15–20 minutes or until all the liquid is absorbed. Check for salt. If you add more, stir and cook for another 2 minutes.

Cook the lamb: heat the *ghee* or oil in a separate wok or large frying pan over medium-high heat. When hot, add the ground lamb.

Stir and fry for 5–8 minutes or until the lamb turns brown and is sealed. Add the onion, ginger and garlic. Stir and fry for 2–3 minutes. Add 2¼ cups of the chick-pea liquid (or water or a mixture of the two) and the coriander, tomatoes, chilies and salt. Bring to the boil. Cover, turn the heat to low and simmer gently for about 45 minutes. Most, but not all, of the liquid should be absorbed by the meat. If it is not, turn the heat up and dry it off. Add the *amchoor* and stir.

Spoon the chick-peas into a shallow serving dish. Layer the cooked meat on top of the chick-peas. Garnish with the fresh cilantro.

S E R V E S   6 – 8

Mrs Chadda's Chaamp Masala
LAMB CHOPS MASALA

SERVE THIS WITH ANY Punjabi bread and Mustard Greens (page 236).
Note: In the Punjab tomatoes are grated to make a purée.

❧

1 (3 inch) (7.5 cm) piece fresh ginger root, peeled and coarsely chopped
3 tablespoons peeled and coarsely chopped garlic
6–8 lamb chops (1¾ lb/800 g) from the ribs, each about ¾ inch (2 cm) thick; remove all extra fat

1 cup grated or finely chopped tomatoes
2 medium-sized onions, very finely chopped
1 tablespoon cayenne
1¾ cups plain whole milk yogurt, beaten
1½ teaspoons salt or to taste

1 teaspoon ground, roasted cumin seeds (page 269)
1–2 teaspoons Punjabi *garam masala* (page 270)
3 tablespoons lemon juice
2–3 tablespoons chopped, fresh cilantro

❧

Put the ginger and garlic into the container of an electric blender with 2–3 tablespoons water and blend to a paste.

Put the chops, tomatoes, onions, cayenne pepper, yogurt, salt and the ginger–garlic paste into a large wok or large, heavy-bottomed saucepan. Stir and bring to the boil. Turn the heat to low, cover and simmer for 50 minutes or until the chops are almost cooked. Add the ground, roasted cumin seeds and simmer for 10–15 minutes or until the meat is tender and the sauce is thick. Add the *garam masala* and lemon juice. Stir. Sprinkle the fresh cilantro over the top and serve.

S E R V E S   3 – 4

Hoshiyar Singh at the Mohan International Hotel: Murgh Tikka
CHICKEN KEBABS

THIS DISH IS WELL known and well liked in the West. It may be served with drinks, as a first course or as a main dish with a salad and flavored rice.

~

2¼ cups plain whole milk yogurt
¾ cup whipping cream
4 teaspoons salt
1 teaspoon cayenne pepper
2½ teaspoons Kashmiri chili powder (page 264)
1 (1 inch) (2.5 cm) piece fresh ginger root, peeled and grated to a pulp
2 garlic cloves, crushed to a pulp

1 teaspoon cardamom seeds
1 teaspoon cumin seeds
1 teaspoon black peppercorns
¼ nutmeg
1 (2 inch) (5 cm) cinnamon stick
7–8 cloves
2¼ lb (1 kg) boned, skinned chicken, cut into 1 inch (2.5 cm) cubes

2 tablespoons white vinegar
2–3 tablespoons *ghee*, (page 271), melted unsalted butter or vegetable oil

FOR THE FINAL FLAVORING:
1 teaspoon *chaat masala* (page 263)
Lime or lemon wedges

~

Place a strainer in the sink and line it with cheesecloth. Empty the yogurt into it and let it sit for 10–15 minutes. Put the drained yogurt into a large bowl. Add the cream, 2 teaspoons of the salt, cayenne pepper, chili powder, ginger and garlic. Mix. This is the marinade.

Put the cardamom, cumin, peppercorns, nutmeg, cinnamon and cloves into the container of a clean coffee grinder and grind to a fine powder. Add to the marinade. Beat well with a whisk or eggbeater.

Rub the chicken pieces with a solution of the remaining 2 teaspoons salt and the vinegar. Let them sit for 5 minutes. Pat them dry with paper towels. Drop the chicken pieces into the marinade. Marinate for 2 hours or even overnight.

Pre-heat the broiler. Lift the chicken pieces out of the marinade and divide them equally between 4 skewers. Brush with the *ghee* or the butter or oil. Broil about 4–5 inches (10–13 cm) from the source of heat for 3–4 minutes on one side until lightly browned. Turn over and broil for another 3–4 minutes or until the chicken is browned and cooked through. Remove from the skewers and place on a serving plate. Sprinkle the *chaat masala* over the top and serve with the lime or lemon wedges.

SERVES 4–6

Hoshiyar Singh at the Mohan International Hotel: Murgh Patiala
CHICKEN PATIALA

MOST RICH DISHES ARE given royal names. Whether they have any real connection to royalty is often questionable. Such is the case with this dish. Patiala was once an important princely state in the Punjab. Whatever its origins, *murgh Patiala* is quite worthy of being served at a grand dinner with a pilaf and a selection of vegetables. It is fairly mild and gentle.

Skinned melon seeds are sold by Indian grocers. If you cannot get them, use more poppy seeds or chopped raw cashews.

❧

- 6 tablespoons white poppy seeds
- 7 tablespoons skinned melon seeds, poppy seeds or raw cashew nuts
- 4 tablespoons *ghee* (page 271) or vegetable oil
- 1 medium-large onion, peeled and finely chopped
- 2 medium-sized tomatoes, finely chopped
- ⅔ cup plain whole milk yogurt
- 1 (2¼ lb) (1 kg) chicken, cut into about 8 serving pieces
- 1 tablespoon Punjabi *garam masala* (page 270)
- 1 teaspoon ground white pepper
- ¼ teaspoon cayenne pepper
- 1 teaspoon Kashmiri chili powder (page 264)
- 1½ teaspoons salt
- ½ cup whipping cream
- 2 tablespoons golden raisins
- 2 tablespoons blanched, slivered almonds

❧

Put the poppy seeds, melon seeds or cashews into a clean coffee grinder and grind as finely as possible. Put in a bowl and add 5–6 tablespoons water to make a paste. Set aside.

Heat the *ghee* or oil in a heavy, wide saucepan over medium-high heat. When hot, put in the onion and brown lightly. Add the tomatoes and continue to brown until you can see the oil separating from the sauce. Add the seed or nut paste and continue to stir and fry for 2–3 minutes. Put in the yogurt a tablespoon at a time, stirring and frying each time until it is incorporated in the sauce. Add the chicken pieces, the *garam masala*, white pepper, cayenne pepper, chili powder, salt and 1 cup water. Stir and bring to a simmer. Cover, turn the heat to low and cook until the chicken is tender, about 20 minutes. Add the cream, golden raisins and almonds. Mix and bring to a simmer. Cook very gently without covering for another 5 minutes.

SERVES 3–4

ENTRÉE

Amritsari Macchi

AMRITSARI FISH

THIS IS SOLD ALL over Amritsar: fish, either filleted or in steaks, that has been marinated, rubbed with a spicy chick-pea flour paste and then deep-fried. It is crunchy on the outside and very sweet and tender inside. Local river fish such as *rahu*, a kind of carp, or *singhara*, a slimmer, long fish, are generally used but you may substitute fish like salmon or cod, which is superb cooked by this method. Serve it with Mint and White Radish Chutney (page 251).

∾

2¼ lb (1 kg) fish steaks, cut into ¾ inch (2 cm) thick slices; use any fleshy, round fish such as salmon or a smallish cod
1 tablespoon plus 2 teaspoons salt

3 tablespoons cider vinegar
1⅓ cups chick-pea flour
1½ tablespoons peeled and very finely grated fresh ginger root
1½ tablespoons crushed garlic
1 teaspoon cayenne pepper

½ teaspoon ground turmeric
½ teaspoon freshly ground black pepper
1½ tablespoons *ajwain* seeds (page 259)
Oil for deep-frying
Lime wedges

∾

Wash and clean the fish steaks and pat them dry on paper towels. In a shallow ceramic bowl mix the 1 tablespoon salt and the vinegar. Add the fish steaks in a single layer, turning them so that they are coated with this marinade. Marinate for 30 minutes. Remove the fish steaks from the marinade and place on paper towels to get rid of any excess marinade.

Put the chick-pea flour into a bowl. Slowly add 1¼ cups water to make a smooth paste of coating consistency. Add the ginger, garlic, cayenne pepper, turmeric, *ajwain* seeds, black pepper and 2 teaspoons salt to the paste and mix them in. Rub the fish with this mixture and place in a flat dish in a single layer to marinate for 30 minutes.

Heat the oil in a wok or deep frying pan over high heat. When hot, put in as many pieces of fish as will fit in a single layer. Fry for a minute and turn the heat to medium-high. Cook, turning now and then, until the fish is golden-brown and cooked through. Remove with a slotted spoon and drain on paper towels. Do all the fish this way. Serve with the lime wedges.

SERVES 4 – 6

Chicken Patiala (page 231) with Puffed Leavened Breads (page 249).

Jatinder Kaur's Sarson Da Saag
ⓥ MUSTARD GREENS

IF YOU CAN IMAGINE a buttery, meltingly soft, mustard-greens-flavored polenta, this is it. It is Punjab's very own winter specialty, made nowhere else in India. Something of a cross between a dish of greens and polenta, it is always eaten with Flat Corn Breads (page 250) lathered generously with homemade white butter. If a Punjabi farmer comes in for lunch after a hard morning's work in the cold fields to find that his wife has prepared a big warming bowl of these greens, butter glistening at the top, a stack of flat corn breads and a tall glass of *lassi* (yogurt drink), he tends to return to the fields a very happy man. For most Punjabis, this meal is as much yearned for as roast beef and Yorkshire pudding are in England.

The greens must cook slowly and for a long time. The fairly tough stems of the leaves need to turn very soft. If your greens are still a bit watery when you finish cooking them, you can increase the cornmeal flour by 1–2 tablespoons. The coarse purée of greens should be fairly thick, but still soft and flowing.

It is best to use the cornmeal flour sold by Indian grocers. It has just the right texture for this dish and the breads.

In the Punjab a special wooden tool is used to mash the greens in the pan in which they are cooked. Called a *saag ghotna* (greens masher!), it looks somewhat like a wooden potato masher, with a long straight handle attached to a chunk of wood with a rounded base. A whisk, not an electric blender, is the best substitute.

---

8 cups very finely chopped
  spinach
8 cups very finely chopped
  mustard greens
5 tablespoons coarsely
  chopped garlic
4–6 fresh hot green chilies

1½–2 teaspoons salt
About 5–6 tablespoons
  cornmeal flour (page 268)
3 tablespoons *ghee* (page
  271) or vegetable oil
1 medium-large onion,
  finely chopped

1 (2 inch) (5 cm) piece fresh
  ginger root, peeled and cut
  into thin, long slivers
2 medium-sized tomatoes,
  finely chopped
A generous dollop of
  unsalted butter

Combine the spinach, mustard greens, garlic, chilies, salt and 3⅓ cups water in a large, heavy pan. Set over high heat and bring to the boil. Cover, turn the heat to low and simmer gently for 1¾ hours or until even the stems of the mustard green leaves have turned buttery soft. With the heat still on, add 5 tablespoons of the cornmeal flour, beating constantly with a whisk or a traditional greens masher as you do so. Using the same whisk or masher, mash the greens until they are fairly smooth (a little coarseness is desirable). The greens will thicken with the addition of the cornmeal flour. If they remain somewhat watery, add another

tablespoon or so. Leave on very low heat.

Heat the *ghee* or oil in a separate pan or wok over medium-high heat. When hot, put in the onion. Stir and fry until it turns golden-brown. Add the ginger. Keep stirring and frying until the onion is medium-brown. Put in the tomatoes. Stir and fry until the tomatoes have softened and browned a little. Now pour this mixture over the greens and stir it in.

Empty the greens into a serving dish, top with a dollop of butter and serve.

SERVES 6

Mrs Kapoor's Baigan Bharta
EGGPLANT PÂTÉ

EGGPLANT *bhartas* ARE much loved all over the Punjab. It is eaten with Punjabi breads, pickles and tall glasses of cool *lassi* (a yogurt drink) but you may serve it with any Indian meal.

❧

3½ lb (1.5 kg) eggplants
3 tablespoons vegetable oil
1 teaspoon cumin seeds
1 large onion, finely chopped

1 tablespoon peeled and very finely grated fresh ginger root
1 tablespoon very finely chopped garlic
4 peeled plum tomatoes, finely chopped

3–5 fresh hot green chilies, finely chopped
1 teaspoon cayenne pepper
2 teaspoons salt
2 cups fresh cilantro, finely chopped

❧

Prick a few holes in the eggplants. Stand one directly on top of a medium-low gas flame. Hold it with a pair of tongs until the bottom has charred. Lie it down on the flame and move it back and forth until one section is completely charred. Keep turning the eggplant until it is charred on the outside and soft on the inside. Do all the eggplants this way. Hold one eggplant at a time under running water and peel off the charred skin. Collect all the pulp in a bowl and mash it lightly.

If you wish to use the oven to do this roasting, you may, though the *bharta* will not have its traditional smoky taste. Pre-heat the oven to 475°F (240°C). Cut the eggplants in half lengthwise and place them, cut-side-down, on a lightly oiled baking sheet. Bake in the oven for 10–15 minutes or until the eggplants have collapsed slightly. Remove from the oven and spoon out the flesh. Discard the skin. Roughly

chop up the flesh and set it aside.

Heat the oil in a wok or wide, preferably non-stick pan over medium-high heat. When hot, put in the cumin seeds. Let them sizzle for 20 seconds. Put in the onion. Stir and fry until the onion is translucent. Add the ginger and garlic. Stir and fry for another 2–3 minutes. Add the tomatoes, chilies, cayenne pepper and salt. Stir and fry for 2 minutes. Turn the heat to medium-low and continue to cook for another 7–8 minutes or until the tomatoes are soft. Put in the eggplant pulp. Stir and fry for 5 minutes or until the vegetables are melded together.

Add the fresh cilantro, stir and remove from the heat.

S E R V E S   4 – 6

Mustard Greens (page 236) with Flat Corn Breads (page 250).

Promila Kapoor's Gobi Aloo

Ⓥ CAULIFLOWER WITH POTATOES, BANQUET STYLE

CAULIFLOWER AND POTATOES ARE cooked together throughout the Punjab and there are many recipes for this delightful combination. Here is one that is used for parties and banquets. Serve it with Flaky Breads (page 245) and a yogurt relish or as a part of any North Indian meal.

❧

1 large cauliflower
2–3 medium-sized potatoes, peeled
8 tablespoons vegetable oil
3 medium-sized onions, finely chopped

1 (2 inch) (5 cm) piece fresh ginger root, peeled and cut into very fine slices and then into very fine slivers
2 medium-sized tomatoes, grated or very finely chopped
¼–½ teaspoon cayenne pepper

½ teaspoon ground turmeric
1½ teaspoons ground coriander
1–1½ teaspoons salt
½ teaspoon Punjabi *garam masala* (page 270)
½ teaspoon ground roasted cumin seeds (page 269)

❧

Break the cauliflower into medium-sized florets. Cut the potatoes lengthwise into halves and then cut each half lengthwise into roughly 3 pieces to get chunky chips.

Heat the oil in a wok or frying pan over medium heat. When hot, add the potatoes and fry them until they are medium-brown and just barely cooked through. Remove with a slotted spoon and drain on paper towels. Put the florets into the same oil and fry until golden and just barely cooked through. Remove with a slotted spoon and drain on paper towels. Remove all but 3 tablespoons of the oil from the wok or frying pan. Put in the onions and stir until they are light brown. Put in the ginger

and continue to stir and fry until the onions are medium-brown. Add the tomatoes and keep frying until they turn soft and darker and the oil seems to separate from the sauce. Add the cayenne pepper, turmeric, coriander and salt. Stir and fry for a minute. Put in the potatoes and florets. Stir to mix gently. Sprinkle a tablespoon of water over the vegetables. Cover. Turn the heat to low and cook gently for 3–5 minutes. Uncover. Add the *garam masala* and ground roasted cumin seeds. Stir gently to mix and turn off heat.

SERVES 4–6

Karele Pyazaa
STUFFED BITTER MELONS

I HAVE NEVER NEEDED any special incentive to eat bitter melons (*karela*), having loved them since I was a little girl. They are, indeed, bitter, as their name suggests, but that is part of their attraction. Of course, everyone in India (and much of East Asia as well) believes that they cleanse the blood and help fight off cancers but that is part of folklore and I can only pass this information on, not substantiate it. The melons are, perhaps, an acquired taste, like olives, but once you fall under their spell there is no getting away. The melons are sold by Indian and Asian grocers. Serve these melons with any Indian meal.

2¼ lb (1 kg) small bitter melons *(karela)*, page 261
6 tablespoons salt
3–4 medium-sized onions, peeled and coarsely chopped

2 teaspoons *amchoor* (page 259)
1 teaspoon freshly ground black pepper

1 teaspoon cayenne pepper
½ teaspoon ground turmeric
1 cup vegetable oil

Scrape the skins of the bitter melons so thoroughly with a sharp knife that all the ridges are removed. Pick up a melon and, using a small, sharp knife, make a slit lengthwise down one side from top to bottom, being careful not to cut it in half. Do all the melons this way. Rub salt inside the slits and all over the skin. Leave in a colander for 30 minutes. Rinse thoroughly, squeeze out excess moisture and pat dry on paper towels.

Put the onions into the container of an electric blender and blend to a smooth paste. Add the *amchoor*, black pepper, cayenne pepper and turmeric to the onion paste. Blend for a second to mix. With a teaspoon, stuff the melons with this mixture and tie a string around each one in 2 or 3 places, depending on size, to hold in the stuffing.

Heat the oil in a wok or large frying pan over medium-low heat. When very hot, lay down the melons, stuffed-sides-up, and fry one side for 7–9 minutes or until browned. Turn the melons over and fry gently until the opposite side, too, is brown. This will take another 7–10 minutes. With a slotted spoon, lift the melons out of the oil and drain them on paper towels. Cut off the strings before serving.

SERVES 4 – 6

Ma Di Dal/Dal Makkhani
Ⓥ CREAMY SPICED BEANS

MORE THAN HALF OF the Punjab's population is vegetarian and for them, after wheat, nothing is more important than beans. This dish in a simpler form (without the cream, garlic and tomatoes as well as the final *tarka* of onions) is served with plain breads (*rotis*) at Sikh *gurdwaras* (temples) to any one who asks for food. In this simple form, it also bubbles away for hours in all *dhabas* (fast food joints), in monstrous, narrow-necked pots, stirred every now and then with huge paddles. It can be enriched as orders come in. This enrichment can consist of a simple *tarka* of onions and cayenne pepper in *ghee*, in which case it is called *ma di dal* with *tarka* or it can have cream added to it as well as the *tarka* or a generous dollop of butter, in which case it is called *dal makkhani* (buttery beans).

White butter is butter that is churned at home or on farms and is without additives or coloring. Good, unsalted butter is the best substitute. Serve with a Punjabi bread, any meat in this chapter, a Punjabi vegetable, a yogurt relish and a pickle or chutney.

1 cup whole black *urad* beans (page 261)

⅓ cup red kidney beans (page 260)

4 teaspoons peeled and very finely grated fresh ginger root

4 teaspoons crushed garlic

2 medium-sized tomatoes, grated or finely chopped

2 teaspoons cayenne pepper or to taste

2–3 teaspoons salt or to taste

6 tablespoons freshly made white butter, if available, or any unsalted butter

½ cup whipping cream

2 teaspoons Punjabi *garam masala* (page 270)

FOR THE FINAL FINISH OR *tarka*:

A generous dollop of unsalted butter

or

3 tablespoons *ghee* (page 271) or vegetable oil

1 smallish onion, cut into very fine half-rings

1 teaspoon cayenne pepper

2–3 tablespoons chopped, fresh cilantro (optional)

Wash the 2 types of beans and drain. Cover with water and leave to soak overnight. Drain. In a large pan, combine the beans with 2½ quarts water and bring to the boil. Cover, turn the heat to low and simmer gently for 3–4 hours or until the beans are quite tender. With a potato masher, beat or mash about half of the beans lightly until they form an exceedingly coarse purée. Half the beans should remain whole. Add the ginger, garlic, tomatoes, cayenne pepper, salt, butter, cream and *garam masala*. Cook very gently for another 30 minutes, stirring occasionally.

The beans may be served just this way with a final dollop of butter at the top. They are also very good with a *tarka*. For this, heat the *ghee* or oil in a small pan or small frying pan over medium-high heat. When hot, put in the onion. Stir and fry. When the onion is a rich, reddish-brown, put in the cayenne pepper. Immediately lift up the pan and empty its contents into the pot with the beans.

Garnish with the fresh cilantro, if desired, before serving.

S E R V E S   6

Amritsari Dal
ⓥ AMRITSARI BEANS

THIS IS ANOTHER BEAN and split pea dish that is served at Sikh *gurdwaras* (temples) and in all Punjabi homes as part of everyday meals. This is best eaten with a Punjabi bread and a selection of vegetables and pickles. If meat is desired, any of the lamb or chicken dishes in this chapter may be served.

¾ cup whole black *urad* beans (page 261)

Generous ½ cup *chana dal* (page 260)

1½ teaspoons salt or to taste

2 tablespoons very finely chopped garlic

2 tablespoons peeled and very finely chopped fresh ginger root

3 tablespoons *ghee* (page 271) or vegetable oil

1 teaspoon cumin seeds

1 medium-large onion, finely chopped

4–5 fresh hot green chilies, seeded and finely chopped

2 medium-sized tomatoes, finely chopped

1 teaspoon Punjabi *garam masala* (page 270)

A generous dollop of unsalted butter to garnish (optional)

A handful of coarsely chopped, fresh mint or cilantro (optional)

Wash the combined *urad* beans and *chana dal* and drain. Cover with water and leave for 2–3 hours. Drain and put in a large, heavy pan with the salt and 3½ pints water. Bring to the boil. Turn the heat to low and skim any scum off the surface. Add 1 tablespoon each of the garlic and ginger. Cover and simmer for 2 hours or until the *urad* beans and *chana dal* are soft. Whisk them until they are smooth.

Heat the *ghee* or oil in a separate wok or large pan over medium-high heat. When hot, put in the cumin seeds. Let them sizzle for 15 seconds. Put in the onion. Stir and fry until the onion is golden-brown. Add the remaining ginger and garlic and continue to fry for another 5–6 minutes. Add the chilies and tomatoes and stir and fry until the tomatoes are soft. Add this spice mixture to the *urad* beans and *chana dal*, stir and continue to cook over low heat for another 30 minutes or until the *dal* is fairly thick and smooth. Sprinkle the *garam masala* over the top and mix it in. Garnish with a dollop of butter and the fresh mint or cilantro, if desired.

SERVES 4–6

Bhatura
Ⓥ PUFFED LEAVENED BREADS

RATHER LIKE NORTH INDIAN *pooris*, these are puffed, deep-fried breads. The difference is they are made with white flour and have leavening and yogurt in the dough making them slightly spongy. They may be eaten with any split peas, beans and vegetables and are also delightful with kebabs inside them and with Ground Lamb with Chick-Peas (page 228).

❧

3 cups plus 2 tablespoons all-purpose flour, plus extra for dusting
Scant ½ cup semolina (*sooji*, page 277)
½ teaspoon baking powder

¼ teaspoon baking soda
1 teaspoon salt
2 tablespoons plain whole milk yogurt
2 teaspoons sugar

2 tablespoons *ghee* (page 271) or unsalted butter
Vegetable oil for deep-frying

❧

In a large, shallow bowl, mix together the flour, semolina, baking powder, baking soda and salt. Whisk the yogurt, ¾ cup water and sugar in a separate bowl. Make a well in the center of the flour mixture and slowly pour in the yogurt mixture, mixing as you do so, until it is fully absorbed. Knead this dough until it is pliable but firm. Cover with a damp cloth and let it stand for 15 minutes.

Melt the *ghee* or butter and mix it into the dough. Knead for another 5 minutes. Cover with a damp cloth and let the dough rest for 45 minutes. Break the dough into 1¼ inch (3 cm) wide balls. There should be about 18.

Heat the oil in a wok or large frying pan over high heat. While it heats, dust your rolling surface with flour. Flatten one ball in the flour. Roll the ball out with a rolling pin, dusting it

with flour when needed, until you have a disc about 5 inches (13 cm) in diameter. Lift up the disc carefully, without allowing it to fold up, and slip it into the hot oil. It should sink to the bottom and rise immediately. Quickly flip it over. Keep tapping it lightly with a slotted spoon, pushing it down gently into the oil as you do so. It should puff up within seconds. Turn it over after 30 seconds and fry for a further 20–30 seconds or until it is golden and crisp. Remove with a slotted spoon. Rest briefly on paper towels to drain and then put on a plate. Cover with a domed lid or inverted bowl. Make all the *bhaturas* this way and serve immediately.

MAKES ABOUT 18 BREADS

From Kesar-da-Dhaba, Amritsar: Ghiya Raita
Ⓥ ZUCCHINI RAITA

THIS VERY SIMPLE YOGURT relish is offered at one of the oldest fast food joints in the walled city of Amritsar. Serve it with any Indian meal or eat it by itself. It is made with *ghiya* (bottle gourd) in Amritsar but I find that very lightly cooked zucchini make a good substitute.

2 medium-sized zucchini

1¼ cups plain yogurt
½ teaspoon salt or to taste

2 tablespoons finely chopped, fresh mint leaves

Peel the zucchini and cut them in half lengthwise. Scrape out the seeds with a spoon and grate the remaining flesh.

Bring 2½ cups water to the boil in a small pan. Put in the grated zucchini. Boil rapidly for 10 seconds then drain thoroughly in a strainer. Let the zucchini sit in the strainer until they are cool enough to handle. Squeeze out as much moisture as you can. Set aside.

Put the yogurt into a bowl. Beat lightly with a fork or whisk until it is smooth and creamy. Add the salt and mix it in. Add the fresh mint and the zucchini. Stir to mix, making sure that all the zucchini strands are well separated.

SERVES 4

Shalgham, Gajar Aur Phoolgobi Aachar
Ⓥ CAULIFLOWER, TURNIP & CARROT PICKLE

AT ITS SIMPLEST this may be eaten with Flaky Breads plain or stuffed (pages 245–8), but you may also serve it with grand Indian meals.

❧

1 cup mustard oil

1 small onion, finely chopped

1 tablespoon fresh ginger root, peeled and cut into very fine strips

1 teaspoon finely chopped garlic

½ medium-sized cauliflower, cut into large, chunky florets

1 medium-sized turnip, peeled and cut into 1 inch (2.5 cm) cubes

2 carrots, peeled and cut into 1 inch (2.5 cm) sections and then in half lengthwise; if too thick, quarter lengthwise

2 teaspoons Punjabi *garam masala* (page 270)

1½–2 tablespoons cayenne pepper

4 teaspoons ground cumin

2 tablespoons brown mustard seeds, lightly ground in a clean coffee grinder

1 tablespoon salt

⅔ cup sugar

½ cup white vinegar

❧

Heat the mustard oil in a wok or large frying pan over medium-high heat. When hot, add the onions. Reduce the heat to medium and cook until the onions are light brown. Add the ginger and garlic and stir and fry for 1 minute. Put in the cauliflower, turnip and carrots. Stir and fry for 30 seconds. Add the *garam masala*, cayenne pepper, cumin, mustard seeds and salt. Stir for 1 minute. Mix the sugar with the vinegar and add to the vegetables. Stir and fry for another 30 seconds. Remove from the heat and leave to cool.

Transfer the pickle to sterilized jam or pickling jars. Cover the lids with cheesecloth, secured with rubber bands, and keep the jars in a dry and, if possible, sunny place for 2 days to allow the pickle to breathe, and so that any excess moisture is dried up. Shake the pickle jars every now and then.

On the third day remove the cheesecloth and seal the jars with tight fitting lids. Leave unrefrigerated in a warm, sunny spot in the house. The pickle should be ready in 4–7 days. It is ready when it has turned sour. It can now be refrigerated.

Stir well before removing from the jar.

MAKES 3¾ CUPS

Radha Anand's Seviyan
ⓥ VERMICELLI PUDDING

A MUCH LOVED DESSERT made with what Punjab has in abundance: milk.
Angel hair or capellini pasta would also work well instead of vermicelli.

❧

1 tablespoon *ghee* (page 271) or melted unsalted butter
3 oz (85 g) fine vermicelli, angel hair or capellini

pasta, broken up into 3 inch (7.5 cm) pieces
5 cups whole milk
¼ cup blanched and slivered almonds

⅔ cup sugar
8 green cardamom pods
2 tablespoons golden raisins
2–3 drops *kewra* water (page 272)

❧

Heat the *ghee* or butter in a large wok or frying pan over medium heat. When hot, add the pasta and stir-fry until it is golden-brown. This should take about 5–6 minutes. With a slotted spoon, remove the pasta and place on paper towels to absorb excess fat.

Bring the milk to the boil in a heavy based saucepan. Add the pasta. Turn the heat to low,

add the almonds and sugar and stir. Meanwhile, peel the cardamom pods, discard their skins, and add the seeds to the milk as well as the golden raisins. Simmer for 30 minutes, stirring often, until the mixture is thick. Remove from the heat and add the *kewra* water. Serve warm.

SERVES 4

Cauliflower with Potatoes, Banquet Style (page 240)
and Amritsari Beans (page 244).

Sunil Vijayakar's Rabadhi

Ⓥ CREAMED MILK PUDDING

THIS DELICIOUS INDIAN DESSERT quite justifies the time taken to prepare it.

---

3 quarts (12 cups) whole milk
1⅔ cup sugar

4 tablespoons shelled, unsalted pistachio nuts, skinned and roughly chopped

2 cardamom pods, lightly crushed
2–3 drops *kewra* water (page 272)
2–3 drops rose water
Fresh rose petals (optional)

Bring the milk to the boil in a large, heavy saucepan, over medium-high heat. Turn the heat down slightly so that the milk does not bubble over and continue to boil for another 30 minutes, stirring constantly. Continue to cook the milk, stirring every 3–4 minutes, for another 45 minutes. The consistency should now be grainy and thick. Add the sugar, pistachio nuts, and cardamom pods. Continue to stir and cook for another 10–15 minutes. The mixture should be fairly thick by now. Remove from the heat and add the *kewra* and rose water.

Place in a bowl. Cover and refrigerate for a couple of hours before serving. Garnish with rose petals, if desired.

SERVES 4 – 6

SPECIAL INGREDIENTS

Available in Indian grocery stores.

AJWAIN (OR AJOWAN) SEEDS

These small seeds look like celery seeds but taste more like a pungent version of thyme. (A student of mine compared it to a mixture of anise and black pepper!) Used sparingly, as their flavor is strong, they are sprinkled into Indian breads, savory crackers and numerous noodle-like snacks made with chick-pea flour. They also add a pleasant thyme-like taste to vegetables such as green beans and potatoes and to roast meats.

AMCHOOR (GREEN MANGO POWDER)

Unripe green mangoes are peeled, sliced and their sour flesh sun-dried and ground to make *amchoor* powder. (The dried slices are also used in Indian cookery but not needed for recipes here.) The beige, slightly fibrous powder, rich in vitamin C, is tart but with a hint of sweetness and is used as lemon juice might be. It is particularly useful when sourness is required but the ingredients need to be kept dry, such as when sautéeing spiced potatoes. As the powder can get lumpy, crumble it well before use.

ANARDANA (POMEGRANATE SEEDS)

Sour, dried pomegranate seeds used mainly in Punjabi cooking to give sourness to foods. They are sometimes crushed or ground before use. You may do this in a mortar or else grind them for a second or two in a clean coffee grinder.

ASAFETIDA

The sap from the roots and stem of a giant fennel-like plant dries into a hard resin. It is sold in both lump and ground form. Only the ground form is used here. It has a strong fetid aroma and is used in very small quantities both for its legendary digestive properties and for the much gentler, garlic-like aroma it leaves behind after cooking. (James Beard compared it to the smell of truffles.) Excellent with dried beans and vegetables. Store in a tightly closed container.

ATA
See *Chapati flour*.

BAY LEAVES
These dried leaves are added to scores of Indian rice and meat dishes for their delicate aroma. Sometimes they are lightly browned in oil first to intensify this aroma, using the "*tarka*" technique (page 286).

BEANS AND PEAS, DRIED
All beans should be picked over and washed in several changes of water. Store in tightly closed jars.

Chana dal: The Indian version of yellow split peas but with better texture and a very nutty flavor. Comes hulled and split. It may be cooked by itself or it can be soaked and cooked with rice or vegetables or meat. In the south, it is used as a spice. It also goes into many Indian snacks of the "Bombay Mix" variety.

Chana dal, roasted: This is *chana dal* that has been roasted. It is actually edible at this stage. It is often ground and used to bind all manner of ground meat kebabs. It can also be fried and put into snack foods or used to thicken sauces.

Kidney beans, red: Known as *rajma* in the Punjab where they are eaten most, these are the red kidney beans that are sold by most supermarkets.

Masoor dal (red split lentils): A hulled, salmon-colored pea that turns yellow after cooking.

Moong (or mung) dal: These yellow split beans are sold both with and without skin by almost every Indian grocer. The skins are green, the flesh yellow.

Mung beans, whole: The same bean as above, only whole. It is these beans that are sprouted and sold as bean sprouts. Indians half-sprout them and also cook them whole.

Toovar dal (also called arhar dal): A dull yellow split pea with an earthy taste. It is sold in its plain form and in an "oily" form which is darker. The latter is rubbed with castor oil. This oil needs to be washed off.

Urad beans, whole black: Small, black-skinned oval beans that are pale yellow inside. Their texture is somewhat glutinous. You can buy them from all Indian grocers. Ask for whole *urad* or *sabut urad*. In the Punjab, where they are much loved, they are known as *ma di dal*.

Urad dal: A small, pale yellow split pea that is used, among other things, to make all manner of South Indian pancakes. It has a slightly viscous texture. It is also used as a seasoning. It is South Indians who seem to have discovered that if you throw a few of these dried, split peas into hot oil, using the *"tarka"* method, the seeds will turn red and nutty. Anything stir-fried in the oil afterwards will pick up that nutty flavor and aroma.

BITTER MELONS (KARELA IN MOST OF NORTH INDIA)

One of the many bitter vegetables loved in India, these look like members of the marrow family except that their green skins are ridged like that of an alligator. To prepare *karela*, the ridges are first scraped off leaving a smooth skin, and the melon is then rubbed with salt and set aside. Some of the bitterness flows out with the salty water. Indians consider them very good for cleansing the blood and for diabetes. Here in the U.S. they are mainly available in Asian markets.

BLACK PEPPER

Native to India, whole peppercorns are added to rice and meat dishes for a mild peppery-lemony flavor. Ground pepper was once used in large amounts, sometimes several tablespoons in a single dish, especially in South India where it grows. The arrival of the chili pepper from the New World around 1498 changed that usage somewhat, though it still exists. In some South Indian dishes peppercorns are lightly roasted before use to draw out their lemony taste.

BLACK SALT (KALA NAMAK)

This fairly strong-smelling rock salt is used in many of North India's snack foods. It is sold both ground and in lump form by Indian grocers. If you buy the lump form, grind what you need in a clean coffee grinder. Store in a tightly lidded jar.

CARDAMOM

Cardamom pods: Small green pods, the fruit of a ginger-like plant, hold clusters of black, highly aromatic seeds smelling like a combination of camphor, eucalyptus, orange peel and lemon. Whole pods are put into rice and meat dishes and ground seeds are the main flavor in *garam masala* (page 270). This versatile spice is the vanilla of India and used in most desserts and sweetmeats. It is also added to spiced tea and sucked as a mouth-freshener.

Cardamom seeds that have been taken out of their pods are sold separately by Indian grocers. If you cannot get them, take the seeds out of the pods yourself. The most aromatic pods are the ones that are green in color. White ones sold by supermarkets have been bleached and therefore have less flavor.

Cardamom pods, black: Somewhat like the smaller cardamom in flavor, these large black pods have seeds with a cruder, heavier flavor and aroma.

Cardamom seeds, ground: The seeds of the cardamom pods are sold by themselves in both their whole and ground forms. This powder can be put into rice dishes, desserts and Indian-style meat dishes.

CASHEW NUTS

These nuts traveled from the Americas via Africa and India all the way to China. It might be useful for you to know that all so-called "raw" cashews have been processed to remove the prussic acid in their outer shells. They are grown commonly on India's west coast and are used in pilafs, desserts and even made into *bhajis* and curries.

CAYENNE PEPPER

This hot powder is made today by grinding the dried, red skins of several types of chili peppers. In India, and in Indian grocer shops in the West, it is simply called chili powder. But since that name can be confused with the

Mexican-style chili powder that also contains cumin, garlic and oregano, I am using the name "cayenne pepper" in all recipes. Even though chilies came from the New World, India today is the largest producer and one of the largest exporters and consumers. When adding to recipes, use your discretion.

CHAAT MASALA

There are many versions of this throughout North India. Here is a Punjabi version.

Makes about 5 tablespoons

4 teaspoons lightly roasted and ground cumin seeds

1½ tablespoons *amchoor*

2 teaspoons cayenne pepper

1 teaspoon finely ground black pepper

¾ teaspoon finely ground black salt

1 teaspoon salt

Mix all the ingredients thoroughly, breaking up any lumps. Store in a tightly lidded jar.

CHAPATI FLOUR

Very finely ground whole wheat flour used to make *chapatis*, *pooris* and other breads. Sold by all Indian grocers.

CHAROLI NUTS

A tiny nut that tastes a bit like hazelnut. Used in rich meat sauces and in sweets and stuffings.

CHHANA

A fresh cheese made by curdling milk. Used for making many Bengali sweets. See the recipe on page 173.

CHILIES, WHOLE, DRIED, HOT, RED

When whole dried chilies are added to Indian food, it is generally done through the *"tarka"* method (page 286). A quick contact with very hot oil enhances and intensifies the flavor of their skins. It is that flavor that Indians want. (Mexicans traditionally do this by roasting their chilies.)

Then, if actual chili-heat is desired, the chilies are allowed to stew with the food being cooked. The most commonly used dry chili is a cayenne type. To remove seeds from dried chilies, break off the stem end and shake the seeds out. Rotating a chili between the fingers can help. Sometimes it is necessary to break the chili in order to get all the seeds out.

There is a variety of red chili, known frequently as the "Kashmiri chili," that is known for the bright red color it imparts, rather like good paprika. Since it is not always easy to get in the West, I often use a combination of cayenne pepper and paprika in my recipes.

CHILIES, WHOLE, FRESH, GREEN AND RED

The fresh green chili used in Indian cooking is of the cayenne type, generally about 3 inches (7.5 cm) long and slender. Its heat can vary from mild to fiery. (Stupid bees, it seems, unthinkingly cross-pollinate different varieties that grow in proximity to each other.) The only way to judge the heat is by tasting a tiny piece of skin from the middle section. (Keep some yogurt handy!) The top part of the chili with more seeds is always the hottest, the bottom tip, the mildest. The hot seeds of the chili are never removed in India but you may do so. Use whatever chili you can find. The *jalapeno* is thicker skinned and hotter than the Indian chili. Use discretion. Also wash your hands well after handling chilies. If you touch your eyes, mouth or nose without washing, they may burn.

Red chilies are just ripe green chilies. However, their flavor is slightly different, though their intensity can be exactly the same.

Chilies are a very rich source of iron and vitamins A and C. To store fresh red or green chilies wrap them first in newspaper, then in plastic and store in the refrigerator. They should last several weeks. Any that begin to soften and rot should be removed as they tend to infect the whole batch.

CHILI POWDER, KASHMIRI

This is powder made from a long Kashmiri chili that is relatively mild in taste but which, like paprika, gives off a lovely, deep red color.

CILANTRO, FRESH

This is the parsley of India. It is ground into fresh chutneys, mixed in with vegetables, cooked with chicken and used as a garnish.

Generally just the delicate, fragrant, green leaves are used though South Indians often throw the stems into soupy *dals* for extra flavor. The cilantro should be very well washed first. When fresh green cilantro is called for, chop up the top of the plant where the stalks are slender. From the lower half, where the stalks are thicker, you will have to pick off the leaves.

When you buy fresh cilantro, the best way to keep it is to stand it in a glass of water, cover it with a plastic bag and refrigerate the whole thing. Break off the leaves and stems as you need and keep the rest refrigerated. The water should be changed daily and dead leaves removed.

CINNAMON

Used mainly for desserts in the West, cinnamon, often in its "stick" form, is added to many Indian rice and meat dishes for its warm, sweet aroma. This inner bark from a laurel-like tree is also an important ingredient in the aromatic mixture *garam masala* (page 270).

CLOVES

Indians rarely use cloves in desserts but do use them in meat and rice dishes and in the spice mixture *garam masala* (page 270). They carry the pungently aromatic cloves as well as cardamom pods in tiny silver boxes, to use as mouth-fresheners when needed. For the same reason cloves are always part of the betel leaf paraphernalia that is offered as a digestive at the end of a meal.

COCONUT, FRESH

When buying a coconut, look for one that shows no signs of mold and is free of cracks. Shake the coconut. If it contains a lot of water it has a better chance of being good. People generally weigh a coconut in each hand and pick the heavier of the two. In the West it is always safer to buy an extra coconut just in case one turns out to be bad.

To break open a coconut, use the unsharpened side of a cleaver and hit the coconut hard all around its equator. You can hold the coconut in one hand over a large bowl while you hit with the other. Or you can rest the coconut on a stone while you hit it and then rush it to a bowl as soon as the first crack appears. The bowl is there to catch the coconut water. Some people like to drink it. I do. This coconut water, by the way, is not used in cooking. But it is a good indication of the sweetness and freshness of the coconut.

You should now have two halves. Before proceeding any further, cut off a small bit of the meat and taste it. The dreaded word here is "rancid!" Your coconut should taste sweet. If it is lacking in sweetness, it can be endured. But it must never be rancid or moldy inside. Now remove the tough outer shell by slipping a knife between it and the meat and then prising the meat out. Sometimes it helps to crack the halves into smaller pieces to do this. This meat now has a thin brown skin.

To grate fresh coconut: If your recipe calls for freshly grated coconut, peel the skin off with a vegetable peeler or a knife, cut the meat into small cubes and throw the cubes into the container of a food processor or blender. When you blend you will not get a paste. What you will get is something resembling grated coconut. You can freeze what you don't use. Grated coconut freezes very well and it is a good idea to keep some at hand.

As a substitute for freshly grated coconut, you can use unsweetened, dried coconut which is sold in most health food stores. Here is how you do this: To get the equivalent of 8 tablespoons of freshly grated coconut, take 5 tablespoons unsweetened, dried coconut and soak it in 4 tablespoons water for about an hour.

COCONUT MILK

This is best made from fresh coconuts but is also available canned or may be made using powdered milk, unsweetened, dried coconut or blocks of creamed coconut. No prepared coconut milk keeps well – this includes canned coconut milk after the can has been opened. Its refrigerated life is no longer than two days.

Using fresh coconut: First you prise off the flesh as suggested above. Whether you peel the brown skin or not depends on the dish. If it needs to look pale and pristine, remove the skin. If not, leave it on and grate the meat in a food processor or blender (see page 265). To make about 1½ cups coconut milk, fill a glass measuring jug to the 2 cup mark with grated coconut. Empty it into a blender or food processor. Add 1¼ cups very hot water. Blend for a few seconds. Line a sieve with a piece of muslin or cheesecloth and place it over a bowl. Empty the contents of the blender into the sieve. Gather the ends of the cloth together and squeeze out all the liquid. For most of my recipes, this is the coconut milk that is needed. It is sometimes referred to as thick coconut milk. If a recipe calls for thin coconut milk, the entire process needs to be repeated using the squeezed-out coconut and the same amount of water. If you let the thick coconut milk sit for a while, cream will rise to the top. That is why I suggest that you always stir the coconut milk before using it. If just the cream is required, then spoon it off the top.

Canned coconut milk: This is available at most Asian grocer shops but the quality varies. There is a brand which I like very much and use frequently. It is *Chaokoh* and is a product of Thailand. It is white and creamy and quite delicious. As the cream tends to rise to the top in a can as well, always stir it well before using it. Sometimes, because of the fat in it, canned coconut milk tends to get very grainy. You can either purée it for a second in a blender or else beat it well.

I find that whereas you can cook a fish, for example, in fresh coconut milk for a long time, canned coconut milk, which behaves differently is best added toward the end. Canned coconut is very thick, partly because it has thickeners in it. As a result, many of my recipes require that canned coconut milk be thinned before use.

Powdered coconut milk: You can now buy packets of powdered coconut milk from Oriental grocers and supermarkets. Their quality varies from good to poor, the poor ones containing hard-to-dissolve globules of fat. Emma brand from Malaysia is acceptable. Directions for making the milk are always on the packets. The process usually involves mixing an equal volume of powder and hot water and stirring well. Unwanted lumps should be strained away. This milk is best added to recipes towards the end of the cooking time.

Using unsweetened, dried coconut: Put 2 cups unsweetened, dried coconut into a pan. Add 2½ cups water and bring to a simmer. Now pour the contents into the container of a blender or food processor and blend for a minute. Strain the resulting mixture through a double thickness of cheesecloth pushing out as much liquid as you can. You should get about 1½ cups of thick coconut milk. If you repeat the process with the same amount of water again, using the left-over coconut, you can get another 2 cups of thin coconut milk.

Using creamed coconut: Available in block form, this can also be turned into coconut milk. I do not advise that you do this if you need large quantities of milk. However, if just a few tablespoons are required you can, for example, take 2 tablespoons creamed coconut and mix them with 2 tablespoons hot water. The thick coconut milk that will result should only be put into dishes at the last moment.

CORIANDER SEEDS

These beige, ridged seeds are sweetly spicy and cheap. As a result they are very commonly used in a great deal of Indian cookery. They are often the major part of many spice mixtures. In Maharashtra in western India, they are combined with cumin, shredded coconut and other spices, then dry-roasted and ground to make a delicious "black *masala*" that is used with both meat and vegetables. In the southern state of Kerala, they are combined with fenugreek seeds, black peppercorns and red chilies, dry-roasted and used to flavor dishes of prawns (shrimp) and lobster. In the north, coriander, cumin and turmeric are a common trinity used in hundreds of dishes.

To dry-roast coriander seeds: Put the required quantity into a small, heated cast-iron frying pan. Stir and roast for 2–3 minutes until the seeds turn a few shades darker and emit a roasted aroma. To grind the seeds, it is best to use a clean coffee grinder or other spice grinder.

CORNMEAL FLOUR

There are many grades of cornmeal flour. The one used for tortillas (*masa harina*) is perhaps the closest to the Indian variety. It is really best to buy this flour from Indian grocers where it is called *makki ka ata*. Store as you would any flour, in a tightly closed tin. It is not the same as plain cornmeal.

CUMIN SEEDS

These look like caraway seeds but are slightly larger, plumper and lighter in color. Their flavor is similar to caraway, only gentler and sweeter. They are used both whole and ground. When whole, they are often subjected to the "*tarka*" technique (page 286), which intensifies their flavor and makes them slightly nutty. When ground, they are used in meat, rice and vegetable dishes. Cumin seeds can also be dry-roasted first and then ground. This version is sprinkled over many snack foods, relishes and yogurt dishes.

Ground roasted cumin seeds: Put 3–4 tablespoons cumin seeds into a small, heated, cast-iron frying pan. Keep over medium heat. Stir the cumin until it is a few shades darker and emits a distinct roasted aroma. Grind in a clean coffee grinder and store in a tightly lidded jar.

CUMIN SEEDS, BLACK

A rare and therefore more expensive form of cumin with sweeter, smaller and more delicate seeds. Their mild pungency is perfect for the aromatic mixture of spices known as *garam masala* (page 270). The seeds can also be lightly dry-roasted and sprinkled whole over rice pilafs.

CURRY LEAVES, FRESH AND DRIED

These highly aromatic leaves are used in much Indian coastal and southern cookery. They are always used in their fresh form. They are now increasingly available in the West. You could use the dried leaf if the fresh is unavailable. Its aroma is very limited. Indian grocers sell both fresh and dried curry leaves. They come attached to stalks. They can be pulled off their stalks in one swoop. Keep curry leaves in a flat, plastic bag. They last for several days in the refrigerator. They may also be frozen, so when you do see them in the market, buy a lot and store them in your freezer.

FENNEL SEEDS

They look a bit like cumin seeds but are much plumper and greener. Their flavor is decidedly anise-like. In Kashmir they are often ground and used in conjunction with *asafetida* and powdered ginger for a host of fish and vegetable dishes. In north and western India, the whole seeds are used in pickles and chutneys and snack foods. Using the "*tarka*" technique, they are also used in the stir-frying of vegetables, particularly in Bengal (eastern India), where they are part of the five-spice mixture called *panch phoran* (page 275). Fennel seeds can be dry-roasted and then eaten after a meal as both a digestive and mouth-freshener. To grind fennel seeds, just put 2–3 tablespoons into a clean coffee grinder or other spice grinder and grind as finely as possible. Store in an air-tight container.

FENUGREEK SEEDS

It is these angular, yellowish seeds that give many commercial curry powders their earthy, musky "curry" aroma. In most of northern India they are used mainly in pickles, chutneys and vegetarian dishes. In western, southern and eastern India, they are used in meat and fish dishes as well (such as the *vindaloo* from Goa). They are a part of the Bengali spice mixture, *panch phoran.*

GARAM MASALA

This spice combination varies with each household though the name seems constant. "*Garam*" means "hot" and "*masala*" means "spices" so the spices in this mixture were traditionally those which "heated" the body according to the ancient *ayurvedic* system of medicine. They all happened to be highly aromatic as well. Commercial mixtures tend to cut down on the expensive cardamom and fill up with the cheaper coriander and cumin. Here is how you make a classic ground mixture: combine in a clean coffee grinder 1 tablespoon cardamom seeds, 1 teaspoon cloves, 1 teaspoon black peppercorns, 1 teaspoon black cumin seeds, a 2 inch (5 cm) cinnamon stick, ⅓ nutmeg and a curl of mace. Grind to a fine powder. Store in a tightly closed jar and use as needed. Many people add a bay leaf to the mixture. Generally, though not always, *garam masala* is sprinkled towards the end of the cooking time to retain its aroma. The *garama masala* spices can also be used whole. If two or more of them are used together, they are still loosely referred to as *garam masala.*

Punjabi garam masala: *Garam masalas* vary in different parts of India. Here is one that is commonly used in the Punjab.

5 tablespoons coriander seeds

3 tablespoons cumin seeds

2½ tablespoons black peppercorns

2½ tablespoons black cardamom seeds

1½ teaspoons green cardamom seeds

1 (2 inch) (5 cm) cinnamon stick

4–5 cloves

About ⅙ nutmeg

Put the coriander and cumin into a cast-iron frying pan over medium heat. Stir until very lightly roasted. Empty onto a plate. Allow them to cool slightly, then put them and the remaining ingredients into a clean coffee grinder and grind as finely as possible. You may need to do this in more than one batch. Store in a tightly lidded jar.

GARLIC

Some Indians (Kashmiri Hindus, the Jain sect) do not touch garlic but the rest of the country eats it with pleasure. It is an important ingredient in meat sauces which often require that onion, garlic and ginger, the "wet" trinity of seasonings, be ground into a paste and then be fried in oil until dark and thick. In parts of Saurashtra in western India, garlic, salt and dried red chilies are pounded together to make an everyday condiment.

GHEE (CLARIFIED BUTTER)

This is butter that has been so thoroughly clarified that it can even be used for deep-frying. As it no longer contains milk solids, refrigeration is not necessary. It has a nutty, buttery taste. All Indian grocers sell it and I find it more convenient to buy it. If, however, you need to make it, put 1 lb (450 g) unsalted butter in a pan over low heat and let it simmer very gently until the milky solids turn brownish and cling to the sides of the pot or else fall to the bottom. The time that this takes will depend on the amount of water in the butter. Watch carefully toward the end and do not let it turn. Strain the *ghee* through a triple layer of cheesecloth. Homemade *ghee* is best stored in the refrigerator.

GINGER, FRESH

This rhizome has a sharp, pungent, cleansing taste and is a digestive aid to boot. It is ground and used in meat sauces (see *Garlic*) and in drinks. It is also cut into slivers or minute dice and used when stir-frying potatoes, green beans, spinach and other vegetables. When finely grated ginger is required, it should first be peeled and then grated on the finest part of a grater so it turns into pulp. When a recipe requires that 1 inch (2.5 cm) of ginger be grated, it is best to keep that piece attached to the large knob. The knob acts as a handle and saves you from grating your fingers.

Ginger should be stored in a dry, cool place. Many people like to bury it in dryish, sandy soil. This way they can break off and retrieve small portions as they need them while the rest of the knob generously keeps growing.

JAGGERY

A form of raw, lump, cane sugar. It is sold in pieces that are cut off from larger blocks. You should look for the kind that crumbles easily and is not rock-hard. It can be found in Indian grocer shops or substitute brown sugar.

KALONJI (NIGELLA)

Most Indians associate these black, tear-drop-shaped seeds with *tandoor* oven breads (they are sprinkled over the top), with pickles, with Bengali food and the Bengali five-spice mixture, *panch phoran* and with certain North Indian vegetarian dishes. Their oregano-like taste is quite strong so they should be used with some discretion.

KEWRA ESSENCE

This flowery essence comes from a variety of the screwpine plant. In Muslim Indian cooking it is used in banquet-style dishes of rice and meat and in desserts. It may even be sprinkled on breads though this is usually done not with the concentrated essence but with the lighter *kewra* water which is sold in larger bottles. *Kewra* is also available as a syrup which is mixed with ice and water to make a summer drink.

Kewra water: This is a more diluted version of *kewra* essence.

KOKUM

This is the pliable, semi-dried, sour and astringent skin of a mangosteen-like fruit (*Garcinia indica*) that grows along India's coast. It is used for souring, rather like tamarind. It can sometimes be a bit salty as well so use a little care. Store in an air-tight container to prevent drying out. When *kokum* is used in a dish, it is rarely eaten. It is left either in the pan or in the serving dish.

MACE, SEE NUTMEG

MELON SEEDS, PEELED

These are used to thicken sauces, especially for meat dishes.

MUSTARD OIL

This oil has the same characteristics as the seeds it comes from. When raw, it smells hot and pungent. When heated, the pungency goes into the air (you can smell it in your kitchen) and the oil turns sweet. It is used in Bengali and Kashmiri cookery, and in most oil pickles. It is also good for a massage!

MUSTARD SEEDS, BROWN

Of the three varieties of mustard seeds, white (actually yellowish), brown (a reddish-brown) and black (slightly larger, brownish black seeds), it is the brown that has been grown and used in India since antiquity. To confuse matters, the brown seeds are often referred to as black. When shopping, look for the small, reddish-brown variety although, at a pinch, any will do. All mustard seeds have Jekyll and Hyde characteristics. When crushed, they are nose-tinglingly pungent. However, if they are thrown into hot oil and allowed to pop using the "*tarka*" method (page 286), they turn quite nutty and sweet.

In India, both these techniques are used, sometimes in the same recipe. Whole mustard seeds, popped in oil, are used to season vegetables, beans, yogurt relishes, salads and rice dishes. Crushed seeds are used to steam fish, in sauces and in pickles.

MUSTARD SEEDS, HULLED AND SPLIT

Brown mustard seeds are hulled and split and made into what Indians call a *dal*. This spice is mainly used for pickling. The best substitute is coarsely ground brown mustard seeds.

MUSTARD SEEDS, WHOLE, YELLOW

The European mustard seeds are also used by Indians when a milder flavor is desired. Sometimes brown and yellow mustard seeds are mixed for a special effect.

NUTMEG AND MACE

Nutmegs are the dried seeds of a round pear-like fruit. Mace is the red, lacy covering around the seeds that turns yellowish when dried. Both have similar warm, sweetish and slightly camphorous flavors though mace has a slightly bitter edge. Both nutmeg and mace are used here in the *garam masala* mixture (page 270). A nutmeg breaks easily. Just hit it lightly with a hammer to get the third needed for the *garam masala* recipe. Indians almost never use nutmeg for desserts and drinks.

OIL

For most of the recipes in this book, I would recommend using peanut or corn oil. If oil is used for deep-frying, it can be re-used. Skim off all extraneous matter with a skimmer and then drop a chunk of ginger or potato into it and let it fry. This chunk will absorb many of the unwanted flavors. Strain the oil when it is cool enough to handle through a triple thickness of cheesecloth or a large handkerchief. Let it cool completely and then store it in a bottle. When re-using, mix half old oil with half fresh oil.

Olive oil: This is only found in Goan recipes because of that area's Portuguese heritage. Its use is now quite rare as almost no foreign oil is imported.

PALM SUGAR

This is a delicious, raw, honey-colored lump sugar used in much of coastal India. It is sold by Southeast Asian grocers both in cans and in plain plastic containers. It comes in lump or fairly flowing forms. The best substitute for it is either Indian sugar cane jaggery (make sure it is not rock-hard) or brown sugar. It keeps well if tightly covered. Refrigeration is not needed.

PANCH PHORAN (5-SPICE MIXTURE)

This very Bengali spice mixture consists of fennel seeds, mustard seeds, fenugreek seeds, cumin seeds and *kalonji* mixed in equal proportions.

PAPRIKA

Not generally used in Indian food. I use it frequently in place of red chilies in order to give the dishes their traditional red color. Paprika tends to darken as it sits in glass bottles. Since I use it only for the color, it is important that you use good quality paprika that is bright red.

POPPADOMS

Also called *papar*, these Indian wafers are made out of dried split peas and are sold either plain or studded with black pepper (or garlic or red pepper) by Indian grocers. They should be deep-fried for a few seconds in hot oil or toasted. They are served with most Indian vegetarian meals. They are also good with drinks.

POPPY SEEDS, WHITE

Only the white seeds are used in India, mainly to thicken sauces.

PRAWNS (SHRIMP), DRIED

These are sold in plastic packets at Chinese and all Southeast Asian grocer shops and are best when pinkish in color. Price is often an indication of quality. They should be rinsed off and then soaked for 5–10 minutes in hot water before being lifted out of the water and ground. They add a tremendous amount of concentrated flavor to the dishes to which they are added. They last well if kept in a well-closed plastic container in the refrigerator. I have used these prawns (shrimp) instead of the very tiny ones found in Goan markets.

RICE

Many varieties of rice are used in Indian cookery. There is the protein-rich, partially milled "red" rice used along the Konkan coast south of Bombay. Then there is "boiled" rice. This is the original par-boiled rice that predates Uncle Ben and must have been the inspiration for the rice Uncle Ben produced in 1943. Along India's southern coasts, "boiled" rice has been produced for centuries. The process of boiling the rice before it is husked and milled not only makes the grains tough and indestructible but it also pushes the B complex vitamins into the inner kernel. This rice is used not only for everyday eating in the south but also to make a variety of pancakes, cakes and snacks.

Then there is basmati rice, the pearls of the north. It is a very fine, long-grain, highly aromatic rice grown in the foothills of the Himalaya mountains. The better varieties are generally aged a year before being sold. This rice is now being grown in America as well.

RICE FLOUR

This is made from ground rice and is sold by most East Asian, Southeast Asian, Indian and Pakistani grocers.

SAFFRON

I have only used leaf saffron in this book. These are the whole, dried saffron threads, the stigma of the autumn crocus. Look for a reliable source for your saffron as it is very expensive and there can be a great deal of adulteration. Indians often roast the saffron threads lightly before soaking them in a small amount of hot milk to bring out the color. This milk is then poured over rice, in dishes such as *biryani*, to give it its orange highlights.

SAMBAR POWDER

Makes 1¼ cups.

This powder, which uses split peas as spices, is used to make the South Indian dish called *sambar*. It can be stored in a tightly closed jar for several months.

1 teaspoon vegetable oil

5 tablespoons coriander seeds

1 teaspoon mustard seeds

1 teaspoon *moong dal*
½ tablespoon *chana dal*
½ tablespoon *urad dal*
1 teaspoon fenugreek seeds
1 teaspoon black peppercorns
¼ teaspoon ground *asafetida*
1 teaspoon cumin seeds
20 fresh curry leaves (optional)
12 dried hot red chilies

Heat the oil in a large, heavy frying pan or a heavy wok over medium heat. Put in the coriander seeds, mustard seeds, *moong dal*, *chana dal*, *urad dal*, fenugreek seeds, black peppercorns, *asafetida* and cumin seeds. Stir and roast for 3–4 minutes. Add the curry leaves if using. Stir and roast for another 5 minutes. Add the dried chilies and continue stirring and roasting for 2–3 minutes or until chilies darken. Remove spices to a plate.

When the spices have cooled, put them into a coffee grinder in small batches and grind as finely as possible. Store in a tightly closed jar.

SEMOLINA

This is wheat ground to the texture of grain cornmeal or polenta. It is sold by Indian grocers as *sooji* and really has no good substitute. The supermarket semolina tends to be far too fine for Indian pilafs and *halvas*.

SESAME SEEDS

You may use white sesame seeds or the beige ones for all the recipes in this book.

To roast sesame seeds: Put a small, cast-iron frying pan to heat over medium-low heat. When hot, put in 1–3 tablespoons sesame seeds. Stir them around until they turn a shade darker and give out a wonderful roasted aroma. Sesame seeds to tend to fly around as they are roasted. You could turn down the heat slightly when they do this or cover the pan loosely. Remove the seeds from the pan as soon as they are done. You may roast sesame seeds ahead of time. Cool them and store them in a tightly lidded jar. They can last several weeks this way though I must add that they are best when freshly roasted.

To roast and lightly crush sesame seeds: Roast the seeds as suggested above. Now put them into the container of a clean coffee grinder or spice grinder and whir it for just a second or two. The seeds should *not* turn to a powder. You may also crush them lightly in a mortar.

SHALLOTS

These are used routinely in South India in place of the larger onion common to the north. In places like Goa, they hang in kitchens like long ropes, to be plucked at will.

STAR ANISE

A flower-shaped collection of pods. Brownish-black in color, this spice has a decided anise flavor. It is used frequently along India's western coast where the trade with China started in ancient times. Store in a tightly lidded jar. If a pod of star anise is called for, think of a pod as a petal of the flower and break off one section.

TAMARIND

The fruit of a tall shade tree, tamarinds look like wide beans. As they ripen, their sour green flesh turns a chocolate color. It remains sour but picks up a hint of sweetness. For commercial purposes, tamarinds are peeled, seeded, semi-dried and their brown flesh compacted into rectangular blocks. These blocks need to be broken up and soaked in water. Then the pulp can be pushed through a strainer. This is tamarind paste.

To make your own tamarind paste: Break off 8 oz (225 g) from a brick of tamarind and tear into small pieces. Put in to a small non-metallic pot and cover with 2 cups very hot water, and set aside 3 hours or overnight. (You could achieve the same result by simmering the tamarind for 10 minutes or by putting it in a microwave oven for 3–5 minutes.) Set a sieve over a non-metallic bowl and empty the tamarind and its soaking liquid into it. Push down on the tamarind with your fingers or the back of a wooden spoon to extract as much pulp as you can. Put whatever tamarind remains in the sieve back into the soaking bowl. Add ½ cup hot water to it and mash a bit more. Return it to the sieve and extract as much more pulp as you can. Some of this pulp will be clinging to the underside of the sieve.

Do not fail to retrieve it. This quantity will make about 1½ cups of thick paste. All the calculations for my recipes have been done with this thick, chutney-like paste, so do not water it down too much. Whatever paste is left over may either be put into the refrigerator where it will keep for 2–3 weeks or it can be frozen. It freezes well.

TURMERIC

A rhizome-like ginger, only with smaller, more delicate "fingers," fresh turmeric is quite orange inside. When dried, it turns bright yellow. It is this musky yellow powder that gives some Indian dishes a yellowish cast. As it is cheap and is also considered to be an antiseptic, it is used freely in the cooking of beans, vegetables and meats. Both the fresh and the dried form are used in India. In the West, we generally get the dried powder. If you have access to Indian grocers, try using the fresh rhizome. A 1 inch (2.5 cm) piece of fresh turmeric is equal to about ½ teaspoon of ground turmeric. Just like ginger, it needs to be peeled and ground. This grinding is best done with the help of a little water in an electric blender.

EQUIPMENT

WOK

Known in India as a *karhai*, this is an all-purpose utensil that may be used for steaming, simmering, stir-frying or deep-frying.

A wok is traditionally a round-bottomed pan. Because of its shape, flames can encircle it and allow it to heat quickly and efficiently. It is most economical for deep-frying as it will hold a good depth of oil without needing the quantity a straight-sided pan would require. It is ideal for stir-frying as foods can be vigorously tossed around in it. As they hit nothing but well-heated surfaces, they cook fast and retain their moisture at the same time.

Choosing a wok: What kind of wok should you buy? A traditional Indian wok is generally made out of cast-iron but any wok will do. Advances are being made all the time and every year seems to bring new woks into the market place. Traditional woks of good quality are made either of thin tempered iron or carbon steel. The ideal wok is 14 inches (35 cm) in diameter and fairly deep. (Saucer-shaped shallow woks are quite useless.) A round-bottomed wok works well on a gas burner. A new, somewhat flat-bottomed wok has been invented for people who have electric burners. I cannot say I love it. Instead I have opted for a yet newer invention in my country house in the USA which has an all-electric kitchen. This is an electric wok – but a very special one. It is the only electric wok I know which heats very quickly, becomes *very* hot and allows foods to be both stir-fried and simmered, though I must add that it is better for stir-frying than it is for simmering.

Seasoning a wok: The iron and carbon steel woks leave the factory coated with oil. This needs to be scrubbed off with a cream cleanser. Then a wok needs to be seasoned. Rinse it in water and set it over a low heat. Now brush it all over with about 2 tablespoons vegetable oil. Let it heat for 10–15 minutes. Wipe the oil off with a piece of paper towel. Brush the wok with more oil and repeat the process 3–4 times. The wok is now seasoned.

Do not scrub it again; just wash it with hot water and then wipe it dry. It will *not* have a scrubbed look. It will, however, become more and more "non-stick" as it is used.

Wok accessories: For use on a gas burner, a wok needs a stand that not only stabilizes it but allows air to circulate underneath. The perfect stand is made of wire. The collar variety with punched holes seems to kill free circulation of heat and should not be used on gas burners.

When you buy a wok, it is also a good idea to invest in a curved spatula, a steaming tray and a lid.

CAST-IRON FRYING PANS

I find a 5 inch (13 cm) cast-iron frying pan ideal for roasting spices and a large one perfect for pan-grilling (pan-broiling) thin slices of meat. All cast-iron frying pans can be heated without any liquid and they retain an even temperature. Once properly seasoned, they should never be scrubbed with abrasive cleaners.

BLENDER AND COFFEE GRINDER, MORTAR AND PESTLE

In India, pestles and grinding-stones of varying shapes, sizes and materials are used to pulverize everything from cumin seeds to dried hot red chilies. I find it much easier to use an electric blender for wet ingredients and a clean electric coffee grinder for dry ones. For small quantities, you might still want to use a heavy mortar and pestle.

GRATER

The Japanese make a special grater for ginger and Japanese horseradish which produces a fine pulp. It has tiny hair-like spikes that are perfect for their purpose. If you ever find one, do buy it. Otherwise use the finest part of an ordinary grater for grating fresh ginger.

DOUBLE-BOILER

This is simply one pan balanced over another. The lower pan holds boiling water and allows the ingredients in the other pan to cook very gently. Double-boilers are available from good kitchenware shops but can be easily improvised.

ELECTRIC RICE-COOKER

Its main use is to free all burners on the stove for other purposes and make the cooking of rice an easy, almost mindless task. I do have one and use it only for plain rice.

DEEP-FAT FRYER

For those who are afraid of deep-frying, this is a godsend. Because it has a lid that closes over all splattering foods, this piece of equipment also helps to make deep-frying a painless, safe and clean task.

RACKS FOR GRILLING FISH

Hinged double racks are useful for grilling fish over charcoal. The fish lies sandwiched between the two racks and can be easily turned and basted. Many types of hinged double fish racks are available in the West, some even shaped like a fish. Most of them are sold by kitchen equipment stores. I find them exceedingly useful.

THALI

This is a round, flat metal tray with raised sides used as a plate for eating and as a tray for serving and also for other kitchen uses such as steaming.

Thalis can vary in size from about 6 inches (15 cm) to almost 3 feet (90 cm) in diameter. Stainless steel *thalis* are sold by most Indian grocers.

TECHNIQUES

TO PEEL, DEVEIN AND CLEAN PRAWNS (SHRIMP)

In the United Kingdom, these instructions and illustrations apply to the large uncooked prawns known as Pacific or king prawns. These are usually sold frozen and in the shell, but with the heads already removed. In the rest of the world, they apply to the common prawns (shrimp) that are sold, fresh or frozen, with the heads often removed in the West. If frozen, defrost. (a) First, peel off the shell and, with it, the tiny legs. (b) Pull off the tail. (c) Make a shallow cut down the back. (d) Remove the fine digestive cord which runs along the length of it.

It is always a good idea to wash off prawns (shrimp) before cooking them. I think this makes them taste sweeter. To do this, put the peeled and deveined prawns (shrimp) into a bowl. Add about 1 tablespoon coarse or kosher salt for every 1 lb (450 g) of prawns (shrimp) (unpeeled weight). Rub the prawns (shrimp) with the salt. Wash off the salt. Repeat this one more time. Drain the prawns (shrimp) well and pat them dry. They may now be covered and refrigerated and are ready for cooking.

TO CLEAN SQUID

Twist off the head (with the tentacles). The inner body sac will probably come away with it. If it does not, pull it out. Discard the sac and the hard eye area, which you may have to cut off with a knife. Retain the tentacles. If possible pull off some of the brownish skin on the tentacles. (You may safely leave this on, if you wish.) Peel the brownish skin from the tube-like body. Discard this skin and pull out the smooth inner cartilage. The squid can now be washed and used.

MARINATING

Meats are often cut up and put into marinades before they are cooked. A marinade tenderizes meat and injects it with all the flavors and aromas of its myriad ingredients. The meat can then be broiled or quickly stir-fried while retaining the tastes of all its seasonings.

SPICE PASTES

Most curry-style dishes require that a spice paste be prepared first. To this
end, fresh and dried spices are ground on grinding-stones. We in the West
have to use blenders and coffee grinders to make our lives easier. Once the
pastes are made, they often need to be fried in oil to get rid of their raw
taste. As they fry, sprinklings of water are frequently added to prevent
burning and sticking. Sometimes yogurt and chopped tomatoes are added
to the pastes to make a rich sauce.

DRY-ROASTING

Spices are often dry-roasted before use. It is best to do this in a heavy cast-
iron frying pan which has first been heated. No oil is used: the spices are
just stirred around until they brown lightly. Roasted spices develop a
heightened, nutty aroma. They can be stored for several months in an air-
tight jar though they are best when freshly roasted.

"*tarka*" (POPPING SPICES IN HOT OIL)

The "*tarka*" technique, known by many other names such as *baghaar*,
chhownk or "seasoning in oil" is quite unique to India. First, the oil has
to be very hot. Then, spices such as mustard seeds or cumin seeds are
dropped into it. They pop and sizzle. Their whole character changes in an
instant. They get much more intense. Their flavors change. Then, either
this flavored oil is poured over cooked foods or foods are added to the oil
and cooked in it. Since four or five spices can go into a "*tarka*," they are
often added to the hot oil in a certain order so that those that burn easily,
such as dried chilies, go in last. The flavor of each is imparted to the oil.
In the case of the chilies, the flavor comes only from the browned skin of
the chili. Any food cooked in this oil picks up the heightened flavor of all
the spices.

Doing a "*tarka*" takes just a few seconds so it is important to have all
spices ready and at hand. A "*tarka*" is sometimes done at the beginning of
a recipe and sometimes at the end. Beans, for example, are usually just
boiled with a little turmeric. When they are tender, a "*tarka*" is prepared
in a small frying pan, perhaps with *asafetida*, cumin seeds and red chilies,
and then the entire contents of the frying pan, hot oil and spices, are

poured over the beans and the lid shut tight for a few minutes to trap the aromas. These flavorings can be stirred in later. They perk up the boiled beans and bring them to life. Sometimes "*tarkas*" are done twice, both at the beginning and end of a recipe.

COOKING COCONUT MILK

When cooking fresh coconut milk, care must be taken that it does not curdle. Stir it constantly as it cooks. Canned coconut milk does not behave in quite the same as fresh coconut milk as it often has thickeners in it. I often add it only towards the end of the cooking period and then just bring it to a simmer and leave it at that. If I wish to simmer it for longer periods, I thin it out first with water or stock.

STEAMING

Steaming is used for cooking anything from the rice cake, *idli*, to Bengali fish. Just as every home in the West has a roasting pan, so every home in South India tends to have a steamer. Steaming cooks gently and preserves flavor.

One of the most satisfactory utensils for steaming is a wok because its width easily accommodates a whole fish, a casserole or a large plate of food. Use a wok with a flat base or set a round-based wok on a wire stand. Put a metal or wooden rack or a perforated tray into the wok. (You could use a small inverted tin can instead.)

Now pour in some water. Bring it to a gentle boil and lower in the food so it sits on the rack, tray or can. The water should stay about ¾ inch (2 cm) below the level of the food that is being steamed. Extra boiling water should be kept at hand just in case it is needed to top up the level.

Cover the whole wok, including the food, with a domed wok lid or a large sheet of aluminum foil. The domed lids are preferable as condensed steam rolls down the sides instead of dripping on the food itself.

If you like, you can also invest in the many-tiered bamboo or aluminum steamers sold in Chinese markets.

DEEP-FRYING

You need several inches of oil in a wok or frying pan and a good deal more in a deep-fat fryer in order to deep-fry. The oil must be heated to the required temperature before you drop in a single morsel of food. Properly deep-fried foods are not at all greasy; the outside is beautifully crisp while the inside is completely cooked.

Oil that has been used for deep-frying may be re-used. Let it cool completely and then strain it. Store it in a bottle. When you cook again, use half old oil and half fresh oil. Oil that has been used for frying fish should be re-used only for fish.

GRINDING SPICES

Many recipes call for ground spices. In India, spices are generally bought whole and then ground as needed. They have much more flavor this way. You probably already know the difference between freshly ground black pepper and ground pepper that has been sitting around for a month. The same applies to all spices. In India, the grinding of spices is generally done on heavy grinding-stones. We, in our modern kitchens, can get the same results without the labor by using an electric coffee grinder. It is best to grind limited quantities so that the spices do not lose their flavor. If you wipe the grinder carefully after use there will be no "aftertaste" of spices to flavor your coffee beans.

Buying ground spices is perfectly all right as long as you know that they will be less potent as time goes on.

MAKING THICK SAUCES

Many of India's meat, poultry and fish dishes have thick, dark sauces. My mother always said that the mark of a good chef was his sauce which depended not only on a correct balance of all the ingredients, but the correct frying (*bhuno*-ing) of these ingredients.

There is no flour in these sauces. The "body" comes, very often, from onions, garlic and ginger. The rich brown color comes from frying all these ingredients properly. Very often, a paste of one or more of these ingredients is made first. In India, this is done on a grinding-stone but in Western kitchens it can be done easily in food processors and blenders, sometimes with the aid of a little water.

Once the paste has been made, it needs to be browned or the sauce will not have the correct flavor and color. This is best done in a heavy pan, preferably non-stick, in a *generous* amount of oil. Remember that extra oil can always be spooned off the top once the dish has been cooked.

ADDING YOGURT TO SAUCES

Yogurt adds a creamy texture and a delicate tartness to many sauces. But yogurt curdles when it is heated. So when Indian cooks add it to their browning sauces, they add just 1 tablespoon at a time. After a tablespoon of yogurt has been put in, it is stirred and fried until it is absorbed and "accepted" by the sauce. Then the next tablespoon is added.

PEELING AND CHOPPING TOMATOES

Many of my recipes call for peeled and chopped tomatoes. To peel tomatoes, bring a pan of water to a rolling boil. Drop in the tomatoes for 15 seconds. Drain, rinse under cold water and peel. Now chop the tomatoes, making sure that you save all the juice that comes out of them. In India, tomatoes are very rarely seeded. Many people do not even bother to peel them though I do feel that this improves the texture of a sauce.

REDUCING SAUCES

Sometimes meat is allowed to cook in a fairly thin, brothy sauce. Then the lid of the pan is removed and the sauce reduced over fairly high heat until it is thick and clings to the meat. The meat has to be stirred frequently at this stage, so that it does not catch and burn.

COOKING CHICKEN WITHOUT ITS SKIN

In India the skin of the chicken is often removed before cooking. The flavor of the spices penetrates the chicken much better this way and the entire dish is less fatty. It is very easy to remove the skin. Just hold it with paper towels so that it does not slip, and pull!

BROWNING MEATS

In India, cubes of meat are not generally browned by themselves. Instead, they are browned with the sauce. However, in the West many meats release far too much water as they cook – Indian meats tend to be very fresh and have far less water in them. So to avoid this problem I brown my meat a few pieces at a time in hot oil and set them aside. Once I have made the sauce, I add the browned meat cubes (and all the good juices that come out of them) and let them cook.

MAIL ORDER SUPPLIERS

The following suppliers offer a mail order service.

THE UNITED STATES
Culinary Alchemy Inc., P.O. Box 393, Palo Alto, CA 94302;
(650) 367 1455

India Spice and Gift Shop, 3295 Fairfield Avenue, Bridgeport,
CT 06605; (203) 384 0666

Seema Enterprises, 10618 Page Avenue, St Louis, MO 63132;
 (314) 423 9990

Foods of India, 121 Lexington Avenue, New York, NY 10016;
(212) 683 4419

INDEX

Page numbers in *italics* refer to illustrations.

H

Haddock:
  easy fish fillets in a traditional mustard
    sauce, 156–7
  fish stew, 25
  yogurt fish, 152–3
Hakimji, Samina, 86
Halibut:
  fish stew, 25
  yogurt fish, 152–3
Halva, 224
Handva, 51, 76–7
Hilsa:
  tamarind fish, 154
Hinduism, 56
Holi, 60
Hooghly River, 142
Hotel Saravana Bhavan, Madras, 181, 209

I

Idada dhokla, 52
Idi appam, 13, 178–80
Idlis, 176, 177, 180, 181, 204–5
Indus Valley, 215
Ingli poli, 44–5
Ingredients, 259–79
Islam *see* Muslims

J

Jaggery, 272
Jahangiri, 181
Jainism, 56–7, 58, 60
Jalebi, 181
Jalkhabar, 140, 141
Jasdan, Rajmata of, 72
Jhol, 138

K

Kachchh, 57
Kadhi, 53, 79
Kadiya hoya dubh, 216
Kaitha chaka pachadi, 45–6
Kala namak, 261–2
Kalappam, 13
Kali, 140
Kalonji, 272
Kanchipuram, 177
Kannava varitiyathu, 31
Kansara, Mrs Kumud, 62–3, 67–71,
    74–85, 88–9
Kapoor, Mrs, 237
Kapoor, Promila, 220, 225, 240
Karela, 261
  stuffed bitter melons, 241
Karele pyazaa, 241
Kari, 61, 64–5
Karimeen fishermen, 14
Kartarpur, 221
Kassim, Mohammad, 60
Kaur, Jatinder, 236, 250

O

O'Brien, Errol, 143

Oil, 274

    mustard oil, 136–7

Okra:

    deep-fried okra in batter, 199, *211*

    mixed vegetables with coconut, 32

    okra with dried prawns (shrimp), *115*, 116

Olan, 17, 34

Olive oil, 274

Olives:

    duck risotto, 124–5

Onions:

    crispy chick-pea flour noodles with onions and chilies, 63

    fish on a bed of potatoes, onions and tomatoes, 111

    potatoes with mustard seeds and onions, 200

    spicy steak, 146

    steamed peanut diamonds in a garlic-onion sauce, 72–3

Osanay samaray, 97, 120–1

P

Palitana, 57, 58, 60

Palm sugar, 274–275

Panaji, 92–3

Pancakes:

    chick-pea flour pancakes, 81

coconut pancakes, *127*, 131

pancake cake, 132

pancakes in syrup, *171*, 172

rice and split pea pancakes, 205–6, *206*

Panch phoran, 136, 275

Paneer, 220–1

    spicy fresh cheese snack, 225

Paneer bhurji, 221

Paneer chat, 225

Pao, 96, 97

Papar, 56

Papri, 57

Paprika, 275

Par-boiled rice, 176–7

Parathas, 215, 218, 245–8

Park Sheraton Hotel, 192

Parra, 92

Parvati, 177

Patel, Smita, 56

Patel, Surendra, 54–6

Pâté, eggplant, 238

Paturi, 138

Paunk, 58

Payasam, 12, 48

Payesh, 136

Pazham roast, 47

Peanut oil, 274

Peanuts:

    cilantro and peanut chutney, *79*, 86

    munchable peanut salad, 185

    steamed peanut diamonds in a garlic-onion sauce, 72–3

Peas, dried, 260

Peas, fresh:

    deep-fried stuffed breads, 167–8

Ramji, Shoba, 26, 28, 33, 41, 44–5,
    199–200, 211
Rasam, 176, 181
Rava khichri, 180, 208–9
Ray, Satyajit, 140
Rechad masala, 108
Rechad spice paste, 98, 108
Red kidney beans *see* Kidney beans
Red spinach, 119
Reducing sauces, 289
Relishes:
    stewed tomato relish, *151*, 168
    yogurt with banana and mustard, 84–5
Rezala, 140, 147
Rice, 12, 176–7, 217, 276
    black pepper rice, *70*, 84
    coconut rice, 203
    duck risotto, 124–5
    Goan style pilaf, 123
    rice and split pea pancakes, 205–6, *206*
    rice with yogurt, 206–8
    savory grain cake with mustard and
        sesame seeds, 76–7
    savory rice breads, *21*, 39–40
    savory rice cakes, 204–5
    stir-fried rice with split peas, *151*, 166
    vegetable rice, *26*, 38
Rice-cookers, electric, 283
Rice flour, 276
    steamed rice "crumpets," 127–8
Risotto, duck, 124–5
Rotis, 215, 217, 224, 250–1

S

Sabji jhol, 160
Saffron, 276
Salads:
    munchable peanut salad, 185
    rice with yogurt, 206–8
Salmon:
    Amritsari fish, 234
    easy fish fillets in a traditional mustard
        sauce, 156–7
    tamarind fish, 154
Salt, black, 261–2
Samar codi, 98, 115
Sambar, 180, 181, 182, 202
Sambar powder, 276–7
Sandesh, 144, 173
Sannas, 94–6, 127
Sarabhai family, 53
Sardines, marinated and stewed, 28–9, *34*
Sarkar, Rakhi, 156, 159
Sarson da saag, 236–7
Sauces:
    adding yogurt to, 289
    making thick sauces, 288
    reducing, 289
Saurashtra, 60
Sausages, 96
    duck risotto, 124–5
Savory grain cake with mustard and sesame
    seeds, 76–7
Savory rice breads, *21*, 39–40
Savory rice cakes, 204–5
Selvaraj's stew, 19
Semolina, 277

X

Xacuti, 97, 105–6

Y

Yale, Elihu, 182
Yogurt, 60, 217, 220
  adding to sauces, 289
  chicken kebabs, 230
  lamb chops masala, 229
  lamb cooked in milk and yogurt, 147
  mango curry, 36
  mango yogurt, 89

  marinades, 289
  rice with yogurt, 206–8
  spicy pineapple-yogurt, 45–6
  steamed yogurt, 169–71
  sweet and sour chick-pea flour soup, 79
  yogurt fish, 152–3, *154*
  yogurt with banana and mustard, 84–5
  zucchini raita, 252

Z

Zacharias, Uma and Zac J., 39, 48
Zucchini raita, 252

PHOTO CREDITS

BBC Books would like to thank the following for providing photographs and for permission to reproduce copyright material. While every effort has been made to trace and acknowledge all copyright holders, we would like to apologize should there have been any errors or omissions.

All location photographs Colorific: pages 2, 6–7, 10–11, 15, 50–51, 55, 59, 134–135, 139, 174–175, 179, 183, 214–215, 219, 223 (Raghubir Singh); 90–91, 95 (Dilip Mehta); 99 (Gianfranco Gorgoni).

ACKNOWLEDGMENTS

KERALA:
Selvaraj, Mr A.R. Sunil, Mr Balasundaram, Shoba Ramji, Mr Damodaran, Mrs Bavani, Mrs K.M. Matthew, A.L. Shrinivasa Shenoy, Ajit Edassery, Ms Rolly Sapru, Uma and Zac J. Zacharias.

GUJARAT:
Mrs Kumud Kansara, Deepak Kansara, Nishrin Attarwala, The Rajmata of Jasdan, Niranjana Rao, Samina Hakimji, Sanjay De, N.P. Kaushal, Surendra Patel, Anand Sarabhai, Basil Joseph and Rambhai Bharwad.

GOA:
Jude Sequeira, Sophie Gonsalves, Reza, Maria Fernanda Sousa, Rita Themudo, Arnold Pinto, Anju Timblo, Lalit Mishra, Rui Madre Deus and Maria Fernandes.

WEST BENGAL:
Sonali Basu, Christine Ward, Mrs Dasgupta, Rakhi Dasgupta, Rakhi and Aveek Sarkar, Ann and Bob Wright and Maya.

TAMIL NADU:
Mrs A. Santha Ramanujam, A.C. Muthiah, Dakshin restaurant at the Park Sheraton Hotel, Shoba Ramji and her staff, Mrs C.K. Ghariyali and Hotel Saravana Bhavan.

PUNJAB:
Promila Kapoor, Shashi Mehra, Jatinder Kaur, the Tarlok Singh family, Munim di Hatti, Surjit's Chicken House, Hoshiyar Singh at the Mohan International Hotel, Mrs Chadda, Kesar da Dhaba, Radha Anand and Sunil Vijayakar.

I also wish to offer my deepest thanks to Ravissant and Damania Airways.